ART
INTO
LIFE

BOOKS BY FREDERICK R. KARL

A Reader's Guide to Joseph Conrad

An Age of Fiction

The Quest (a novel)

The Contemporary English Novel

The Adversary Literature

Joseph Conrad: The Three Lives

American Fictions: 1940–1980

Modern and Modernism:
The Sovereignty of the Artist, 1885–1925

William Faulkner: American Writer

Franz Kafka: Representative Man

George Eliot: Voice of a Century

The Collected Letters of Joseph Conrad
general editor and volume co-editor

Biography and Source Studies
founder and editor

FOUR XLIBRIS BOOKS

American Fictions: 1980–2000

A Chronicle of Wasted Time: America in the Seventies

Quest for Biography (Essays)

Five Decades of Literary, Cultural, and Political Opposition
(Essays)

Frederick R. Karl

ART INTO LIFE

The Craft of Literary Biography

etruscan press

Etruscan Press
English Department
Youngstown State University
Youngstown, OH 44555-3415

www.etruscanpress.org

1 2 3 4 5 6 7 8 9 0

Printed in the United States of America

Publisher's Cataloging-in-Publication
(Provided by Quality Books, Inc.)

Karl, Frederick Robert, 1927–2004
Art into life : the craft of literary biography / by Frederick R. Karl.
p. cm.
ISBN 0-9745995-3-0

1. Biography as a literary form. I. Title.

CT21.K37 2004 808'.06692
QBI04-700340

Designed by Elizabeth Woll

Some of the essays in this volume were previously published; acknowledgment of these publications appears on page 297, which constitutes a continuation of this copyright page.

The publication of Art into Life *has been made possible by grants from the National Endowment for the Arts and the Ohio Arts Council.*

NATIONAL
ENDOWMENT
FOR THE ARTS

Ohio Arts Council
A STATE AGENCY THAT SUPPORTS
PUBLIC PROGRAMS
IN THE ARTS 40 Years

For Dolores

Contents

Foreword

IN ADDITION TO authoring biographies of four major literary figures, in the last twenty years I have written two dozen articles and presented several conference papers on the question of biographical writing. In some instances, I even expressed misgivings about how biography is conceived and structured. As an outgrowth of this activity, I created several courses at New York University on biography and biographical writing. Further, with New York University's backing, I started up a series of hardcover volumes in biography, called *Biography and Source Studies*, which now contains six volumes, with at least another six under contract. In these volumes, which I edit and also contribute to, all aspects of biography are covered by selected contributors from various fields of endeavor: mainly literary, but also art history, psychoanalysis, history, music history, and popular culture.

Since many of these pieces, apart from those in *Biography and Source Studies*, are inaccessible to the more general reader, I decided to collect my contributions in one volume as a companion to the reading and writing of biography. Some of my essays are psychologically oriented, but many others take advantage of contemporary critical theory, although without the jargon and the opaque prose. They are of various kinds, from extended commentaries on each of my four biographies—on Joseph Conrad, William Faulkner, Franz Kafka, and George Eliot—to essays that attempt to blend disciplines, then to pieces that analyze contemporary biographies of American and nineteenth-century British subjects. While the coverage is not universal, the sole major omission is commentary on other biographers, like Leon Edel, Park Honan, and Ira Nadel. But since few agree about very much in this respect, it seemed better to let them speak for themselves. My only real complaint about most commentators is their failure to understand how important social and cultural contextualization is for a subject, even when that means prolonging the text and even disturbing the narrative. In several essays, I have taken to fault nearly all the "brief" biographies published in recent years by Viking Penguin because these lives are so skimpy on cultural contexts—by which I mean not only artistic endeavor, but social and political background. Further, in some of these lives, I question the assignment of the biographer to the subject; the lack of fit often works against the material.

The thread that binds most of my pieces is my belief that biography is not "fixed" or set, but a contingent, almost random genre. More akin to fiction than to history, it is less than a novel, but sometimes more than history. It is linked to autobiography (of the writer), frequently full of sound and fury, but signifying significant information. Although biography has been maligned by critical theorists, it serves several important functions, since its narrative establishes how we read an author and not simply how we read a particular work. Biography also helps in some cases to fix an author's reputation—and in others fails; the work, obviously, will be the determining factor in any lasting reputation. Biography worked well with the recent life of Dawn Powell, and the interest in her letters and personal papers, added to her novels, did create a revival of sorts in what had been a forgotten early twentieth-century writer.

Yet biography did not seem to create any stir in a now almost forgotten author, Thomas Mann, once considered an important figure in the century's literary history. The work remained, at least for the contemporary audience, too heavy or out of step with current interests. Yet the spate of Mann lives may well lead to a revival, since major writers seem to reappear in cycles. Mailer was once up, now way down; Hemingway was once the man of the hour, now under reconsideration; Faulkner was once ignored and out of print, now considered America's leading twentieth-century novelist; Kafka forgotten, now revered. In all cases, biography helped influence the repositioning of these writers for both the general reader and university students. Biography accomplished this, not literary theories, not cultural studies. In feminist studies, biography helped bring out qualities in many once-neglected writers: Wharton, Chopin, and, of course, Woolf. Since biography has been with us since Plutarch—the first of the "brief" biographers—we cannot expect it to go away. Recently, the reader-response theorist Stanley Fish has written disparagingly about biographical writing, but for a man of such erudition and reputation he seemed quite ignorant of the complexities of biography as a genre. For example, he said, "Biographers . . . can only be inauthentic, can only get it wrong, can only lie, can only substitute their own story for the story of their announced subject."

This appeared on the *New York Times*'s op-ed page, and it reveals that a careful reader of texts like *Paradise Lost* (one of Fish's specialties) is not necessarily a careful reader in other forms. While he does touch on some of the problems in biography, where speculation (what Fish deems "lying") does enter, he misses how reading the subject as text in biography is not much different from the reading of any text, literary or otherwise. Is biography more "inauthentic" than history as it is recreated by the historian? All criticism of a given text is full of speculation, and as a theorist Fish must know how different theories, including his own, come to very different conclusions. So can biographers confronting the subject as text. What he ignores is how well, or badly, it is done. He appears to have read only those which are badly done.

Introduction

When I look back at the four subjects of my biographies, I wonder what thread, if any, drew them together; or, conversely, what drew me to four such seemingly different subjects, who, on the surface, have so little in common. I am speaking of my biographies of Joseph Conrad, William Faulkner, Franz Kafka, and, more recently, George Eliot. Further, the attraction of Conrad, Faulkner, Kafka, and Eliot cannot be disengaged from my view of biography itself. And that is the subjective nature of the enterprise—what I write about later as countertransference—no matter how diligent the research, regardless of how consciously objective the biographer attempts to be.

Linguists and philosophers speak of *aporia*, which in its Latin and Greek roots signifies doubt and loss. In more contemporary usage, it suggests that one (here the biographer) doesn't know where to begin or end, and, by extension, how to paper over the absences of data. These absences may involve meaning, significant information, or a sense of continuity. The life leaps, whereas the biographer needs a smooth(er) narrative. *Aporia* expresses the dilemma of the biographer confronted with almost unlimited decisions of what part of the subject's life to highlight, what part must remain in shadows, of how to structure a narrative, as well as where to begin and end. When the life is full of holes, then there is both "doubt" and "loss." I found this compelling.

But there is another even more significant element related to biographical writing, which is that the very things we want to know more intimately and more expansively in the subject's life remain unresolved. I was drawn in by the unreliability of the enterprise. In historical writing, one keeps interpreting data, and although there is a subjective dimension to that, the data dominate. In fictional writing, the subject is always at the mercy of the author, who can move his pieces as though on a chessboard. Biographical writing is different. Those very matters which seem to create coherence, a pattern, even a narrative, are often the very things we do not know; and when this occurs, the biographers must speculate so as to create a semblance of continuity and the appearance of coherence. The possibilities appear limitless but are in actuality restricted. It is a tricky business, almost a game, which occurs behind the scenes, in which moves are invented, frequently in desperation—as I shall illustrate later. For the best of biographers make the reader think that the subject is well in hand; that, in fact, the biographer has command, when he or she may be floundering. Covering up is as much a tool of the biographer as being able to fake sincerity is part of a politician's equipment. And often the part covered up as unknowable—for which there are no data—is the very element that might prove conclusive. Absence becomes more dominant than presence.

This point leads into my choice of subjects. For what drew me to each subject—apart from the literary attraction, which is a given—is the fact that what I wanted to know most about the author and his work were the very elements I could not uncover or fully explain. Each of my subjects is the reservoir of several secrets, or absences, which remain buried deeply within their lives and their artistic processes, their intellectual and literary development—buried far outside reach of even such an exhaustive biographer as I, whose books run from 300,000 (for the Eliot) to 600,000 words (for the Conrad and Faulkner). I am not speaking of those quick, summary-like biographies in the 300-page range, and surely not of the "brief" Viking Penguin biographies, now appearing, of the 150-page variety. I am concerned with those which purport to be inclusive, all-knowing, fully coherent. They aim to provide a seamless line between subject and life, between life and work.

For example, what I really wanted to know about Conrad in several critical areas remains cloudy, ambiguous, ultimately unknowable. When he was twenty, as is now well known, he attempted suicide, a real effort, in which he put a gun to his chest and pulled the trigger. The bullet missed all vital organs (a neat trick even for a professor of anatomy) and exited at his back. Conrad suffered a couple of ugly wounds fore and aft, along with the danger of infection, but no other damage. He recovered rapidly, and never again attempted suicide, although he was depressed and despondent for much of his life—what we would call a chronic depressive. Yet missing here is the sequence of events and thoughts that went through young Conrad's mind—he was not then "Conrad," but Konrad Korzeniowski—what brought him to this act of finality (gambling debts? a broken love affair? a sudden failure of nerve?).

What we know of the event derives from his uncle's letter to a friend in which the act was passed off as a duel, but it was a suicide attempt, and was ascribed possibly to more socially acceptable reasons, like gambling debts. The entire episode became shrouded in mystery and was, in fact, not known during Conrad's lifetime, except by his uncle and the friend to whom he wrote. Yet it has enormous implications for our understanding of the author, since everything that happens in the early years of a major writer has significance, and not to be ignored is that Conrad has at least twelve suicides in his fiction, as well as numerous other acts of violence. The biographer is left guessing, especially if he plans a psychological portrait. In my case, I filled in with possibilities—but these are speculations offered up and accepted by the reader who is eager for a narrative that seemingly explains everything.

There is, in effect, no satisfactory explanation—and perhaps not even an unsatisfactory one. There is no coherence to this event, since it was not repeated, and nothing truly significant led up to it. There is no narrative, except the biographer's own story and arrangement of his material. *Caveat lector*.

Yet this is only the beginning with Conrad. For then we enter thickets of possibilities, without any clear explanation. Polish-speaking, fluent in French from childhood, Conrad decided at twenty-one to enter the British sailing fleet, not knowing any English. He proceeded to learn the language from other sailors and from extensive reading of English novels and some nonfiction—Dickens, John Stuart Mill, Ruskin, others. But when he decided to write, when he was over thirty, and already licensed as a sea captain in the English merchant fleet, expert in both sail and steam, he decided to write in English—a language, incidentally, in which he had such a heavy accent and so mispronounced words that H. G. Wells and Max Beerbohm, among others, parodied him. This was, nevertheless, the language he chose to write in, and he stuck to it as his sole means of livelihood when, after twenty years, he gave up the sea. One of the great mysteries in Conrad biography lies here: what brought him to English? We can speculate that his Polish was rusty and not literary; that his French, while fluent, was not literary French; and that English allowed him expression in a language and a people he admired. All that possibly rings true. But his English grammar was shaky, his punctuation often strange, and his grasp of idiom, while remarkable for a foreigner, was often incorrect for a native and unsteady for a writer. The entire question of language in Conrad is shrouded in mystery; for, even as his English usage improved, underneath one senses a heavy Polish and French construction. In editing Conrad's letters, which were spontaneous samples of his writing, I have repeatedly seen how his usage falls into non-English constructions, into difficulties with positioning adverbs and adjectives, which often goes back to Polish usage.

At one point, Conrad said simply and finally that if he had not written in English he would not have written at all; but we know that was overstated, because his letters to his friend and relative by marriage, Marguerite Poradowska, indicate that he was willing to write in French and, in fact, collaborate with her, an already-established writer. Where is the biographer in all this? Other questions remain speculative and, essentially, unknowable: why did Conrad choose for a wife someone so beneath him in class and knowledge? Was it plain loneliness, which is a distinct possibility? Was it a desire to dominate, as he did? Was it part of a sense of his own inferiority and unworthiness, which he often felt? Was it connected to his difficulty overall with women, including those in his fiction? To what extent, we ask, did his choice of a poor, uneducated, underprivileged woman affect his presentation of fictional women? Was there a connection between the fact his mother died when Conrad was seven and his choice of a woman who could mother him? His letters to his wife well into the marriage when he was away or ill are those of a supplicant child seeking solace from a maternal figure. In another area, what led to his complete nervous collapse after he finished *Under Western Eyes*, a breakdown so complete he lost control of language and reverted to mumblings in Polish, his English forgotten? His wife listened, helpless to decipher his words. None of these questions have satisfactory answers, and this, rather than discouraging me, drove me deeper and deeper into the Conrad psyche. I hoped that if I delved far enough I could perhaps come into contact with the wellsprings of his talent, with what made Conrad into a great writer.

WHEN WE COME to Faulkner, the great wonder of the man and the writer for us lies in the period from the late 1920s to the middle to late '30s, a period of about ten years when he wrote several books unequaled in American literature in number and immensity since Henry James at the turn of the century. In order of publication, we find *The Sound and the Fury* in 1929, *As I Lay Dying* in 1930, *Sanctuary* in 1931, *Light in August* in 1932, and *Absalom, Absalom!* in 1936, plus two short story collections and a lesser novel, *Pylon*. The question

I raised for myself was: How did this man, a dropout from school, with at best a scattered education, some hit or miss reading in modernist texts, come to write these books? Further, how did his man go from being a mediocre and derivative novelist with his first two books—not negligible, but also not particularly noteworthy—to the author of several canonical novels in American literature, books which in many respects turned the whole nature of the American novel from realism and naturalism into the kind of disjointed, fragmented modernism associated with Joyce and Eliot? Still further, we ask, how could Faulkner reach into himself so profoundly, so richly and extensively, when he was bedeviled by the need to generate income, by time spent in Hollywood on scripts he detested, by a marriage which from the beginning was farcical in its mismatch of partners? It was, after all, on their honeymoon that Faulkner's wife, Estelle—already heavily dependent on alcohol and, we suspect, drugs—attempted suicide by striding into deep water and not turning back, even while Faulkner was sitting on the beach and revising *The Sound and the Fury*. Right after their marriage he wrote *As I Lay Dying*, turning himself into Agamemnon and Estelle into Clytemnestra—not exactly a tribute to marital bliss. Yet with all this pressing upon him, with imminent economic ruin facing him, the disruptive nature of Hollywood duty, his obvious helplessness as a script writer, and, of course, his heavy drinking—a constant throughout most of his life—Faulkner created great books. For the biographer, this was supreme material—not the man himself, but those books and the man's mysterious relationship to them.

Once again, as with Conrad, as later with Kafka and Eliot, I was drawn toward those elements in a great writer's life and work which cannot be fully probed, or if probed, cannot be resolved. The biographer amasses the evidence—and evidence is not lacking in Faulkner's life—although the exact nature of Estelle Faulkner's suicide attempt (like Conrad's) is muffled, and the exact nature of their marital wars has been tamped down by the family. But we know enough to set up our coordinates and even to create a narrative based on solid documentation. Faulkner was himself close-mouthed about this, but we can read back from the books certain patterns and repetitions—the horrors of marriage, the martial struggle between men and women—to see where he was emotionally and psychologically in this time frame; and of course we do know about the heavy drinking, both his and Estelle's, an almost suicidal act which took no heed of danger.

With this and other material in mind, I then asked where those books came from, from what psychological and social patterns—and this became, for me, the biographical question and helps explain why I entered into Faulkner's life and work. The nature of the man's life itself, tortured, emotionally deprived, self-destructive, did not particularly interest me except—and I emphasize *except*—as it led into the work. I wanted to arrive at that meeting point and to explain the writer, notably the writer of *Absalom, Absalom!* that novel of overarching greatness.

Yet the more I probed, the more evidence I gathered, the clearer it became that I was not going to penetrate Faulkner's sudden burst of creative energy. My evidence was large and varied: Faulkner did come from a literary family (his great-grandfather wrote a famous novel); Faulkner's mother, Maud, was a reader, and when he was growing up she had introduced him to many classics, including those of Joseph Conrad; Faulkner as a young man was friendly with Phil Stone, who was educated at Yale and who introduced his friend to many modernist works; and Faulkner had revealed some verbal dexterity in his first two novels and in a few lines of the poetry he wrote in his early twenties. But little of this added up. What I found seemed like discrete data, and it became biographically challenging because it would remain unresolvable.

I then worked through influences on Faulkner—T. S. Eliot, Flaubert, and Conrad, for example—and I charted his knowledge of disruptive, dysfunctional family life in and around Oxford, Mississippi, his Yoknapatawpha; but none of it accounted for *The Sound and the Fury* or the understated brilliance of *As I Lay Dying* or surely not for the complex and profound *Absalom, Absalom!* Yes, one could cite the Civil War as the backdrop for that novel, since Faulkner grew up in the post–Civil War South and was present at annual triumphalist celebrations of the South's loss. He was saturated with the war, pride deriving from honor and chivalry, but he was also aware of the injustice done to the slaves and the insidiousness of racial relationships between black and white; further, the unresolvable difference in their ways of life and yet their common humanity—he was aware of all this and it fed into *Absalom, Absalom!* But how was I to explain his clipped, oblique, often difficult approach to the material; to the complexities of his time sequencing; to the interruptions in the dialogue; to the recreating of history and memory as part of a literary narrative; to the presence of certain characters, like Thomas Sutpen, the man on horseback—a figure conjured out of memory; and all the rest, including history based on memory and memory itself based on speculation? My very biographical quest was at once difficult and yet compelling, driven by the need to create a narrative and some coherence around what could remain problematic even after my heroic and valiant 600,000 words tried to explain how Faulkner the man became Faulkner the artist.

MY INTEREST IN Franz Kafka goes back more than thirty years, and I waited to write his biography, or possibly a critical study, until I felt mature enough. Kafka probably creates more problems for a biographer than any other literary figure, dead or alive, for whom there is a substantial paper trail. The difficulty with writing a biography of Kafka begins in the pre-stage. It starts with the awareness that the reader will already have his or her Kafka: a personal Kafka whose story he thinks he knows. Everyone, in this regard, owns Kafka, perhaps because his name has given a word to the language, Kafkaesque, possibly as much misused as used. Kafka is the iconic literary figure of the twentieth century, and even though he died in 1924, he is in some respects an emblem of the century.

Getting at his original materials, his manuscripts and notebooks, I had been warned, was an impossibility—blocked by his niece. But amused by a letter I wrote her, she granted me the privilege of consulting several manuscripts at Oxford's Bodleian Library. Yet a biography of Kafka involves far more than manuscript study or immersion in his life; it involves, also, intimacy with Prague, where he was born and lived, and with the politics and ethnic conflicts of the Austro-Hungarian Empire. I spent considerable time in Prague in 1989, still under the communists, as a guest of the government and as a lecturer at Charles University, on contemporary American fiction. During my time there, I followed the footsteps of Kafka, from his places of residence to where he worked in an accident insurance company. My aim was to create some coherence in a life that seemed to consist of disconnected pieces: for instance, the man who detested his parents and yet lived at home nearly all his life; the man who claimed he was close to suicide on several occasions and yet was a very successful employee, promoted several times, favored by his employers, and this for a Jew in a company that did not usually hire Jews; the man who lived for his art, who sacrificed all for writing, and yet who believed his "scribblings" were of little value. Except for the few things he published during his lifetime, he asked his friend, Max Brod, to burn all of his, Kafka's, manuscripts. This man who wanted to leave nothing behind, no trail, left diaries and other personal notes so detailed that we can follow almost a day-to-day existence for him. This same man, whose behavior appeared heterosexual, filled his notebooks with homoerotic images and scenes, especially the desire to be penetrated by knives in the stomach and elsewhere. He reveled in the fantasy of a blade entering his body and then being twisted and twisted. The pain he would suffer was almost orgasmic.

Yet the more I entered into Kafka's life, the more elusive he became. Contradictions led not to resolution but to further contradiction. This became for me a supreme test as a biographer; for nearly everything I needed to know about Kafka blocked connections. I decided to go after him on several fronts: Prague, of course, for without Prague and its history (and the role of Jews and the Golem in it), no one can begin to understand Kafka; then his placement as a German-speaking Jew, a minority within a minority in the mainly Catholic,

Czech-speaking, nationalistic population (Kafka's relationship to his Judaism becomes a rich source; from there, a close examination of his fiction, interwoven with his notebooks, diaries, and other pieces which the general public knows little about.) Further, I needed to locate him within the cauldron of Middle and Eastern European politics; and still further, I wanted to identify him with the movement we have come to label Modernism, with the other great writers, painters, and composers of his time in Paris, Berlin, Munich, and Prague. Yet Kafka was elusive, always ready to slip away, and that was the appeal. I don't know if I caught him—I don't know if that is possible; but I do know that I encircled him, and from that, I hope he came alive.

WHEN I CAME to George Eliot, the problems were both different from and overlapping with those I'd encountered before. Eliot, clearly, did not prove so elusive as Kafka, or even Faulkner and Conrad, but she proved as challenging. Since my interest was still in areas of biography for which we must make decisions and resolutions even when we lack documentation or a clear story, I saw in Eliot an excellent example. That she was the greatest woman novelist of the nineteenth century in English and, with Dickens, one of the two greatest of her century, did not mean her life could be easily penetrated. Usually, the greater the writer, the more unmanageable the biography becomes. Further, Eliot was more than a novelist; she was one of the two or three most capacious intellects of the period in England. She absorbed the century in all its fullness, in religion, philosophy, the hard sciences, social ideas, and literature. Perhaps only John Stuart Mill or Thomas Carlyle could rival her; but her learning was wider than theirs, since she seemed able to assimilate whatever came before her eyes.

Who was she and how did she get like that? The questions seem simple; the answers are quite complicated. Later in this volume, I speak of writing Eliot's biography, but here I can sketch in a few of the problematical areas. Born near Coventry, she had a relatively uneventful childhood as the daughter of a homemaker and a father who administered a large estate and was also a master carpenter and something of an architect. Eliot's family enjoyed no educational background and, except for Eliot herself, were not readers. Yet from an early age—she was baptized Mary Anne Evans—she showed great intellectual promise, and her father—it was left to fathers—permitted tutors and access to serious books. She was also deeply religious, pious, really priggish about her Church of England beliefs. She read deeply, was chiefly self-educated; and she was, in terms of brainpower, clearly a freak of nature; there is no other way of explaining her rapid intellectual development as a young woman, an inadequacy the biographer has to confront. She absorbed everything, in whatever field, and she mastered foreign languages, seven of them before she died—Latin, Greek, German, French, Italian, Spanish, and Hebrew.

One of the significant problems in writing Eliot's biography is finding in this uneventful background some sense of development, some way of explaining how she became George Eliot. A good part of my interest in Eliot was the need to find coordinates in the first twenty or twenty-five years that would explain who she was and what she became. One of my strongest points came to be that, increasingly, she felt herself smothered—she often herself used such images and metaphors—as she grew from her teenage years into a young woman, even while she continued to respect, even revere, her powerful, opinionated father. She was caught in a bind familiar to many nineteenth-century women: she admired her father (although not her mother), and yet she saw how provincial his ideas and social world were. Our own generations usually come to this conclusion at the university; Eliot came to it on her own, later supported by close Coventry friends. And this conflict drove her—her fear was real, palpable, nearly unbearable—that all her potential talents, as yet unfocused, would come to nothing.

She bit deeply into religion, and then began to move away from formal belief, an act of defiance which her father found unacceptable in their small community. Her first real rebellion—

the first of many—came in her early twenties in her refusal to attend church, and even though she eventually made peace with Robert Evans, she was desperately trying to find ways to break through her narrow world, and to emerge. Evans by now, in the 1840s, was ill with the ailment which would kill him eventually, but Eliot found herself the sole nurse, her brothers and sister having married. She was in effect experiencing a death watch, aware that her own life would be strangled—she was approaching thirty, almost middle age—until her father died, and yet she still respected and admired him.

Her sole piece of work had been a translation from the German of Strauss's *The Life of Jesus*. Otherwise, she felt useless, neurasthenic, wasted, headed nowhere. For the biographer, this period is both a bonanza and a challenge. We have plenty of facts, we know her despair, but what we don't know is what promises she made to herself, how she planned to use her freedom, just how desperate she was, how helpless and full of anger, hostility, even self-hatred. These are the intangibles; and yet I was forced to build upon them to explore how she moved along. We do know, after all, that she came through, she succeeded, she became George Eliot. Hindsight encourages us. But the journey was not easy, was not linear or continuous, did not take a predictable course—and yet, as we have emphasized, the biographer needs certainties, a sequencing of events, explanations. How do we get started? How do we understand her? We find the question of *aporia* again—evidence, but meaning what?

Several clues exist to explain what she was undergoing as she attempted to emerge: she suffered from several ailments—headaches constantly, perhaps disruptive menstrual periods, stomach upsets—and these indicate she was not succumbing or surrendering, but struggling to exist on her terms. Fighting back meant suffering. She changed her name, a small matter as yet, from Mary Anne Evans—the Anne with an "e"—to Mary Ann Evans, without the "e." We know this meant something to her because it foreruns several name changes, of which George Eliot later as her professional name was only one. Mary Ann gave way, in turn, to Marian, the French version.

Renaming becomes an indication, to me, that she was fighting within to find something distinctly hers, to resist the smothering which she felt until almost thirty.

Once Evans died, she was left with an inheritance that was insufficient to live on. Enormous decisions for a woman in her time had to be made: she moved down to London, settled in with the publisher John Chapman and his wife and mistress, and possibly became physically intimate with him. Through the London scene, she met Herbert Spencer, the philosopher, sociologist, and Darwinian—she threw herself at him, and he utterly rejected her. She pleaded to be accepted, misidentifying this life-long bachelor as marriage material. He found her ugly, physically unappealing. Then she met George Henry Lewes, and the largest decision of her life was at hand.

The biographer requires certain points of reference in the subject's life that seem definitive—or in another way, the biographer *makes them definitive* by selecting them out of a welter of other details. The encounter with Lewes and the eventual elopement was the deciding point for Eliot—the way in which she went from Marian Evans (now that, in 1854) to George Eliot four years later. Lewes was the most unlikely of choices: messily married, with four sons by his wife, but also responsible for the growing family his wife was acquiring with her lover, Thornton Hunt, son of the poet Leigh Hunt. Lewes could not obtain a divorce because he had accepted the illegitimate children as his own; thus, in the eyes of the law, condoning his wife's adultery. Further, Lewes had the reputation of a philanderer, a lightweight in intellectual matters, and was, himself, considered the ugliest man in London—the Carlyles referred to him as a monkey face, an apelike creature. Physically unprepossessing, he had a reputation that had been scarred, aside from the impossibly messy marital situation. He did not seem like a suitable companion for the thirty-five-year-old Marian Evans, especially since by casting her fortunes with him, she was putting her reputation in peril. Had the liaison not worked out, she would have been deemed the worst sort of scarlet woman, and though the companionship lasted for twenty-four years, until Lewes's death, she remained an outcast to many households, even while admired and revered as a great writer.

For the biographer, Eliot's decision to go off to Germany with Lewes is a goldmine, but it also raises the very questions I mentioned before, those questions which cast into doubt the entire biographical enterprise. For while we know the facts of Eliot's decision, we are not certain of what went into it: her rebound after the rejection by Spencer—possibly; the fact her own career in subediting and article writing was at an impasse—possibly; her age, at close to thirty-five—possibly; her recognition she had reached the limits of what a woman under traditional constraints could do and sought a dramatic breakthrough—possibly; an infatuation with the witty and clever Lewes—possibly; and then the great unknowns—the intuition every great artist has that something is looming and needs to be released, although the mode of release may be irrational, illogical, even on the surface self-destructive. I found this in Conrad, Faulkner, and Kafka, and now I decided to pursue it in Eliot.

I was still seeking to probe and uncover those elements which remain subsurface, hidden, the talents buried deeply within, what challenges the biographer to become both detective and analyst. I sensed that Eliot—still Marian Evans—at close to middle age in nineteenth-century terms, had to emerge in her own right, however dramatically and potentially traumatically, or else wither. Her departure with Lewes was not so much an act of desperation, although some of that was present, as it was her decision to reinvent herself, transform or perish. Although she did not then consciously realize her potential for fiction writing, it was somehow there; she needed to create the conditions for it to be released, and in this area Lewes helped. Whatever else his past had been, he remained supportive and, as far as we can determine, faithful.

With that, I had my four subjects and their innumerable biographical problems. The challenges they presented went to the heart of the biographer's craft. They became the framework or scaffolding for all my other writings on biography. A selection of these pieces follows and includes as well several long article-reviews of other biographies. I begin with my contribution to *American Imago*, the journal devoted to psychoanalysis, on Kafka and countertransference. Countertransference is not talked about much in biographical circles—it is a kind of dirty secret because it is so subjective—but it posits something obvious: that the biographer imposes himself or herself on the subject. The complications from this are enormous, and I try to single out a few of the problems it creates. Countertransference is an essential part of the unknowables existing in biographical writing: the relationship of biographer as analyst to the subject as analysand. Any biographer who remains unaware of this profound connection, and the role it will play as the biography evolves, proceeds at his own peril.

From this follow essays on the writing of each of my biographies. Then I continue with some more general pieces working in and out of my themes of uncertainty, choice, indecision, and the unknowable. These essays range over a period of thirty years and include published articles as well as several unpublished talks at conferences. What follows these are article-reviews, some concerned with contemporary subjects, some with recent biographies of nineteenth-century English novelists, and some with the first fruits of the Viking Penguin "brief" biographies, those in the 150–160-page range. For the latter, I examine the problematics of such a phenomenon—Proust, Mozart, and other giant figures "done" in 40,000 words or so, most without notes, all without index, none based on original research, many by nonbiographers. My main object: what does this mean for the future of serious biography? Can the long, "definitive," originally researched biography continue to exist, or is this kind of tabloid biography a sign not of the future but of now?

(Since all routes lead back to my four biographies, there is, inevitably, some small overlapping among the essays.)

ART
INTO
LIFE

A WAY TO READ BIOGRAPHICAL WRITING

Dr. Louise Kaplan, an editor at *American Imago* (a journal devoted to psychoanalytic culture), asked me to contribute to one of two volumes focusing on transference and countertransference in biographical writing. Based on my own experience, I chose to write about countertransference in interpreting Franz Kafka's stormy relationship to his parents, but especially to his mother, Julie. My aim was to see how this affected the direction of his life and work. Previous biographers have emphasized Kafka's strained relationship to his father, Hermann; but I found his anger and dismay at his mother equally significant for him, and perhaps more central to the formation of his fictional ideas than those linked to Hermann. He felt that in her deference to her husband she neglected him, Franz, emotionally and psychologically; that she sacrificed him in order to placate her husband; and that the wounds were palpable, profound, and ever present. None of this neglects the presence of Hermann in Kafka's life, but suggests that Julie's behavior went deeper. This view of Kafka shifts the ground considerably from previous biographies and opens up what has always been of great significance to me—countertransference in biographical writing—whereby the biographer imposes personal values, beliefs, emotional responses, and childhood experiences on the subject.

In the Struggle between You and Kafka, Back Yourself

"In the struggle between you and the world, back the world" —KAFKA

IT IS AN article of faith in all Kafka biography that his lifelong struggle was with his father. Franz, who was named after the Austro-Hungarian emperor Franz Joseph, seemingly became weak, passive, fearful, impotent when confronted with the physically large, forceful, demanding, apparently omnipotent father, Hermann—a godlike figure in the Prague household. Kafka of course wrote about this personal agony, we recall, in his now very famous "Letter to His Father," in 1919, when he, Franz, was thirty-six years old. The son's attack came on several fronts: that at mealtimes his father was disgusting—especially his cleaning out of his ears with a toothpick; that his father brought Franz and his sisters up by means of irony—which suggests disrespect, condescension, verbal hostility; that Hermann resented nearly everything Franz tried to do, and particularly mocked his very mild sexual escapades; that Franz stammered or "hesitated" because of the father; that the shape of the family, in fact the map of the world, was dominated by the father's large presence; that the images of extreme violence in Kafka's work—for example, in "In the Penal Colony" or in numerous notebook entries—are perceptions of Franz as his father's chosen victim; that Hermann spoke of the children in the past, as if they were no longer in the home, or else dead, humiliating them by failing to acknowledge their presence; that Hermann created sexual disgust in the son, no more than when they undressed together at bathing establishments—Hermann built on a large scale, Kafka with an almost skeletal frame.

This Oedipal battle continued throughout Kafka's adult life (he died at forty). It is a given that some dimension of son-father relationships not only dominated Kafka's mature personal life but influenced, perhaps more than anything else, his writing life. The demons, the ghosts and spectral presences, the forces of mysterious domination which squeeze through every situation, the desire for and yet fear of authority, the emphasis on impotence alongside the persistent desire to break into one's own potency—all these seem related to the father's effort to efface the son and the son's futile jousting to survive, but of course transformed, transmuted, as if the powers of the paternal God could be filtered through the son's needs.

And yet what if the biographer does not see it this way at all? What if Kafka's own narrative is read differently? What if the biographer probes Kafka contertransferentially, so that the biographer's own perception of parental authority (despite quite different consequences) informs his sense of Kafka's life?

The battle now shifts its grounds; but, as Joseph Conrad once said about other twisted relationships, "where to?" This biographer has argued that the real conflict in Kafka's life came over his mother and her role in the marriage. We know with certainty from Kafka's notebook and letters, from his handling of female characters in his fiction, from his comments to his fiancée Felice Bauer, and from his overall difficulty with women that his relationship with his mother, Julie, was strained, and that one of the reasons was her utter and complete devotion to Hermann. She worked in his fancy goods store, she played cards with him in the evening, she raised the children and kept the home going. To his dismay, Kafka saw his more-accomplished and better-spoken mother giving herself completely to Hermann so that while the husband could play a divinity in the home—we have the son's perception for that!—Julie played acolyte. The father demanded; she served. Furthermore, Kafka sensed that he and his three (younger) sisters had been neglected. In his *Letter*, he accused his mother of playing the "beater" in a hunt and driving Franz back into Hermann's trap. The image is murderous. When I asked Kafka's niece about this—she was fourteen when Kafka died in 1924—she considered it a possibility; but as the last keeper of the Kafka flame and legend she did not wish to create any ripples in the standard Oedipal drama. Julie's devotion of course made her a model middle-class wife in the waning decades of the Hapsburg Empire, but also was the source of her son's revulsion.

But was I putting down Julie Kafka as a clear response to my own experiences with an unstable, problematic mother? And how and why was I doing it? After all, my mother was the dominant figure, the father passive, almost nonexistent, a reverse of the Kafka household; the two sets of parents as it were coming from opposite directions. And the consequences were themselves quite different—in my case, a conventional marriage and family life, no discernible difficulties with women.

Yet I perceived the destructive powers implicit in my mother's behavior, and even though I set myself against her at every juncture, she became in some curious way the mirror image of Julie Kafka, the latter reticent, the former self-centered, self-serving, a force for chaos. Unlike Julie, who went along with everything Hermann demanded of her, my mother set herself not only against her husband (not too difficult to accomplish) but against the better interests of her children. In her distaste for life itself and in what I later sensed was a profound depression, she demanded center stage through a series of calculated moves: a constant changing of households, cities, even sections of the country, so that I attended a dozen grammar schools and was, on several occasions, farmed out to relatives; a long-running "sickness" which was attributed to nerves and which made her, vocally, a potential suicide—announcements I took seriously; a persistent sequence of verbal attacks on my father as a failure in every aspect of his life, especially in financial terms, but, as I came to recognize later, in sexual terms as well; a constant pairing of myself and my older sister in ways that were not helpful: her looks and my brains, and how lucky that it had turned out like that.

She considered the household a place for warfare, a battle between her and the world. She was always full of "what ifs"—what if she had married some of the successful men who had courted her—mainly fantasies, I discovered; what if she had not fallen into such a loveless marriage (a typical marriage among immigrants and immigrants' children); what if she had used her looks (she was quite pretty) and brains (not too evident) to advance herself, instead of being entrapped; what if she went to work (she never did) and asserted herself; and so on? She lived to tear down, probably because she was so miserable with her life, so depressed, and yet unable to see that much of it was her own fault. Whatever was bad—and nearly everything was—she made worse, so that my sister escaped into marriages and I escaped, through the good fortunes of a war, into the navy.

All this was good preparation, perhaps not for life, but for the future biographer. The main pitfall awaiting me was not one of transference, but of countertransference, that emotional tie that develops between biographer and subject and often leads to the former placing a subjective template on the latter. Whether we use Freudian terms or Erikson's "idealization" and "unconscious identification," the danger was that I would seek formative dimensions in my subjects' lives that validated a mother-oriented family, whether the mother was dominant or passive. Freud cited countertransference (*Gegenübertragung*) to indicate how analysts may respond to patients; but he was primarily interested in transference, as he later came to understand and accept it. Yet countertransference was implicit in analyst-patient relationships, and more than merely present in biography. The biographer shapes, retells, imposes, reinvents, creates continuities; he or she is always *there*. In psychobiography, such as Freud's own *Leonardo Da Vinci*, it is critical.

In volume II of his Standard Edition (London: Hogarth Press, 1957, 139–51), Freud speaks of biographers as fixated on "their heroes" for a special reason: that the "hero" has his/her being in the writer's own emotional life. Once the selection is made, the biographer "idealizes" his hero, seeing the latter as fitting in for the child's sense of his own father; as a consequence, the biographer erases those traits and even deeds which taint the idealized portrait, and obliterates human weakness, human error, even pivotal events. But Freud does not account for many of the lives written now which are presented, not as idealizations, but negatively, displaying the avidity with which biographers undermine their subjects. With these, we have countertransference: acts of anger, vengeance, and scorn visited upon a subject.

My Kafka biography clearly presented me with harder choices than I had had with Faulkner and Conrad, or would have later with George Eliot. To put it in literary terms, there was the Kafka story—the raw materials of his life and cultural contexts which most of us agree upon—and the plot—my own intervention, to give coherence, continuity, and some degree of closure. Plot or retelling was my act of countertransference, and with Kafka, as we shall see, it was problematical. I had to be aware at every moment of what I was doing, or else I could easily have slipped into radical manipulation and distortion.

With Conrad, his mother, Ewa, died when he was still a small child, and then his father, Apollo, followed a few years later. He was an only child, taken in by relatives and friends of the family until he left Poland for France and the merchant marine just short of his seventeenth birthday. His mother existed mainly in memory, as someone sacrificed to his father's political ambitions. Apollo Korzeniowski saw himself as a romantic, a revolutionary, a patriot; and his activities against Czarist Russia in effect destroyed the family while making him something of a legendary figure. Conrad's childhood was deeply linked to Polish-Russian historical events and to left-wing politics which he later abjured and wrote about scornfully. His mother worship, accordingly, was intermingled with Polish history and Polish striving for freedom, and it existed not so much in the way he consciously arranged his life (in my reinvention of it) but in a young child's sense of a "missing" figure, an absence, an incomplete family. Many of Conrad's novels can be read this way; but for this biographer, interesting as the example may be, there was little here of either transference or countertransference.

For Faulkner, there was so clearly mother worship on the writer's part that for the biographer the lines were evident. Physically, emotionally, even to personal traits, Faulkner resembled Maud, not the burly, coarse, rough father, Murry. She was a huge influence on the developing writer, offering him books, reading to him when he was growing up, encouraging the son who was "different." Faulkner's hostility to Murry was also so clear that it did not require more than the usual care in defining a son-father relationship; the facts were obvious, and there seemed no powerful undertow. All the biographer had to worry about was not to make Murry—a fighter, drunkard, a loser as husband, father, and businessman—into a monster. In other words, the problem for the biographer here was not to overdetermine the father as someone worse than he was, while at the same time emphasizing Faulkner's devotion to his mother.

The struggle for identity in each case was not made into the war that Kafka envisaged. While Conrad's mother as holy saint worked unconsciously on his fiction and his creation of women, and while Faulkner's devotion to Maud influenced both his life and fiction, we do not have that conscious laying out of a battleground which Kafka insisted upon. Here, in his life, we have an intertwining of several elements, all of which created special problems for the biographer.

To complicate matters, Kafka himself perceived his family life as male-driven, as energized and terrorized by a father who was both dominant and in some personal ways despicable. In actuality, Hermann was little different from most Teutonic fathers, and his shtetl-oriented Jewishness did not take the hard edge off his patriarchal demands; in fact, his Jewishness and the somewhat precarious position of Jews in the waning years of the Hapsburg Empire may have enhanced his need for authority. (As a reminder, we must not forget the critical time and place of Kafka's early life, even as we try to sort out psychological problems.)

The problems here were oceanic for the biographer since my countertransference was based on a crossover, a household which was completely mother-driven. How was I to handle Kafka's diatribe against his father in the *Letter* and in numerous other comments in his correspondence, epigrams, aphorisms, not to speak of fictions like *The Metamorphosis*. Here, in 1912, the father is viewed as a killer of the son; the battle is not heroic, but pitiable, when the son is transformed into vermin so as to change the rules of the challenge. In my own case, while my father was physically present some of the time, he was defanged and declawed, marginalized, a beaten figure by the time I was old enough to observe. He was struck down not only by life (the Depression years, a lack of business sense, an uneducated, narrow outlook) but by my mother. Here, before I wrote my first word about Kafka, I was up against an inner struggle, which was how to achieve some degree of objectivity in a situation where my own feelings and conditioning were completely different from my subject's. Or were they? Was there convergence?

But before citing numerous passages in which Kafka asserted how his mother "deserted" him, one must probe more searchingly into the argument for countertransference. One strategy would be roundabout: to neutralize Kafka's perception of Hermann as bully and beast by arguing that in the father the writer-son had found a "character" in his life, and that this character gave him the basis of an agon, someone to push against throughout both his personal and writing life. As such, Hermann Kafka was a figure in the Kafka theatre—we must not forget that Kafka and Kafkaesque are theatrical, acting-out qualities, becoming part of what we used to call "the theatre of the absurd." Hermann was the prime player here, perhaps operatic, a *basso profundo*, his voice booming through the apartment, his authority prefigured in his shadow as much as in his actual presence. As in opera, he was the bad guy, the one who might have had the woman for a time, but one who was bound to lose out eventually. Sometimes, the *basso profundo* is the king or emperor, but even so, he takes a hit, or comes upon a bad end. His very voice is an indication he will be perceived as part of the devil's kingdom.

So Kafka "starred" Hermann in his drama of muscular pathology. In this argument, the son needed the father as a way of highlighting his own failings and, in so doing, shaped that conflict which gave him something to push creatively against. This is, all in all, a reasonable argument, and not one to be dismissed easily. It in part undermines a transferential strategy, since it shifts the ground from psychology, pathology, even impotence, to matters of art and aesthetics. In this view, Hermann is what his son *chose* to make him, an imaginatively created figure in a typical lower-middle-class family caught on the cusp of a disintegrating empire. As Hermann waxes and wanes, so the point goes, so went the Empire, slackening off as Franz Joseph became a sick king, one of the sick old men of Europe. Kafka, then, had his own version of Franz Joseph in the household, not an emblem but a flesh and blood character whom he could berate, fight, and throw himself against. Once so imagined, the scene mutes the distinction between conscious and unconscious.

The compelling part of this argument is that it reveals how a creative person works. But it is insufficient for Kafka, and it too conveniently loses sight of the mother. We know that the obvious parent, the alpha figure, is not necessarily the real agent in these transactions between parents and children. Julie made Hermann possible, as we see in Kafka's own words repeated so often as to become a text. As we noted, the mother is a beater trapping Franz in Hermann's snare—the mother's seeming kindness only made Hermann's brutishness more pronounced; the mother never manifests that she understood Franz or had any idea of what he was up to; the mother assumed her son was like other young men and needed only a regular schedule, nutritious food (Kafka was a picky eater), warm clothing (he wore summer suits in the Prague winter), and a devoted woman; the mother had nothing left over for the children once she let Hermann squeeze her; and, finally Julie Kafka failed him in the worst area of all—she ruined him for all women, and in time spoke in unison with Hermann's voice.

I was drawn to inadequate mothers—different though they were. Kafka's, in his view, was destroyed by her weakness, her deference. My own was self-serving, obsessive, depressed, with a need to manipulate. Kafka would drive himself to become everything his own mother was not; he pursued bachelorhood the way she pursued marriage. I was now driving hard to interpret his avoidance of all serious relationships with women as his way of avoiding, even negating, Julie. I saw in my own marriage and family how I had set myself against my own mother, and the two situations converged. I pressed on to other convergences, where Kafka and I shared instead of crossing over.

While moving in and out of mothers and mothering, I knew I needed broader areas of convergence. We shared backgrounds, mine the result of Eastern European immigration, his in Prague, with shtetl life not too distant. We both belonged to the same tribe, accompanied by the stressful difficulties of a Jewish family and by bouts of anti-Semitism. Then there was the presence of enormous depression in the family lines—Kafka himself, Hermann, Julie; in my family, suicide by three of my father's siblings and my mother's lifelong slide; and, finally, Kafka's pre–World War I perception of European decline and disarray matched my own perception of post-Vietnam American decline and disarray. I saw in Kafka not only a biographical subject, but an historical figure, and, most of all, a secret sharer. We could communicate when I reinvented him.

Since I had grown up with my mother's depression as an almost physical presence in the household, I was particularly attuned to Kafka's. His was a particular kind, not a clinical or acute condition—he wrote, he worked, he saw friends—but close to what has been called "essential depression," a term coined by Edoardo Weiss. This condition arises when the individual is linked to a relationship he or she cannot forgo. In this view, Kafka gained strength from what was also draining him—a condition we observe in many creative artists and intellectuals, where the paradoxes of existence and of work do not resolve themselves except possibly in the work itself. In Kafka it was particularly intense in that he needed his negative feelings about his mother as a way of strengthening his fight to the death with his father. To put it this way is, once again, to observe the mother as the generative member of the family, the one who gave it the negative energy someone like Kafka could feast off. The father, in this view, was the shield behind which Kafka could disguise his real feelings, which as we have seen he expressed on numerous occasions.

But all this only scratches the surface. For Kafka, the subject becomes intermixed with a huge historical drama, so that the Oedipal drama, however configured, is not enough. The fact he gave his name to an entire way of looking at the world, "Kafkaesque," suggests that he belonged to an era, was identified with it, and perhaps more than any other writer defined it. I had to observe Kafka biographically on several levels: the social-historical, in which the individual experienced the demise of the Austro-Hungarian Empire; the man who was present at the development of Modernism, in which Kafka was the contemporary of Proust, Joyce, Picasso, Kandinsky, Schoenberg; the citizen of Prague itself, not a backwater, but a center for Modernistic culture in literature, music, and painting; the Jew, as part of a minority of a German-speaking minority in Prague—with Jews caught between basically a German-oriented culture and Czech nationalistic aspirations. Here was a narrative and shaping dilemma: how could I pursue his relationship with his mother in a context which cried out for so much historical and cultural reclamation? How could I prevent the individual pathology—if indeed it was that, and perhaps it was not!—from appearing more significant than the huge forces Kafka felt himself moving with and against? How could I locate what I thought was really not sickness, but cultural dislocation of a kind which Kafka was himself able to comprehend only partially? How could I account for the fact that, as Freud writes of Leonardo da Vinci, Kafka could not complete his longer works? So that his three "novels"—really texts, chapters in and out of sequence—are all incomplete? Was this inability to finish his work part of the dislocation? Was it connected to his feelings about his mother, his father, the couple as a whole?

Did it, perhaps, fit into some sense of a declining empire, one rotting from corruption within? What relationship did "Kafkaesque" have to any of this, but particularly to Kafka himself as a boy and young man, then as a grown man so attached to someone he disliked that he lived with her for most of his life? With this, my engagement to my subject became far more difficult, more entangled with my own background, feelings, responses—nearly all of which went in very different directions from Kafka, not only in achievement but in personal life.

Freud warned on several occasions about the countertransference that occurs between biographer and biographee. "They [biographers] frequently select the hero as the object of study because, for personal reasons of their own emotional life, they had a special affection for him from their very outset" (*Da Vinci*, p. 109). Freud is of course attempting damage control, to undercut attacks on him for romanticizing da Vinci. He cautions that the idealization of the subject is almost inevitable, for biographers strive "to enroll the great man among their infantile models, and to revive through him, as it were, their infantile conception of the father" (p. 109). Yet such an investigation has its dangers, leading into what Freud labeled "pathography," and he warned against that mode in which the subject's ills supersede his achievements. When such pathologies subvert a holistic view, inevitably the biographer sensationalizes his material.

Freud says that with pathography one "never obtains an understanding of his [subject's] importance and his attainments, and that it is therefore useless mischief to study in him things which could just as well be found in every Tom, Dick and Harry" (p. 108). He then equivocates, saying that pathography does have its uses, since it never tries to "make comprehensible the attainments of the great man" (p. 108) and therefore should not be blamed for failing to do so. In one large respect, Freud has worked himself into a hole; he indulges in pathography in his reading of da Vinci—the cultural meaning in the mouth symbolism, the homosexuality, the yearning for the mother's kisses, and the like—and then tries to ease out of it by asserting he wasn't trying to assess da Vinci's achievements. Pathography seems acceptable if he does it, but is not to be encouraged.

A countering argument is that we can work through pathography and countertransference, as we must, in what should be the very model of biography: one in which we measure both the private dimensions of a great or interesting subject *and* the public achievements. Then while pathography becomes unavoidable, countertransference is not merely a "happening"; it is acknowledged and becomes a given in all biography. We come to recognize that every biographical subject is an abstraction, even a living one. Every biographer looks into a mirror image with a distorted narrative, one whose perspectives and vanishing points he must mediate between himself and his subject. What he or she sees in that mirror image is not "reality" or "truth." Instead, we have perceptions, and perceptions involve choices, choices influenced by how we perceive ourselves, our attitudes toward friends and toward work, our sense of success or failure, our peace or war with parents and siblings. In my own case, my struggle (in the main successful) against a difficult and unstable mother influenced, first, my choice of Kafka as a subject, then influenced further my shaping of his attitudes and some of his life's choices. But, of course, matters went further than mothers and one's attitude toward them; they went into questions of Kafka's fiction, his achievements, most of all into how he turned what seemed defeat into great victory.

There is pathography in any reading of Kafka, but to see him as pathological is completely off the mark. His mother did not sink him. He held a responsible position in an insurance company—and became one of the few Jews to be promoted in an anti-Semitic Prague—and he worked his way through a large body of fiction and nonfiction (diaries, notebooks, letters, incidental writings) before he died at forty. He also had a wide circle of friends, including several of considerable achievement—Franz Werfel, Max Brod, Hugo Bergmann, others. What was most attractive about Kafka—and one could possibly say something similar about Samuel Beckett—was that despite his sense of defeat, his extreme pessimism, his culture of failure, he was able to produce work which belied that feeling. Running through his notebooks and letters is an even more persistent pessimism than we find in the fiction; a sense of himself as doomed in a world that was, in effect, "Kafkaesque."

Yet none of this self-definition as a loser, as someone lacking *Affekt,* as a person unable to make meaningful contacts with women, none of this stopped him. The culture of defeat and disappointment, in fact, nourished his ambition and determination to produce great writing—an ideal which he felt he always fell short of and, therefore, the reason why he asked Max Brod to destroy most of his manuscripts after his death. While my own personal life followed a far more conventional course, my sense of how the world worked shaped my view of Kafka. Broadly formative was my growing perception that one always had to save oneself, or the abyss—what my parents in their poverty, narrowness, and sheer unhappiness presented at every turn—would claim me. I not only understood Kafka's effort to keep afloat, I made sure that this became my theme: that every blockage simply became another obstacle he had to overcome.

One area I had difficulty reconciling was Kafka's sexuality. Here points of identity, as far as I could consciously determine, ended, since my own was conventionally heterosexual. Kafka, too, was in practice heterosexual, and yet a recurring insistent image in his notebooks is of a knife being thrust into his lower body and then twisted. He expresses great pleasure at the pain, the anguish, the finality of it. It is repeated in some of the fiction, the knife thrust at the end of *The Trial*, the needle machine in "In the Penal Colony," and elsewhere. The insistence of the knife thrust suggests a homoerotic experience, the phallic knife, the thrusting and probing, the obviousness of it all, but there is no other indication of homoerotic, no less homosexual, interest on Kafka's part. Unconsciously, perhaps, but in all his conscious acts—and they proved few—his sexual activity was heterosexual. Not that it was easy for him—it was in fact very difficult, and his experience throughout most of his adult life was with casual pickups (shopgirls eager to earn a little extra money) or with professional prostitutes. I could not resolve the issues here, and countertransference no longer seemed to apply.

When it did come to a woman whom he was engaged to twice over a five-year period, Kafka feared her, feared the relationships, feared that a sexual attachment would undermine his concentration on his writing—so it all appeared. He seemed caught in some kind of active-passive ambivalence, pursuing Felice, then rejecting her when she came within reach. Felice became in this respect an emblem of the woman as destroyer of talent, blocker of creativity, subverter of imagination and real achievement, part Medea, part Medusa. I interpreted much of this ambivalence about women—once again not my own—to his feelings about Julie Kafka, however much Kafka had to distort his mother to create this unconscious model.

That image of Julie as "beater" looms large. Kafka sees her as the real killer, Hermann as the torturer. We recall the defining work in Kafka's career, the writing of "The Metamorphosis" in 1912, his breakthrough year. The son is to be sacrificed so that the parents can thrive. Julie as "beater" is, clearly, not an insight that occurred to Kafka in 1919, when he wrote the *Letter*, but was a snowballing of perceptions which hardened into fact, from the earliest stages of Julie's mixture of kindness and neglect. All those cooks, housemaids, and governesses the Kafka family employed simply became stand-ins for the indifferent mother.

With her agenda elsewhere, Julie, although present, was an absent mother—for the child, locating an absent but present mother becomes difficult. I found the problematics here very appealing and, of course, as a biographer will do, turned it into thematic material in my book. If Julie was the beater, Hermann the beneficiary, and Franz the prey, as Kafka perceived himself, so he would portray his protagonists as prey, hunted, victims of "Kafkaesque." In this respect, everything he wrote was both an extension of and revenge upon that archetypal woman, Julie.

Yet this is still not the whole story. Much remains shadowy, barely touched upon above. Julie Kafka, while on the surface stable and functioning with intense labor, was subject to heavy bouts of depression, possibly because her life from childhood on had turned her into a slavey. I wondered about her depression, but could not discover any clear definition of her bouts, how often they occurred, how acute they were, how chronically depressed she might have been while she functioned as homemaker and storekeeper. This is information I desperately wanted, since it would have been congruent with my own mother's persistent depression and her destructive efforts to break through with self-defeating schemes—moving constantly, furnishing and refurnishing apartments for only brief stays, turning the household into a battle zone of charges and countercharges, expressing to one and all how vile her life was. Julie apparently repressed whatever had marked her as a female victim, but the depressive episodes—however intense or extended—were the price she paid.

As often happens in biography, what we want to know the most is what we lack evidence for. How did Kafka resolve those sexual ambiguities cited above? In his work, we must observe. How did he deal with his "absent" mother? In his work, we must respond. How did he handle his sense of marginality? In his work! How did my own response to Judaism color my view of his? Would I follow Max Brod and see Kafka pursuing transcendental ideas, spiritual forms, coming closer and closer to a Hebrew God? Would I impose my own loose, secular relationship to Jewishness on Kafka, distorting perhaps a yearning in him for the transcendental? Here I encountered a battle between countertransference and transference.

Was Kafka getting to me even while I thought I was imposing on him? Right here we enter thickets of perception and misperception, a meeting of all the unresolvables a biographer of a complicated figure is capable of.

I was a thoroughly assimilated American and saw Eastern European Jewry—my immediate background—as part of another planet. And then Kafka—amidst general anti-Semitism plus German-Jewish distaste for Eastern European Jews—showed that the latter had something very human to offer. Despite its roughness and hardship, the shtetl was a community. Jews pouring out of Poland and Russia enjoyed large families, they displayed affection for each other, they seemed close-knit and comfortable with each other: the family against the world. Zionism itself made sense, given the history of Europe's treatment of its Jews. (As a note, long after Kafka's death, his three sisters were swept up in Germanic cleansing and all perished in the camps.)

I was forced into a strange compromise. There was Jewishness, and there was Judaism—and between them a gulf existed. Brod saw Kafka as yearning to bridge that gulf and to become one with some generic Jew; but I saw his ambiguity as simply another unresolved element in the writer, the very thing which made him so compelling. He confronted all the unresolvables, and still refused to succumb, until consumption turned him into a corpse. His defiance was measured by his response to "Kafkaesque"; he recognized the limits of man's choices, and yet he insisted to the end on choice. I wanted him not as a hero, but as a valiant protagonist in a vast Freudian-like drama, where tragedy is both out there and internalized. Like every other Kafka biographer, I had created my own Franz.

THE FOUR BIOGRAPHIES

Kafka, Conrad, Faulkner, Eliot

My interest in Kafka as a possible book subject threads through my entire publishing career of over forty years. From the time I first taught Kafka in a college classroom (*The Metamorphosis* and "In the Penal Colony" at the City College of New York), I had considered him as a primary subject for research, although not necessarily as a biographical subject. I wrote about Kafka early in my career, on spatial and temporal considerations in *The Trial* and *The Castle,* but a fuller treatment awaited, I felt, more mature years when I knew more. I waited until a 1985 book, my *Modern and Modernism,* caused me to research broadly the middle-European world of culture and history. Kafka was, of course, a looming figure in this study. I worked on other projects for a few years before attempting a full-dress biography. I needed to brush up on the German language, and this I did at NYU, where I was then a professor. After a visit to Prague, where I lectured on American literature at Charles University and walked the city in Kafka's steps, I was, finally, ready. All along, I felt some trepidation since a Kafka biography had not previously come from someone in English and American literature (it being the provenance of German specialists); but I had mastered the literature, the language, and the history, and my own ancestral background from Eastern Europe provided some assurance.

Writing Kafka's Biography

My recent biographies of Franz Kafka (1991) and George Eliot (1995) would appear to have little in common with Janet Malcolm's gossipy discussion of Sylvia Plath biographies in *The Silent Woman* (1995, first published in the *New Yorker*, 1993, 1994). But my own experience in dealing with two such disparate subjects forced me to confront many of the charges and countercharges Malcolm leveled against Plath biographers, and especially those judgments she rendered on biography itself. These judgments are driven by her personalized "use" of Plath biographers, nearly all of whom she attacks as saturated in self-interest, venial needs, and their own brands of retroactive revenge on Ted Hughes, Plath's husband at the time of her suicide, and his sister Olwyn, the Cerberus guarding the door of the Hughes-Plath estate. It is unfortunate that she attempted remarks on biography when her real subject was a kind of pit bull attack on those whom she accuses of themselves "using" Plath for their own ends.

Malcolm does have some penetrating comments about individual Plath biographers and their studies of the poet. She recognizes that the air around Plath is supercharged, since she filled many roles: as female victim, as object of feminist wrath, as failed wife, as minor poet attempting to seem major by co-opting themes she had not earned (like Nazism and the Holocaust). But Malcolm argues against biography itself as pretending one thing while proving another. She speaks of it as a "transgression," by which she means that the biographer covers his or her tracks with a show of research and scholarship while all the time providing voyeurism and busybodyism. This transgressive nature of the biographical process gives the enterprise "an appearance of banklike blandness and solidity" (p. 9).

Still pursuing how biography works, Malcolm states that letters give the biographer something "real," and when the latter quotes from letters, only then does he or she "share with his readers his sense of life retrieved" (p.110). As we shall see, letters are notoriously *unreliable*; they are as fictional as autobiography, with which they share the subject's perception of himself. They are not history, they are not *the* truth, they are not even honest memory. They must be read as fictions of a sort, not as documents or data. Quite contrary to what Malcolm says, letters—like diaries and journals—are among the most deceptive materials we have in biography; and they must be handled not as documentation but as part of the "fiction" the subject has made of his life.

Malcolm carries her argument further and superficially seems to be making a shrewd point when she says that in a work of nonfiction—i.e., biography—we "almost never" know the truth of what happened, whereas in fiction, we assume, the author can be trusted when he or she presents narrative, character, or situation. This is, of course, a willful misreading of both nonfiction and fiction. The question is not whether one or the other asserts the "truth" or who is to be believed. Quite differently, the question is how creatively we read both genres, because in neither do we have firm guideposts. The author of fiction, whether in third-person or first-person narrative, stream of consciousness, or whatever variation, is not to be trusted—or else the fiction is so low-level it has little or no resonance, ambiguity, or spark. Similarly, in nonfiction, we all know that history is an approximation, as is biography—all the books on Plath suggest that!—but because of several factors some are more reliable than others.

In biography, what are these factors? I will draw my illustrations from my writing of Franz Kafka's biography in particular, inasmuch as a Kafka biography is as ambiguous, uncertain, and outside ordinary guidelines as one can go. The reason for this is not paucity of material—letters, observations, documentation, diaries, and the like—but the difficulty of attempting some coherent portrait as a result of one's labors in the archives. Furthermore, if one is writing an in-depth critical biography, as I was (and no one had in English before me), then the inclusion of Kafka's work into the arena creates still another slippery dimension. Just as Kafka's novels and stories (as well as his sayings, paradoxes, diary entries, various letters) seem to slide away even as one digests them, so, too, their introduction into the life creates a Sisyphus-like task, at least in the biographer's perception.

To digress, when I completed my biography of George Eliot—obviously a very different kind of writer and person—I felt that I was reasonably sure of her. My work on the mountain of letters, my reading of her manuscripts and published work, my contextualization of her life as it cut through mid-Victorian England, all gave me a solid foothold on the material and, by extension, on the person. I felt that she was "doable," to the extent that any large-sized and major figure, literary or otherwise, is doable. We make assumptions here that are more sanguine than the situation may call for, but in certain ways we do feel that some tasks are achievable, while others may not be. Eliot, I believed, fell into that first category.

I had little of that certainty with the Kafka, and that is why I have chosen to use this biography as a response to Malcolm's attack on the genre. I did not want to make my answer to her overheated charges too easy, which I could have done with the Eliot biography. With Eliot, I could have shown how much she, Malcolm, muddies the biographical waters, adding nothing to the genre in general and, in fact, merely using her position at the *New Yorker* as a way of "getting at" various Plath biographers. The Kafka biography brings everything out in the open and does not permit that neat Malcolm "transgression," which has about it a whiff of evil, the poison of the Garden.

I will back up, since the Kafka venture was not the usual three-four-five years a biographer spends on his subject, but closer to an entire professional career. Possibly because of my own background, more likely because of my reading, I began, more than thirty-five years ago, to measure literature by the standard I had developed from reading Kafka. My first entry into his world came under almost perfect conditions: in a dark part of the Butler Library, when I was a student at Columbia College, I read *The Metamorphosis*. In those dimly lit passageways between the stacks, there were no sounds, no interruptions, little light. Kafka's pathologically real world—perhaps made more real because the setting accentuated the pathology—gave him an aura; and nearly all my subsequent reading in modern literature was nourished by images from *The Metamorphosis*. Strikingly, at the time of this reading, I was taking Columbia College's famed humanities sequence, the first parts of which involved close readings of Greek classical drama. And rather than seeing Kafka as somehow separated from this overwhelming literature, I perceived him—in my inchoate way—as linked, in particular, to dramas by Sophocles and Aeschylus. He did not possess their fully mature grounding, but he did have a sense of the tragic qualities of life, to the extent he could mock tragedy and, in fact, work through it. The "pathology" I observed in the Prague writer was, in some respects, the pathology that existed among the most exalted of the Greek protagonists: their decision to escape themselves even at the cost of self-destruction, and, most of all, their fated recognition of what they had done or become. More than two thousand years later, I found their descendant in Gregor Samsa.

During my years at Columbia, I moved along Kafka's body of work—never in courses, always on my own, through *The*

Trial, *The Castle*, the major stories. I knew nothing of his letters, diaries, or fugitive jottings. I also knew nothing of Kafka biography (Brod's was not available in English), and I possibly did not know that his background was Czech. I did know he wrote in German and was Jewish, although those factors in themselves meant little or nothing to me. Only later did I consider the geography and the racial/religious aspects—but by then I was more than a Kafka reader; I was a Kafka scholar.

Although I published an early article on space and time in *The Trial* and *The Castle*—when such matters were still not commonplace—my first real grappling with Kafka and the Kafka "question" came when I wrote *Modern and Modernism: The Sovereignty of the Artist 1885–1925*, in 1985. This study, a general look at the Modern movement in its broadest sense, combining literature, music, and painting, situated Kafka as a touchstone. While I included extensive remarks on the most important Kafka works, his appearance was as much a shadowy presence as a major player. In nearly everything I perceived as part of Modernism—strategic and innovative techniques, experiments in language, narrative discoveries and manipulation, deconstruction of character and plot—I saw the face of Kafka staring back at me and my material. Obviously, other figures were equally significant—Kandinsky, Schoenberg, Proust, Joyce, and the earlier French poets—but Kafka was the driving force.

With this long study of Modernism, I moved my center of interests temporarily from English and American literature into the world of central-eastern Europe. And I began to study in some detail the workings of political, social, racial, and ethnic systems quite distinct from those in England and America. I noted the importance of Prague, although many when comparing it with Vienna, Paris, and Berlin still considered it a backwater. I perceived that Prague was in some respects more interesting than the other cities because of the way its population was split, and, primarily, because of its German-Jewish minority, who were caught between a majority of Czech nationalists, with their emphasis on the Czech language, and those who were German but not Jewish, with their allegiance not to Czech nationalism but to the culture deriving from Vienna. The latter was the hub of the Austro-Hungarian Empire which had gobbled up the Bohemian land mass including Prague. Without being fully aware of it, I began to see Kafka biographically: not only as a writer, but as a writer in a particular culture which helped to explain what I had once thought was pathology. That condition was really not sickness, but cultural dislocation of a kind which Kafka was himself able to comprehend; Kafkaesque took on significance from this cultural context.

Kafkaesque, in fact, began to dominate my thoughts, not the trivial sense of the term, but its fuller meaning suggesting a world of dissociation, dislocation, schizophrenia, a world with its own rules, guidelines, its own forms of behavior that are not amenable to human will. Once again, I linked Kafka and Kafkaesque to Greek tragedy, emanations from the world of demons and witches and the supernal. Kafkaesque seems to have a will of its own, destructive of human endeavors. I ran across Kafka's witty saying that in the struggle between you and the world, back the world. Here was something inexorable, fated, even as the human spirit in Kafka's fiction refuses to be silenced. I had my paradigm for Modernism and, beyond that, for much of the twentieth century. Kafkaesque in our century has replaced the now old-fashioned fate or destiny or even circumstance and happenstance. It has become the representative adjective of our times, even when it is used in puerile fashion (as, I missed my bus; the mess was Kafkaesque).

Kafkaesque, I found, need not be completely negative, or inhuman. A common misapprehension makes the term a cover for all the ills of the world. On the contrary, for Kafka himself the adjective described conditions that brought out the Sisyphus-like qualities in himself. Without Kafkaesque, Kafka could not have been able to energize himself to confront all the terrors welling up from beneath, or to face all the bureaucratic-cultural frustrations he saw as inevitable. The word also gives us, as readers, a means of coming to terms with the Austro-Hungarian Empire in its dying phases, Robert Musil's Kakania (shitville). Kafkaesque becomes here an historical term, a means of reading the past. After Kafka's death, we have turned the word into "the way of the world." It is not only history; it contains the sociology and psychology of a period. It fits in quite well with Freud, another master of paradox and conundrum. We recall that even while Kafka had a horror of Sisyphus—he recoiled from the "bachelorhood" of this martyred figure—he also found in his suffering something heroic, substantive, redemptive. Kafkaesque, accordingly, as I began to come to grips with the word, does not always mean surrender to a horrendous destiny; it becomes something to battle against.

The idea of finally doing a Kafka biography was sneaking up on me, and my coming to terms with the deeper meaning of Kafkaesque was no small contributor. After *Modern and Modernism*, however, I became involved in another very long project, postponing any Kafka work. The new project was a biography of William Faulkner, certainly different ground, a very different kind of research, and very different results. The Faulkner biography was the natural outgrowth of my attraction to his body of work and to my growing immersion in American fiction of the twentieth century. More than a decade had passed since Joseph Blotner's monumental two-volume biography of Faulkner, and with some new material and many fresh ways of reading the writer, I felt another life was in order. Most of all, I came to see linkages between Faulkner and Kafka, linkages that lay in the shadows, bindings of an attenuated kind: with the Czech writer's placement in the death of an Empire and Faulkner's in a South still caught in the death of a hoped-for autonomy, with their sense of common defeat, and with their desperate struggles to reinvent themselves amidst confusion. If Kafka was the historian of his old world, Faulkner, in my view, was the historian of his—both writers caught in a spiral of anguish, ignominy, defeat, the annihilation of an old order that papered over permanent fissures.

What made the two readily compatible was their alertness to history, even though Faulkner's was more direct than Kafka's. But the latter's more angled perspective on history was present, in his fables, allegories, paradoxes, puzzles, even in his stories of animals intersecting with humans. Both writers were, in one regard, victims of history, whether the American South or the Austro-Hungarian Empire; and as a corollary, both were heroes of history, having discovered ways to see their way clear through language, wit, cynicism, and irony.

Having come through the Faulkner experience, I was prepared now for the Kafka. I emphasize how, contrary to Malcolm's glib words, I was not caught in any transgressive action; I would not appeal to any prurient or puerile interest in Kafka, while hiding behind "an appearance of banklike blandness and solidity." I even came to resent her stereotyping of bankers as bland, when, in the 1980s, which I assume Malcolm was aware of, they turned out to be some of the biggest outlaws this country has ever known. They were spectacular gunslingers, only not with guns but with their depositors' money. No. I was not hiding anywhere. I was seeking nothing less than to read Kafka as a "representative man," as someone who kept up a most ordinary position in Prague life while harboring a great imaginative vision which, while filling personal needs, caught the final days of the Empire.

I found I needed some governing or magisterial concept to hold my vast material together. History was one way, psychology another, cultural contexts a third; but I needed something more personal, and for that I co-opted Emerson's "representative man." I called Kafka our representative man of the twentieth century, although that might not be acceptable to everyone. Unlike Emerson's person, Kafka's marshals his weaknesses so forcefully and so wittily he becomes a pillar of strength. He is a man whose seeming passivity and inaction disguise tremendous reserves of inner power. He is marked by a seeming dissociation of self, his being and becoming heading, as it were, in different directions. He lacks unity, or integrity; he divides and subdivides. And yet, withal, he does not collapse or surrender. He has fitted himself to the century, appearing as a victim when in reality he is a survivor.

I WAS READY to begin. I always make part of my preparation for a biography a close comparative analysis of the author's manuscripts with his or her completed text. I look in particular at the alterations, using the revisions as a way of reading into the writer as well as into the text itself. Often, cancelled passages, or pages, revisions of phrases and lines, rewrites of all kinds provide revelations—literary, of course, but also psychological. It is the biographical quest for ways in which the writer reveals what the final text fails to provide.

The way to Kafka's manuscripts was torturous, and I was told to forget about it. Several obstacles stood in my way. First, there was Kafka's niece, Mrs. George Steiner (not *that* Steiner); then there was Sir Malcolm Pasley, the dean of Kafka textual scholars, who had underway a definitive or authoritative edition of Kafka's works; and then there was the fact that the manuscript of Kafka's *The Trial* had just been sold, for close to two million dollars, and was to be housed in the Schiller National Museum in Germany for analysis by Sir Malcolm's team of textualists. I was, in this game, not even a player; and Kafka scholars told me I could expect rejection at every level. The manuscripts I wanted to see at the Bodleian Library in Oxford, England, could not be touched without permission from Mrs. Steiner and Sir Malcolm.

I had faced something of this situation before when I was working on Faulkner's biography. The writer's daughter, Jill, refused to see me or even answer my letters, although I had introductions to her from people she knew and trusted, such as Joseph Blotner. Her refusal meant I could not gain permission to quote from any of the manuscripts, but it did not inhibit me from spending long weeks and months with the material at the University of Virginia and University of Mississippi libraries. In addition, I had access to private collections, most notably the superb collection of L. D. Brodsky. Jill Faulkner's failure to acknowledge me was hardly fatal; it simply meant I could not quote directly from the manuscripts. But I was able to paraphrase from manuscript material; and as far as quoting from letters went, they had been collected by Joseph Blotner and published. For those I needed only the publisher's permission, which Random House gave me readily. Withal, what had been blockage on the part of Faulkner's daughter led to no disaster. When I was in Charlottesville for the University of Virginia collection, I even tried one more time to see Ms. Faulkner, who owned a farm nearby; but when I was rejected, I settled for paraphrasing passages from her father's manuscripts and never looked back.

The Kafka situation was different. The manuscripts were situated in the equivalent of Fort Knox, and if I wanted access I would have to get something in motion. My motives were hardly those malevolent ones Janet Malcolm attributes to biographers—for if anything would reveal the "truth" of a writer's life, then his or her manuscripts would. A major failure of Malcolm's study of Plath biography, in fact, is her unfamiliarity with the finer points of her subject's poetry, her inability to read the lines and explicate the tropes closely and cogently; and her overall feeling that biography lies purely in the life, not in the subject's work.

I decided to try. But in preparing to write about Kafka, I had to bring my knowledge of reading German up to another level. At one time, I was fairly fluent in reading the language, but was not bilingual; German was for me a learned language, not something I could call up from childhood or from early conditioning. Except for some Yiddish in my background, I had come to it as an adult, as a graduate student, and became quite adept; but it slipped badly from disuse. What I had to do was, mainly, to regain a vocabulary which would enable me to penetrate into Kafka's irony, alternative and double meanings, his sheer playfulness which often turned grimness into wit and even into broad humor. I knew I would never achieve fluency; but I felt I could reach for some degree of accuracy.

I signed up for an intense review course at New York University's Deutsches Haus, a course of study which involved several hours of class work and about fifteen hours of homework each week. Most of the others in the class were doctoral-level students who had selected German as their degree requirement, or who needed it for a specialty or discipline. Here, I regained my reading fluency, but not, of course, the degree of precision with the language I felt I needed to read Kafka in German. For that, I had to rely on dictionaries, English translations—which I compared carefully with the German text—and my own sense of foreign languages, which included a most useful one, Latin. Overall, I was never completely satisfied with my language skills. One part of my dissatisfaction was connected to my suspicion I was missing subtleties in Kafka himself; the other linked to my need to read through German scholarship, an experience which involved an intensity of application I hope never to repeat.

Through connections and networking—a kind of Kafkan secrecy must remain here—I was given Mrs. George Steiner's address in England. Now something very strange happened. I *did* confuse her with the other Mrs. George Steiner, the wife of *the* critic, *that* George Steiner. Without considering that age differences clearly should have made such confusion impossible, I went ahead. In my letter to her, I spoke of how my oldest daughter, Deborah, had been a campmate of her daughter, also Deborah, and of how my daughter, at a French camp, had taught her daughter to sail. It was an intimate, cozy, amusing letter, written in an offhand manner, eschewing that special pleading that usually accompanies requests for information or permission. I employed none of that "I would be very grateful if," or "Let me thank you in advance for," or "I hate to bother you, but." I wrote her as though we had been friends for twenty years, since her daughter and mine had attended camp together and become close friends.

Of course, I had the wrong Mrs. George Steiner—my Deborah and *the* Steiner Deborah fitted into another scenario altogether; and their close friendship had in fact ended when *that* George Steiner went into his vitriolic stance and wrote a nasty review of my Conrad biography because he was trying to strike back at my then publisher, Farrar, Straus & Giroux. His review had clouded everything between the young people, and yet when I wrote for the Kafka material, to the other Steiner family, I had decided that the wife was not implicated in the poisonous emissions of her husband. The other Steiner, Kafka's niece, responded that she did not know me, that she had no daughter named Deborah, that she wished my Deborah well, and that she found my letter so amusing (her characterization) she would do what she ordinarily never does. She gave me permission to consult the Kafka manuscripts at the Bodleian, although *The Trial*, in German hands, remained outside this permission. At the Bodleian, I would find manuscripts of *The Castle*, the notebooks, also several stories, including one I wanted to see more than any other, "The Judgment."

She indicated how it would all come around. She gave me the address of Sir Malcolm Pasley; I made a copy of her letter and wrote to him. He agreed to meet me at the Bodleian at a certain hour on a certain day and to guide me through the Kafka material. Once he had done that, he would leave me to work with the material as long as I wished. I then built my trip to England as the first stage in my Kafka research, the final stage of which would bring me to Prague for an extended stay. I planned to go from the manuscripts themselves to the streets of the city which so infused Kafka's outlook and work. For that final stage, I made arrangements, through a friend, to give some lectures at Charles University in Prague on contemporary American fiction, which I knew would be a popular topic. Since this was early 1989, Prague was still under the Communists, and it was the Communist government which formally invited me to come, to lecture, and to stay in a hotel set aside for foreign visitors, very possibly the better to bug them. But first came the Bodleian.

My wife and I arrived in Oxford, where I met Sir Malcolm at the appointed time. Before that, I had gathered all the requisite permissions from the Bodleian itself—my passport for identification, then a special card with my photograph on it for access to the special collections. Sir Malcolm spent about an hour with me, showing me the materials in the archive, and then left me with much of the most important Kafka material in hand—no one came near me for my entire stay in the Bodleian. I had been touched by his magical wand, and that was that. I was given a chair and table in the Duke Humfrey room, a place of such magnificence that I felt for the moment like royalty—Kafka manuscripts in hand, elegant surroundings, absolute quiet, perfect trust.

The notebooks, which became the basis for the diaries, proved of little use; but the stories gave up some secrets, especially the story I wanted to examine in detail, "The Judgment." This story was for me a starting point, for it came in 1912, a point of departure for Kafka; he claimed that he wrote it in an eight-hour shift. It is the first of his mature works, the first to demonstrate how he had assimilated many of the qualities of Modernism: characters who exist only in the foreground; sexual battles that lie well below the surface and have little to do with eroticism; landscapes of desolation, comparable to the urban wastelands of Baudelaire; the spareness and void associated with Mallarmé, but especially that sense of reverie or dream that Mallarmé created between events and reader, what we might call dreamtime; furthermore, conflicts that seemingly have no basis in ordinary or expected life, along with a geometric ordering of people and events; overall, resolutions that, while extreme, appear to be insufficiently motivated or explained.

In "The Judgment," Kafka defined his archetypal story, the conflict between father and son, to the degree the father condemns his son to death by drowning, a Kierkegaardian and Freudian replay of Abraham and Isaac. The son, Georg, with Herr Bendemann's injunction in mind, rushes out to a bridge and lets himself drop into the water. The "traffic" that passes over the bridge is, in German, *Verkehr*, the word for intercourse, and it is unclear in the German text (in English, it is translated as "traffic") whether Georg is condemned to die in traffic or through sexual contact. A third meaning is possible: a transaction, such as a business or commercial deal, also floats through the story, adding layers of complication. But for me the most significant element of the manuscript came in Kafka's handwriting, in the segment in which he describes how Herr Bendemann jumps on the bed just prior to Georg's suicide. The handwriting shows considerable agitation, with the kind of movement we associate with the needles jumping on a lie detector test when the one questioned fudges the truth. From this point on, moreover, the otherwise clean pages become more revised, with crossed-out words, substitute language, some uncertainty. Yet, on the whole, the manuscript of "The Judgment" is remarkably clean, reinforcing Kafka's claim that he wrote it at a fever pitch.

The Bodleian Kafka collection has as its centerpiece the manuscript of *The Castle*. It is relatively clear of corrections, emendations, or vagueness of composition. As with so many other works of Kafka, it seems to have emerged smoothly, but that does not mean he failed to experience difficulty in developing his material. As we can see from comparing the manuscript with published versions, Kafka left plenty of room for rearrangement and other editorial choices. At the beginning there is some revision, indicating hesitation perhaps, or else that desire for perfection which made it impossible for him to complete any of his longer fictions. The revisions involve crossing out and insertions, mainly to achieve greater clarity or more silhouetting of the castle's "foggishness" and inaccessibility. The aim, apparently, was to sharpen ambiguity, to deconstruct any clear narrative line, to create a confusion of the senses. After that, many pages are virtually untouched, although occasionally an entire page is deleted.

Sir Malcolm Pasley's edition of *The Castle* creates several alternatives to the English translation. Pasley's arrangement offers titles, in German, for most of the chapters, but his chief readjustment is in his division of the very long chapter 15 into six separate entities, of which he gives names to five. As a consequence, his edition of the novel contains twenty-five chapters, whereas the English version has twenty. But there are other interesting considerations, perhaps the beginning being the most compelling. One beginning is K.'s arrival at the village, which lies deep in snow, with the Castle Hill hidden, veiled in mist, dark, shadowy. K. stands on a wooden bridge leading from the main road to the village, staring into what Kafka calls "the illusory emptiness above him." But an alternate version of the opening paragraph differs, with the landlord welcoming K. The novel begins, not with the arrival, but *in medias res*, as it were, with K. seeking quarters. The first version seems more attuned to Kafka's way of working, which was to lead into murkiness with certain spatial considerations; but that does not lessen the possibilities of the second version, with the "middle" beginning as the source of the kind of confusion Kafka associated with the castle experience itself.

OVERALL, I WAS energized by my experience with the Kafka manuscripts, and after a brief stay in Paris, my wife and I proceeded to Prague, where we planned to remain for several weeks. As mentioned above, through a professor at Charles University, whom I had befriended when he came to New York on a research trip, I was invited by the then Communist government to be a guest of the Czech state and to give lectures at Charles University in Prague and other university centers. Since I spoke on contemporary American fiction, I drew large crowds made up of advanced graduate students (all my lectures were in English), faculty members from several disciplines, and translators from all over the country who had been translating Heller, Oates, Bellow, Roth, Styron, Mailer, and others into Czech. As I learned, the Communist government permitted such translations of American fiction in limited editions, which usually sold out on publication day.

But lecturing took up only a small part of my time in Prague. Most of it was spent in walking the streets in the footsteps of Kafka. The university had provided me with an interpreter to handle situations in which my spoken German was inadequate and only Czech would do. Incidentally, although Kafka wrote only in German, I did learn enough basic Czech to understand the workings of a language in which he grew up—and which to some extent was used in and around his father's fancy-goods store. The most important thing, however, was to get a "feel" for Prague—as I had earlier experienced Oxford, Mississippi, for my Faulkner biography; I spent several weeks in the Czech city. Prague overwhelms everything in Kafka, and I was especially interested in "The Castle" (Hradčany), a large area overlooking the city and itself very much a castle in its buildings, including the Palace, now the official residence of Vaclav Havel. In one of its winding lanes, called Alchemist Lane (Zlatá Ulička, or Golden Lane), Kafka's youngest sister, Ottla, had a small house which Kafka used as a studio. At No. 22, a plaque announced that the writer "lived" there, a mislabeling, since he wrote there, but lived elsewhere. No. 22 is now a shop aimed at tourists.

But while the Castle area was most redolent of Kafka, no less seductive were the narrow streets of the Old City, the area known as Old Town Square, with the building, the Kinsky Palace, where Kafka's father's store had been located; the much decorated house (Minuta House) where Kafka lived from 1889 to 1896; and the bust of the author—dating from 1986, one of the very few signs of recognition of this famous son of Prague. The Communists of course considered him a hopeless bourgeois, and for the most part he was proscribed. When I mentioned to the students at Charles University that Prague had produced perhaps the most significant writer of the twentieth century, they barely acknowledged him. Their argument was that since he wrote in German, he was part of German, not Czech, literature; and they implied that since he was Jewish, he was part of a foreign, not Czech, culture, although his forebears, as we know, were all Czechs.

In walking Prague, I came across all the places where Kafka lived—a palace where he had rented a room was now the American Embassy site. The insurance company building where he had spent most of his professional life still stood; and the old Jewish ghetto, torn down before the turn of the century, did yield up the Old Synagogue and the Old Jewish Cemetery, where the bodies were layered as many as fourteen deep and the gravestones were angled as though markers in a Mondrian painting. The New Jewish Cemetery, on the outskirts of Prague, where Kafka was buried, was notable for the meticulous way his grave (and his parents') was maintained—as a tourist attraction—whereas the rest of the cemetery was chaotic, strewn, overgrown, The people who would have kept up the graves had all been killed, through Czech complicity with the Nazis.

Despite the Soviet presence, the World War II German occupation, at least for this observer, still hung heavily over the city, especially since the majority of tourists were East German, and the German language was heard in the streets. Particularly compelling was the presence of hundreds of German tourists at an exhibition of children's drawings from Theresienstadt, the "model camp" from which the Germans sent children of all ages to the ovens. The drawings had names and ages attached to them, children of 8, 9, 10, 11. One Prague moment was always the scene of Germans silently moving through the exhibition, viewing the drawings of children their relatives and friends had killed. Prague, then, was strangely still redolent of Kafka in its insistence on itself as the jewel of middle to Eastern Europe and yet as a place of death, first from the Germans and then, in terms of harsh restrictions, from the Soviets. It was the city not only of Kafka, but of Kafkaesque.

During my stay in Prague, I heard that a group of Kafka's letters to his parents, written near the end of his life, was becoming available. This was new material, a biographical coup. They had been discovered, I learned, in a Prague bookstore and were now, with some degree of secrecy, being readied for publication. One of my missions in the city was to find out what was in those letters, since they represented the largest discovery of Kafka material in many years, a real treasure trove, even though they were near the end, not the beginning, of his life and writing career. The publisher was Odeon, and I approached the director through several common friends, the sole way I could operate in these waters. He agreed to see me, and I went accompanied by my interpreter. What ensued was an amusing three-language conversation, in which I, who knew no spoken Czech, communicated with the director in German and English, and he responded to my interpreter in Czech that was then translated for me into English. It worked. I was promised the letters as soon as the published texts appeared; on that the director was adamant, since he feared, despite my disclaimers, that I would scoop him. Several months later I received a copy of a beautifully produced book, with the handwritten letters reproduced on one page, the printed-out German on the other, interspersed with rare photographs from the Kafka archives. In addition, the letters were extensively annotated. If anyone believes that the Communist presence was fatal to Czech culture, this book alone reveals what care and attention to detail a beleaguered Czech publisher was capable of.

I now had my materials at hand. The problems were still of several kinds; these were not matters of research but of shaping, structuring, and even before that, conceptualizing. The material was, in fact, almost limitless, at least as I saw my book. In addition to a critical biography, I wanted to write a cultural history, so that Kafka's life and work were caught in an historical context. And then I wanted to connect Kafka to Modernism, the major movement of his day and one which he helped to bring to fruition. I had my major trope, Kafka as "representative man" of the century. The problem was to find some way to put it all together without forgoing a narrative line. I decided that some loss of narrative was necessary, although I knew that this would not go down well with many readers, including reviewers, who like an uncluttered story line.

There was, however, too much in the way of information, detail, historical and cultural data for me to work it into a "story." The thrust of the biography would have to be throttled when relevant details became necessary; and I did not want to stint on such details and their expanded explanation. My main areas involved Modernism itself, with all its twists and turns and paradoxes; the city of Prague as virtually another character, a parallel figure, as it were, to Kafka; the role of German life, society, and language in Prague as a minority culture within a Czech nationalistic movement; and, finally, but not least, the role of Jews and Jewish life as a further minority within the German minority. Although Kafka was not a practicing Jew and was not a devoted Zionist until near the end of his life, he was intensely Jewish, in both his own way and stereotypically. While he did not put guilt on the literary map, he did associate guilt with Jews in multifold ways that have stuck: Jewish guilt, whether fact or fiction, is the source of amusement in ethnic jokes and the source of motivation in fictions containing Jews. I needed to stress Kafka's Jewishness even while for most of his life he made Judaism itself into a kind of sport he could frolic with.

The nature of the biography, then, demanded that I break with several ground rules implicitly held by most biographers and, of course, most readers—that the narrative of a subject's life should be related chronologically. It is this emphasis which Janet Malcolm holds, whether implicitly or explicitly; when she circles the wagons of Plath biography, she seeks that "story line," even while for her it means a good deal of biographical deception.

Along the way, she cites letters as the means by which the biographer can come "fully into his [the subject's] presence." I hoped to reveal the opposite. I had Kafka letters in abundance, especially the remarkable group to his fiancée (to whom he was twice engaged), Felice Bauer, a collection that runs some 600 pages of book text. Here, once again, I had material that while part of a most significant narrative was, at the same time, matter which needed the kind of explanation and psychological analysis that throttled the narrative line. Revelations here called for extensive criticism: Kafka's obsession with Felice's bad teeth and "revolting" mouth; his denigration of himself as a suitor whom no one in her right mind would want; his appeal to her father to break off the engagement on the grounds that he, his daughter's suitor, would make everyone unhappy; his efforts to break the engagement even while he hung on to the relationship. Withal, he exalted Felice, giving her madonna-like status, far too good for him, out of her mind for contemplating marriage with such a poor specimen of a man. He makes a cultural trope of her desire for heavy, solid furniture, mocking her bourgeois aspirations even while vaunting her magnificent qualities as a woman.

The contradictions, the self-hatred, the fear of any relationship, the revulsion at Felice's person (her teeth, her mouth), his desire to keep himself pure for writing—all of these did not fit well into any narrative pattern. They demanded interruption on both a personal and a cultural scale: as part of Kafka's own response and as part of a more general misogyny which permeated Modernism and its works. But the letters to Felice were only part of the problem; there was the extensive correspondence with members of his family, especially the famous letter to his father, in November 1919, which was not delivered to Hermann Kafka but which remains one of the most significant epistolary documents in all literature. There was no way I could introduce that letter into the chronological narrative and simply allow it to stand there, announced but unanalyzed. That letter was implicit in everything Kafka wrote long before he tried to describe his feelings to his father, and it remained part of Kafka's creative life long after he addressed it.

For instead of seeing the letter as a means of communication, we should view it as an aspect of self-explanation for Kafka; not only a therapy, but an analysis that enabled him to reach into the creative part of himself where he could transcend the elements of self-debasement portrayed there. Calling it therapy is to see it as somehow curative, but to view it as a probing analysis (somewhat similar to Freud's own self-analysis in the later 1890s) is to recognize that Kafka needed it in order to cleanse himself so as to be able to write. *The Castle*, although incomplete, came the following year.

All of this was necessary for my plan, perhaps a more ambitious biography than was possible within the genre. I allowed myself up to half a million words, and the book eventually came in about 100,000 under that. I felt I could get at the "truth" of what happened to Kafka in his cultural context, although I could never be certain that I caught Kafka himself. Janet Malcolm could use this as a wedge for her further comment that in nonfiction (biography, history, journalism), "We almost never know the truth of what happened" (p. 154). She contrasts this with fiction, where we have a far greater authorial certainty. But the confusions here are immense, and they bear on biography, as well as on other genres. I was fully aware in writing about Kafka how slippery he would be: but I never doubted that there was a cultural and historical context, even a chronology of artistic, social, and political events, which gave me solid grounding. Unless we are seeking absolutes, as some form of religious quest, we do accept contexts; and some are more accurate than others, even while the subject may slide around in his or her historical setting. There can be, of course, no scientific proof, but even science often rests on certain assumptions, and what ends up as scientific may start out as intuition and random experimentation.

My suspicion that Kafka could not be completely captured did not mean that all was indeterminate, or that his life was not recoverable in a recognizable setting. Nevertheless, I had to deal with this sense of uncertainty—which, in varying degrees, all biographers share. But, then, fiction writers have their own fears, since the so-called truth of their presentation is based on even shakier premises than is biography. And if the fiction follows some shadowy autobiographical experience, it is even shakier.

All this suggests that while a Kafka biography is not final and can never be final, it can attempt something never tried with him before: a holistic view of him and his part of the century. For me, locating Kafka became coequal with and inseparable from trying to understand him. Yet there were still other problems in "getting at" a figure like Kafka, problems I did not associate with Faulkner or, later, George Eliot. If Kafka was to be my representative man, then there was some commonality between him and myself; there was a bond that went beyond ethnic, racial, and other similarities.

This suggests that I had to disengage my own sympathies, attitudes, beliefs, views of life and culture from Kafka's in ways that I think are more intense than with other subjects. The size of Kafka, for instance, demanded an interface between subject and biographer that the latter would not encounter with a lesser figure. And the cultural context itself, with Kafka located in one of the hot spots of a failing Empire, the Austro-Hungarian, and the demise of the other European empires, Romanov, Ottoman, Hohenzollern, all, was enormous. History was turning Europe over, or Europe was turning history over, and Kafka was at the epicenter, ethnically, racially, culturally, linguistically.

Since that grappling between biographer and subject could become so large, professionally as well as personally, there was the difficulty of distancing. Kafka's problematic response to his Jewishness, for example—when Jews were caught between their own minority status and the rapid growth of Czech nationalism, which was nourished by anti-Semitism—brought into play several scenarios. Relationships with one's parents (his coming from shteltls), with one's beliefs, with what one rejected, with one's attitude toward young childhood and later growth, with the way in which one was formed—all of these became loaded with meaning when the biographer is confronted by Kafka's own struggles in these areas.

And then there was the huge historical question, of what to make of Kafka in the light of further developments in Germany and in Europe in general in the decades after his death. By 1922–23, while Kafka was still alive, Hitler had emerged as head of the German Workers' Party, now renamed the National Socialist German Workers' Party, and had attempted his beer-hall putsch in Munich. The die was historically cast, as it were, and the question is whether or not Kafka was the prophet of the Nazi state and the slaughter of Jews, among several other unwanted types. At least two previous biographers, in English, had discussed Kafka as the prophet of the Nazi era, as *the* writer in the early twentieth century whose work caught the horror in store for racial minorities later in the century. Of course, such an interpretation was difficult to resist. Certainly, Joseph K.'s fate in *The Trial*—the knock on the door, the bureaucratic maze, the rationale of the irrational, the path to doom—would seem to be borne out in the fate of Germany's and Europe's Jews. The death camps seemed, in this view, the inevitable development of all the places where Joseph K. is trapped: office, warehouse, cathedral. So, too, K. in *The Castle* could be viewed as caught in the maze, until his energy and life are extinguished—once again the foreshadowing of how a bureaucracy will eliminate those it considers outsiders.

But tempting as this was, I thought it was a misuse of biography and of history. Kafka's attitudes toward bureaucracy were firmly located in the Austro-Hungarian Empire which controlled its vast territories from Vienna, and in his own observation of the large insurance company where he worked. His hatred of modern technologies, of bureaucracies in which the individual was lost, of all authority, whether state, father, or official, was all he needed to foreshadow what came, without prophesizing the future of Europe. His intense emphasis on the individual in his struggle against authority alone was a theme for the entire twentieth century, although we see it preempted by the Nazis and Stalinists. Kafka did foresee a development which led to the suppression of the individual, although he could not foresee the ways in which it would eventuate. I felt that a biographer had to be very careful, and not enter into forms of voodoo, prophecy, or the reading of innards. Every creative writer is unique and cannot be molded to fit historical or even broad cultural events; he must be seen within his own context, where his conflicts are an outgrowth of that person, in that era, in that particular culture. By rejecting Kafka as harbinger of the Nazi future, I cut across many beliefs, many reputations, and nearly all previous biographical work in English.

Not unrelated to this distancing of myself from other Kafka biographers was my position on his religious beliefs. Max Brod, whose work on Kafka was invaluable in those early days when the writer was ignored, created a strangely disproportionate view of Kafka as a religious writer. If not precisely religious, then Kafka was portrayed as yearning for some religious experience, to be centered on his Jewish background and his interest in Zionism. But the Kafka I discovered was not at all engaged in a religious quest until his later years, when he embraced a secular Zionism and a secular sense of the Hebrew language. Instead, he struggled toward something that he could incorporate into his familiar agon: the conflict between what he hoped to reach and the impossibility of reaching it. And in his early years, he was firmly secular, a socialist (not at all a Zionist), and a mocker of religious values as such. By the time he wrote *The Castle* in 1920, it is possible to observe Kafka yearning, with the castle authorities possibly tropes for godlike figures. Yet I rejected even this, inasmuch as his entire body of work was devoted to the collision between the individual and authority, and authority, divine or otherwise, for him took many forms.

A related point, and not an insignificant one for any biography of Kafka, is whether or not he felt victimized by his fear of authority and his own weakness. In most interpretations of the writer, he is viewed as possibly representative because he was the victim, and the twentieth century is the history of victimization. This is an easy path to follow, since Kafka's protagonists are tortured by a needle machine, or else pursued by demons which end in their death, or further caught in bureaucratic intricacies and behavior they cannot penetrate. Moreover, if we read his diaries and letters, we see he reveled in the role of victim: he play-acted, the Czech Shylock. In the struggle between you and the world, we recall, he told us to back the world—the victim's plea! Nevertheless, I chose to see Kafka quite differently, much of it based on the fact that he handled a difficult insurance position exceptionally well (as one of the very few Jews in a Gentile company), that he dealt with ill health heroically, and, most of all, that he set aside time in an otherwise crowded schedule to write. Writing became for him his identity as a warrior. Instead of becoming a victim, Kafka fought victimization in situations which should have sunk him. His ways of opposing victimization were often weird; but they were *his* means of fortifying a self strengthened by perceived weakness. He was a hero of literature, even though he thought poorly enough of his work to ask Max Brod to destroy nearly everything when he died, at forty.

In these areas, the biographer is caught in choices that will determine the entire thrust of the book. But these are choices every nonfiction and fiction writer must make. The historian selects those events which establish his or her historical point; the psychologist obviously works toward a particular point; and the fiction writer makes innumerable narrative choices for his and her characters. Such decisions are part of the creative or imaginative reach common to all genres; and Malcolm's attack on biography (and autobiography) as dogged by "epistemological insecurity" is an attack on all art. What she attacks is what helps to make it art.

All this returns us to the use of letters, which, like diaries and memoirs, are full of potential roadblocks. The key question is how we use letters, which are almost completely unreliable as insight into the subject unless read psychologically and, as it were, metaphorically, in structuring a biography. Writers toss off letters as personal items which are then contextualized in a biography of another era: the first is a fiction, the latter a nonfiction, a crossing of texts. Even when concerned with business matters, letters are from within, biography from without. Letters are written for the eyes of a correspondent, not for more general usage; and biography is written, not for addressees of the letters, but for strangers who may know next to nothing about the subject. Letters, in fact, come from a different "language," not simply the difference between Kafka's German and my English, but the distinction or shift in uses of language between one era and another. Letters have all kinds of cultural relationships which when cited in another time and place cannot be duplicated. The words may mean something, but the cultural assumptions behind the words are inevitably lost. Then there are the corollary questions about which letters to use, which to relegate to a secondary position, and which to ignore altogether.

In Kafka's case, his persistent irony—which we know from his fiction—also permeated his letters. In trying to make himself as unattractive to Felice Bauer as he could, he wrote of his eccentricities:

> I can stand up to the cold almost better than a chunk of wood. . . . for example, even now in November, not wearing an overcoat, neither a light nor a heavy one, walking around among well-wrapped pedestrians like a lunatic in a summer suit and little summer hat, on principle without a vest (I am the inventor of vestless attire); as for the indescribable peculiarities of my linen, the less said the better. (*Letters to Felice,* p. 30–31)

He tells her he was so weary he wanted to die; and he adds that his irritability is always at the ready. These comments come at a time when Kafka was working on *Amerika*, whose German title translates as "The Man Who Disappeared," or, more correctly, as "The Man Who Was Disappeared." Soon, he would be writing *The Metamorphosis*. If we try to take Kafka's letters to Felice, in this instance, at their face value, we miss their wit, their irony, their poignancy in which he finds himself caught between the chance of bourgeois happiness and the misery of isolated writing. He makes himself into a victim so that he can emerge strengthened by resolve; and he does this by presenting himself as such a poor specimen no sane woman would accept him. And through it all, he is not sure he is doing the right thing. Yet at the same time, he is writing or planning works which remove him even further from the world Felice expected. The complications are immense, and they argue against any easy acceptance of these or other letters as documents or data. The very unreliability of letters is their strength. They are fictionalized as much as the fiction itself.

Kafka biography, it seems to me, is the most problematical in the genre. It incorporates the difficulty of obtaining the materials, the problems of multi-leveled interpretation, the calculated destruction of narrative for purposes of inclusion, the slipperiness of the subject apart from his work, the differences of language and cultural contexts, and the temptation to make Kafka into something he was not, a prophet of the German massacre of the innocents. It forces choices on the biographer which are analogous to the choices a fiction writer must make. Every age will reinvent its own Kafka. There can be no absolute Kafka, no final figure. For someone to attack biography because it lacks truth is beside the point. Each serious biographer gets at something which is asymptotic, with tools as precise and imprecise as in any art, certainly not with the arrogance Malcolm displays toward her subject and the entire genre.

CONRAD'S BIOGRAPHY

My engagement with Joseph Conrad goes back even further than my preoccupation with Kafka. In the 1950s, I completed a dissertation on Conrad as part of the doctoral program at Columbia University, a work called *Joseph Conrad: A Modern Victorian.* In a way, that would ground my observations of Conrad some twenty years later when I decided to write *Joseph Conrad: The Three Lives: A Biography.* Before that, however, I had signed on with a publisher, Stanford University Press, for a "collected" edition of Conrad's letters. His letters had been scattered among several published volumes, and some 2000 others remained unpublished, many ready to vanish into private collections. Eventually, Stanford and I parted ways when it became clear that our original estimate of three large volumes was growing to eight sizable ones, or even more; and I signed on with Cambridge University Press for an edition of eight volumes, of which five have appeared.

In amassing these letters (about 4,000) for Stanford and then for Cambridge, I realized that I had the material for a biography, and in 1975 I sat down to try to write it, the first since Jocelyn Baines's in 1960. In 1979, I turned it in to Farrar, Straus & Giroux, where my editor, Aaron Asher, noting that I had divided Conrad's life into Pole, mariner, and writer, called it "The Three Lives," a most happy title. My main line of argument was that while in several respects Conrad was one of the first of the British Modernists in exploration of narrative strategies, he remained a Victorian in many of his values of steadfastness, integrity, endurance, and self-discipline. This view of Conrad has, I believe, prevailed.

Three Problematical Areas in Conrad Biography

All subjects, I am certain, make difficult demands on their biographers; but, I am equally certain, Conrad poses problems for his biographer that are special. There are areas in Conrad's life which are critical for our understanding of him and his work, and yet these very areas lack the necessary documentation or verification. Or else, in some instances, we have the necessary documentation but are faced with multiple decisions about its use. Thus there are two categories of problematical areas in Conrad biography: *first*, those areas which seem essential to an understanding of the subject, but for which we lack authoritative documentation; *second*, those areas for which we have documentation, but whose possibilities offer so many choices to the biographer that he can create several lives, not simply one.

In the first group, that for which we lack sufficient documentation, we may ask what Conrad was doing during the years he spent ashore. Of the twenty years he went to sea, almost half of that time was spent not on ships but ashore. Or, we may ask, what generated Conrad's decision to leave Poland just short of his seventeenth birthday? We have constructed a house of conjecture around this. Or, what were the factors in Conrad's decision to attempt suicide? We know of the deed, but almost nothing of his frame of mind in the days, weeks, and months before the attempt. In another context, what ingredients went into his choice of English as the language for his writing career? We have sporadic evidence, but it stops short of being conclusive or even satisfactory. Further, how did Conrad in his early and middle years feel about being a Pole? About the attacks directed upon him for his so-called desertion to English life and the English language? We have, once again, some documentation, but nothing definitive. Conrad eluded many of the crucial issues in his correspondence.

What really occurred in the relationship between Conrad and Marguerite Poradowska that led to the virtual silence in the correspondence after 1895? And if the correspondence did not end—we know there were letters—why were these letters suppressed or destroyed? We have convincing arguments, some of them psychologically based, but we lack sufficient hard information. To continue this first group, where we need documentation, how can we explain Conrad's shift from a sea career to a writing career, in a language twice removed from his native tongue? The shift of careers is itself difficult to explain, apart from the language involved. We can make all kinds of explanations and see the change of focus as a gradual, not an acute one, but nevertheless we are left with profound shadows and mysteries. Finally, for this same group of questions, how do we account for the leap that Conrad made between *The Nigger of the "Narcissus"* and his work of the next decade, beginning with *Heart of Darkness* and *Lord Jim*? His preface to *The Nigger of the "Narcissus"* is usually cited as the key document, but it really does not explain the leap; it explains, rather, how Conrad reached that particular point in 1897–98, not how he would go beyond it. In retrospect, it seems to us to have been the base for his further development, but it may not have been that at all.

When we turn to my second group, those problematical areas that result not from lack of documentation but from our difficulty with sifting through it to make biographical decisions, we have, once again, numerous examples. Some of these situations have to do with Conrad's relationships with other writers, which seem critical to his own stability and development. First of these is his association with Ford Madox Ford, the facts of which are solid enough, but whose interpretation has led in several directions: from Conrad's desire to apprentice himself to Ford in order to improve his English to a quasi-homoerotic attachment whose dissolution contributed to Conrad's severe nervous collapse. Another example could be Conrad's relationship with André Gide, a friendship maintained chiefly through correspondence. Gide directed a team of French translators of Conrad's work and, at the same time, offered to the older writer his earlier works, in translation, when Conrad could no longer write at that level of intensity. We can view the association with Gide in several ways. A third relationship we may cite is the one with his wife, Jessie. Although there is sufficient evidence to demonstrate that Conrad remained extremely devoted to her all his life—that the marriage was not an act of infantilism on his part but a shrewd, stabilizing move—nevertheless several commentators have viewed the marriage as lacking substance for Conrad, or as demonstrating his inability to confront real women in his life. Despite all the evidence of stability, the marriage has been given almost unlimited potentiality.

Still in this second group, where documentation is abundant, we have a slightly different kind of example: Conrad's illnesses, which began in childhood and recurred throughout his life in various forms, from physical ailments to ailments close to what Freud and his contemporaries were diagnosing as hysteria. It is possible to enumerate them, even identifying, incorrectly, I feel, an early phase as epilepsy, and then going on to cite malaria, gout, neuralgia, various psychosomatic attacks of one kind or another. Or else, we can perceive the illnesses as another form of infantilism, in which Conrad "played sick" whenever a situation became too difficult for him to face. But still another way is to see the illnesses as forms of preparation, as Conrad retreating into sickness and numbness to gather his forces for an artistic endeavor. We note this process with Virginia Woolf, and it may well apply to Conrad. But whatever decisions his biographer makes, he must confront quite varying interpretations of the same data.

Another example from this second group is the question of literary influences on Conrad, an enormous question in itself. In more recent years, the pendulum has swung toward stressing Polish influences: its literature, history, and general culture. That is all to the good, and yet Conrad himself stressed French literature, and we know that his reading while he was on board ships was heavily in English: Shakespeare, of course, but also Dickens, Cooper, Marryat, other English novelists, including George Eliot. The question of literary influences is a thorny one with all writers, since it involves areas of culture almost impossible to disentangle. Yet with Conrad, we have perhaps the most difficult case of all, spanning three cultures, three literatures, three languages. Also, in the background of his three languages was the presence of Russia, Prussia, and Austria: two more languages, three more cultures. In addition to literary influences, there were several other tremendous pressures on any writer-to-be: Darwin and Marx, Frazer and his ideas about primitive societies, Wagner and his primitive ideas about race and his sophisticated ideas about the arts, Ibsen's immense presence, issues concerning women and their rights. Conrad's imagination was prodded by an array of conflicting influences, some literary, some not: naturalism, symbolism, Polish, French, English romanticism or its remnants, the Wagnerian fever, the ambiguous realism of Flaubert, and so on.

My lists are at an end. If we reach into these episodes, we can construct biographically a Conrad of many coats, many colors, many tones. Put together in different ways, these elements can create a different Conrad for each biographer. Who is the real one? This is a valid question, for it poses an essential biographical query, which is: does the biographer let his material lead him from one point to another without "imposing himself" on it, or does he begin with some thesis, which the life then illustrates? Or does he try to work somewhere in between? I believe that in this age of psychology, biography can no longer be divested of its multiple meanings, which lie just outside of the documentation; the biographer is forced to work with theses, motifs, interpretations, analyses—as tastefully, we hope, as he or she can. He must create not only a life—although he must do that as accurately as possible—but also an understanding of it. He must have some biographical theory functioning in his life, whether it is an examination of the creative function, or an analysis of the writer in his culture. There must be integration as well as deconstruction, interpretation as well as adherence to data. Once this occurs, then biography becomes the sum of "everything," and the biographer finds himself with innumerable choices at every turn of his subject's life. We are now back to the beginning of my paper: those problematical decisions a biographer must make, even while he collects and sifts data for precise and detailed information.

I have selected three areas in Conrad's life to demonstrate how the biographer must "create" his subject's life even when he has a mine of information. My first example will derive from an association, that between Conrad and André Gide. At the second International Joseph Conrad Conference, held at the University of Miami in 1974, I presented a paper, which I later published in *Comparative Literature*, on the relationship between Conrad and Gide and how Gide introduced the older writer's work into the European literary scene. I established, then, the fact that the two met at least twice in Conrad's home in Capel House, near Ashford, Kent; that they corresponded for thirteen years, from 1911 until Conrad's death in 1924, with forty of their letters extant out of a possible fifty or more; that Gide supervised, along with Jean-Aubry, the translation into French of the entire body of Conrad's work; that Gide himself worked on the translation of *Typhoon* into French; that

Gide dedicated his *Voyage to the Congo* "To the Memory of Joseph Conrad"; that, finally, Gide had used an epigraph from *Lord Jim* at the head of book 5 of *Lafcadio's Adventures*.

The lengthy correspondence and the interworking of Gide's career with Conrad's in his last decade are indisputable. We have documentation that establishes how touched Conrad was, initially, to find himself the focus of Gide's attention. We know of the extreme difficulties Gide underwent to make the translations possible, how he had to struggle against Conrad's attacks upon him for assigning women to the job, how he acceded to Conrad's demands for particular translators and even for modes of translation. Yet once we have cited all this, there are nagging questions for the biographer of Conrad. Despite all the evidence, he must find a pattern. Perhaps the most difficult of all decisions would be to assign the association and correspondence to Gide rather than Conrad biography.

Certainly Conrad's earlier biographers did that. Jean-Aubry, Conrad's close friend and a member of the Gide Circle, while filling his biography with personal reminiscences, slighted the Conrad-Gide relationship and only briefly alluded to the correspondence. In a second biography, in which he attempted to update his earlier work, Jean-Aubry quoted from two letters but added little in this area. Conrad's other major biographer, Jocelyn Baines, refers only once to Conrad's association with Gide, quoting two lines from a marginal, published letter. If someone like Jean-Aubry, who knew both parties intimately, has chosen to see almost no significance in the relationship and correspondence, how can I justify my use? I thread the friendship through the final three hundred pages of my biography and make it an important event in Conrad's life, even as his creative powers were waning after *Victory* in 1914.

Let us enter the biographical process to see what possibilities exist. The difference in age between the correspondents—Conrad was twelve years older than Gide and well into his fifties—meant he was beyond any literary influence. Although Conrad was still middle aged, he was old in his feelings, his health, his sense of himself. With no clear influence as a guide, do we present such an association simply as an event; that is, it happened, certain documents support the occurrence, we produce the documents, and let it go at that? Or do we seek in material that might have meant more to Gide than to Conrad something that may have been of meaning to Conrad? If we do, we are leaving our documentation behind. It seems to me that in biography, as in psychoanalysis, everything has meaning; everything leads to some inclusion in the writer's thoughts and imagination, especially when another writer of considerable reputation offers homage. All such detail is of phenomenological importance. Yet this procedure means forsaking documentation and sailing out into foreign waters.

An interrelated question is, how much is permitted to the biographer who is concerned with a creative figure, with the growth of his or her imagination? Does anything go, in the sense that the subject's creative urge can lead to our unrestricted speculation about energy, talent, sources, one's use of those sources? What determines the limitations here, as the biographer moves into Freudian analysis, Jungian archetypes, Eriksonian stages of man, or other psychological tools, all of them imperfect and imprecise as ways of measuring the artistic imagination? I chose to make a good deal of the relationship between Conrad and Gide, although the letters between them with a few exceptions are not of top quality, although Conrad was himself beyond any direct influence from Gide or from the Continent, although the Conrad response was, in fact, mainly to Gide's choice of translators. My strategy was to "create" a scenario for the relationship and correspondence and then fit it into Conrad's life.

One of the perennial problems in Conrad biography is to explain the decline in his work. Some place it in 1910 after *Under Western Eyes;* I locate it qualitatively five years later, after *Victory* and *The Shadow-Line*. In either instance, there appears a recognizable decline in both creative strategies and language after 1915, in the final nine years of his life, beginning when he was still in middle age. Various explanations have been offered, from psychoanalytic interpretations based on Conrad's inability to confront the inner demons after his severe nervous collapse in early 1910, to others based on the war, on the fact that his older son was serving at the front, or to his own poor health and rapid aging. While all of these make sense, we are left with too many imponderables. I introduced the Gide association as a way of either decreasing the imponderables or, possibly, creating more.

When a writer's imagination begins to wane, especially when he is only in his early to mid-fifties, we sense wide gaps in our understanding of the phenomenon and we seek psychological explanations. I propose we can tackle the problem from the other end; that instead of seeking only reasons for the decline, we find reasons for Conrad's ability to keep going in those final years when inner voices were telling him his work was weakening—voices he acknowledged in letter after letter, including those to Gide. I chose to use the Conrad-Gide file as a way of demonstrating how Conrad held on, given the admiration and respect of Gide, given the translations which Gide promised, and given the particular tastes of Gide, which ran to early Conrad. I tried to account for Conrad's reimmersion in materials he had already put behind him, the manuscript of *The Rescue* being the most prominent; such materials reemerge under Gide's praise of his earlier career and Gide's work on translations, which brought back before Conrad the triumphs of his earliest years. I saw this circling back on Conrad's part as an aspect of the Gide influence—not Gide's own work, but the French writer's expressed tastes in Conrad's fiction and the translations themselves, which, as we have noted, offered up Conrad's early fiction for reexamination. In brief, Conrad saw his early career played back to him by way of the translations and by way of Gide's preferences, and he responded with the continuation of *The Rescue* manuscript and a series of novels which circled back to his earliest days, *The Arrow of Gold*, *The Rover*, the incomplete *Suspense*.

This is a curious use of material, and it may be biographically defective, since it makes a mockery of chronology and posits an imaginative thrust on Conrad's part which goes well beyond documentation, into the nature of creativity. I could have detailed the association with Gide in several other ways, of course: as, for instance, Conrad's need to associate with new friends after the split with Ford. Thus, Gide would become part of that second round of friends including Walpole, Jean-Aubry, Curle, Francis Warrington Dawson, replacing Wells, Garnett, Galsworthy, and the earlier group. Another way was to ignore any creative or imaginative thrust and present the association as a straightforward event: Conrad delighted by Gide's interest, Gide paying homage to a writer he admired, their wrangling over the translations as an inevitable disagreement over business matters. A third way, as I mentioned above, was to see the relationship as belonging more to Gide biography than Conrad, since Gide was the initiator and the doer, Conrad the apparent passive element here.

MOVING TO MY second example, a more fundamental episode in Conrad's life and one which has curiously not gained as much interpretation as it deserves is his suicide attempt, when he was twenty. There has been a book devoted to Conrad's exploration of suicide—Jeffrey Berman's *Joseph Conrad: Writing as Rescue*—but little effort to integrate the suicide attempt into Conrad's biography; that is, apart from the numerous suicides, near suicides, potential suicides which appear in his work, all charted by Baines, Meyer, Berman, and others. Jean-Aubry, of course, held to the duel theory, as did Jerry Allen after him. Baines established the fact of the suicide attempt, and to his credit dismissed once and for all the duel theory. But he was not interested in integrating it with Conrad's life, although he points to twelve actual or near suicides. Evidence for the attempt was first turned up as early as 1937 in a Warsaw journal and then when the *New York Times* published an article, "Conrad Once Sought to Take His Life." I am not concerned, however, with the establishment of the event. We can take it for granted. The significant element is what we make of it.

There are several coordinates here, many of them contradictory. Conrad insisted in *The Arrow of Gold* on the truth of his tale: that his fiction was absolutely true to life. But his retelling of early episodes there, with a love affair and duel as substitutes for the actual suicide attempt, is so full of inconsistencies, geographical impossibilities, anachronistic events, and romantic fantasies that we suspect Conrad indulged a family romance. Gun running with Dominic Cervoni, wild adventures and misadventures, the mistress of the Carlist Pretender, the wreck of the *Tremolino* are all run together at the time of the so-called duel, that is, the suicide attempt. Further, we have Bobrowski's letters to Conrad, which speak of gambling debts, of idling and drift, all intermixed, so that the suicide attempt is associated with a kind of Byronic existence whose authenticity is questionable. When Conrad presented it in the figure of Monsieur George, he overlaid events with so much romantic fantasy that fact and fiction cannot be distinguished. Further, according to Bobrowski's letter, Conrad extended an invitation to his creditor, Fecht, an act which suggests he wished to be found in a wounded condition; on the other hand, his attempt was a very real one. Putting a bullet through one's chest, near the heart, is not the same as taking pills and then calling one's doctor.

The possibilities for the biographer are unlimited. Suicide is such an act of desperation—even when it is not so final an effort as Conrad's—that we cannot disentangle it from the writer's imagination. It is part of his thinking even when he is not consciously thinking about it. I think *the least* of the importance of suicide in Conrad's life is the enumeration of suicides and near suicides in his work. These are significant but fail to penetrate the imagination. Far more significant is our attempt to establish what Conrad hoped to accomplish by his suicide, for he apparently intended to kill himself if he could not reestablish his life on different terms. We now enter very difficult terrain, for here the biographer is in the position I suggested above, of moving beyond his documentation into critical decisions with numerous possibilities.

The overriding motif in the suicide, I believe, was Conrad's attempt to remove himself from his uncle's dominance; it was an act of rebellion against someone who was smothering him with love, affection, money, and advice. His situation was, analogously, like that of Beethoven's nephew Karl, who also attempted suicide to escape from suffocating pressures. Intermixed with Conrad's so-called idleness, perhaps his sense of failure, his guilt about family prestige, was his uncle's criticism and his attacks on the paternal side of the family. There was on the uncle's part an effort to efface the father, Apollo, in the living Conrad, and since Apollo was for Conrad such an ambiguous force of good and ill, we have a situation that can be broken up only by an act of extreme aggression.

If he cannot kill the uncle—shades of Hamlet!—then he will kill the uncle within him, which is to say himself. But whatever psychological interpretation we put on the act, it was one of termination: of a situation, a relationship, and even a life. Since Conrad did not attempt suicide again, as far as we know, this one-time effort indicates that he was not a "suicidal type," not a person who seeks in suicide a way out of every frustrating situation. His one effort, then, fits the pattern of someone cutting himself off; and even the invitation to Fecht can be perceived as a way of divorcing himself from his uncle. For Fecht was, as a liaison between Bobrowski and Conrad, an extension of the uncle; he was, further, a living example of everything that Conrad at twenty was not. If Conrad did indeed invite Fecht, Conrad's suicidal act was one of overwhelming aggression against Bobrowski. To contain the connection on its present terms, he would have to extirpate the uncle within himself.

Conrad's decision shortly after this to sail on English ships was based not only on his inability to obtain a French berth, but on a career choice which cut himself off even more dramatically. By leaving France, he left a country with strong historical ties to Poland; by moving to English ships and the English language, he was choosing neutral ground. His uncle would find it difficult to seek him there. What the biographer has wrought with his interpretation has, obviously, moved well beyond the documentation. Yet he has insisted on the primacy of a suicidal act in the conscious and unconscious perceptions of his subject. Conrad was a man of several dimensions, at least dualistic in some of his patterns, possibly more than that. He had established marginality as his mode when he chose to leave Poland just short of his seventeenth birthday, and the suicide effort must be perceived, I believe, as a need for marginality even if that decision led to self-destruction.

Conrad's self-will opened him up to a marginal existence which his uncle could not begin to comprehend, rational and balanced in his thinking as Bobrowski was. Conrad's inner life was turbulent, and I think it is necessary to see that suicide effort as central to that turbulence. When Conrad wrote about this episode in his life in *The Arrow of Gold* he could not project any intensity, and the reason why the prose often fails is that he was being too duplicitous about his past, turning certain realities into fantasy, and then presenting the fantasy as truth. He was caught in contradictions between life and art, and art had to fail him since he could not admit the life. An admission of that life—in a work he called absolutely true—would have meant an intense entrance into his earlier years when even suicide was possible. I think *Lord Jim* makes a more telling impression of this episode, if we read the book as a shadowy existence of Conrad's own journey.

Lord Jim, then, not *The Arrow of Gold*, is a closer analogy to Conrad's life during the period when he attempted suicide; if we seek coordinates for his desperate act, we can possibly find them here. Once again, however, the biographer has left his sources far behind in order to create coherence, or the semblance of it. With *Lord Jim*—both the novel and the character—Conrad indulged role-playing; not only Marlow, but a whole series of roles through which he could locate himself in the text. He identifies with his idealistic subject and yet is capable of demonstrating that he is a bad citizen; he then shifts the terms, from Jim's absolute idealism to those who argue relativism, and finds the latter, the relativists and those who forgive, far less noble than the man who has never learned moderation. Conrad scurries around Jim, seeking this pivot and that, this center or another, trying to discover the coordinates of his behavior. These responses by an author to the delinquencies of his character have their analogy in Conrad's correspondence with his uncle. There, Conrad is a Jim figure, and the uncle is the author trying to fathom from a distance what his delinquent nephew is up to. Yet as Conrad or Marlow moves closer to Jim, even establishing perimeters of behavior for him, he eludes them, slips through, as Conrad slipped through Bobrowski's advice to his own kind of triumph. Jim's desire to die, *his* suicide attempt, succeeds, the consequence of a miscalculation embedded in his own character; and Conrad shaves life that thin, like the bullet that passed through his chest and missed all vital organs. And just as Jim has moved outside anything that Marlow or Stein or the other commentators can comprehend, so Conrad moved beyond his uncle, freeing himself. With this interpretation, the biographer may also be attempting suicide.

INTERPRETING CONRAD'S SUICIDE attempt, the biographer—unless he sticks to chronological and linear sequencing in his subject's life—moves into gray areas indeed. In my third example, we enter even deeper mists and fogs. We have documentation of a certain kind, but it is inadequate, and yet this third example is a real test for the biographer. I am speaking of Conrad's decision to write in English. Connected to this is the question of what impelled Conrad to write fiction at all, but this is too large a subject in present circumstances. It is, also, a subject with considerable documentation that leaves the biographer not much further along than when he started. The question of why Conrad decided to write in English rather than French, chiefly, or even Polish, is associated with the deepest reaches of his imagination and creative ability. Thus, to speak of this subject at all, we must leave behind biographical chronology and venture out. That nagging question arises: to what extent is this matter part of biography, when its real answer lies in personal psychology where no exploration is satisfactory?

One way to look at the question is to say that Conrad was repeating the three languages of his father, Apollo, but reversing their use, so that the father's translating English classics into Polish becomes the son's transference of his Polish thoughts into English. Another, and not dissimilar, view is that his decision to sail on English ships was, in some related way, a decision to master the language of their sailors. Conrad himself spoke in *A Personal Record* of how English first came to him as a source of wonder and power when he heard it spoken by English engineers working on the Saint Gotthard Tunnel in Switzerland. Here, English is connected to a fairyland or mythical presence, for the men—practical and skillful—were involved with a huge hole in the earth; thus English came to him as a kind of privileged moment, a revelatory experience. His first real exposure to the language outside of his father's translations was associated with the wonder of the circumstances in which he heard it. This "wonder," if we exploit it, becomes a biographical detail of some importance, but it is the biographer's construction as much as it is Conrad's.

In this connection, we could view the need to learn and then write in English as somehow associated with the suicide attempt. That is, both are efforts to efface the past and to move on, to escape that part of his heritage which was destructive so that he could do his work. In this sense, the artist, here Conrad, is programmed at birth for certain work, and he must in his developmental stages find the means whereby he can accomplish it. This theory is very seductive for the biographer, since it removes the burden from him to prove something and places it on the subject. In this view, Conrad would expose himself to one difficult situation after another until he had escaped from enough of his past to be able to transform it into literature; his passage through ships and languages, then, would be a working out of destiny, like Aeneas and his vocation to found an empire.

Still another direction, and a profitable one, although also murky, is that Conrad tested out his kind of English as he wrote *Almayer* by writing a certain kind of French to Marguerite Poradowska. Here we enter thickets of possibility. In this sense, Conrad was trying out on Mme. Poradowska, in French, the kind of language—florid, ornate, inflated, very much a language of end-of-the-century decadence—which he was attempting to use in his English novel. If we examine this idea, we see that Conrad's choice of English was a close thing, that it was associated with his knowledge of French, that it was, in fact, almost an English equivalent of French, allowing for the differences in idiom between the two languages. For the biographer, this view means that Conrad only barely edged over into English and had not made a real decision to write in that language, as he always asserted. He did say it was English or nothing for him as a creative writer, but if we see his English developing in the early 1890s, we can assert that he was so uncertain about its use that he had to try out some equivalent in French. Further, we know that Conrad hesitated and was interested in collaboration with his aunt, so that language usage becomes blurred, not at all the clear decision he announced later.

In speaking of his life, Conrad almost always justified the way things turned out. He saw himself, in middle life, as having fulfilled a destiny—the breaking away, the sailing on French and English ships, the rise to a captaincy in the English maritime fleet, the turning to writing and the use of the English language. Conrad saw it all as this way and not any other. But for the biographer each of these decisions cannot be viewed as the hindsight of middle age. Each decision has within it a multitude of possibilities, and the career, as it is perceived from the outside, can obviously go in several directions. What the biographer does know—and here he can be certain—is that his subject turned out well; that each decision fitted into a mosaic of sorts, and the career worked. Or else, there would be no need for a biography. But those decisions that come at crucial moments in the subject's life cannot be trusted to what the subject says about them, even when *he* seems certain. The subject justifies his choice, but the biographer is trying to make sense of a life that was not linear and chronological, a life that moved as much in murk as in clarity.

Conrad's decision to use English, if we can even label it a decision as such, must be perceived as part of his entire shift from Poland to England. That is, like nearly every other biographical explanation of him, it must not be isolated as a detail; we must guide it toward the larger life, as part of the whole. Thus, all his explanations, while true in a limited way, are irrelevant as documentation since they explain *his* hindsight, not what really nourished his intention when the decision was made. English became unknown territory, although familiar as a written language in his father's study; and since Conrad was an explorer, a man profoundly fascinated by geography since childhood, we can posit that language usage—in fact its very difficulties—was associated in his mind with exploration. We recall that Gide, caught up in the Conradian web of language, undertook the translation of *Typhoon*, whose maritime vocabulary was well beyond his command of English; but he, too, was an explorer, and language became part of that unknown territory which he would venture into.

I recognize that I have touched on issues that I cannot pretend to have settled in these brief remarks. I feel, however, that as new material surfaces and new biographies of Conrad are written, the latter cannot be simply a straightening out of the record. Conrad biography is something special, as I have attempted to show, for the material recovered is always outnumbered by great unknowns. We can marshal an immense amount of evidence, and yet the very things we wish to know recede even as we document our materials. I have, I hope, demonstrated that if I could call Conrad a man of three lives, it may be possible to multiply that several times over. Like Jim receding before Marlow's eyes, Conrad, to his biographer, recedes even as he becomes ever more immense.

Conrad's Life and Letters, Letters and Life

The Final Three Volumes

LET ME BEGIN by relating an unpublished letter that Joseph Conrad wrote in the postwar years. One of the things I plan to do here is to reveal how complicated Conrad's life had become in its final ten years or so, as evidenced by his letters—mainly unpublished ones—that will appear in the final three volumes of the *Collected Edition.* Most Conrad criticism and biographical study has focused on the early life, as it should, since Conrad's formation as a writer was unique in the annals of literature. We search out the smallest pieces of evidence of his reading, his associations, his family background, how his ideas were shaped and reshaped, his conception of what it meant to be a writer, his philosophy or ideology, such as it is; and we create out of that a narrative which seemingly locates, even defines, Conrad. Some narratives are more successful than others, although many are too empirically conceived, too grounded in a kind of pragmatism which cannot account for the vagaries in any life, no less than in Conrad's. Letters become part of this narrative and they, too, are unreliable, although we continue to use them, as I will here. But letters can create patterns, designs, new paradigms, so to speak. The final three volumes of Conrad's letters—coming at a time when it is generally agreed that he was closing down fictionally—reveal that he was very much alive to all aspects of his life, work, and reputation; but more than that, we see him interpreting and reinterpreting his life as his earlier fictional efforts burst upon him, in translations, collected editions, and his own use of earlier work to energize later fictions. The last three volumes give Conrad a sense of completion that perhaps we did not recognize before, focused as we were on earlier success and later decline. Memory, return, awareness of origins, all characterized the later years.

Now the letter: I will quote extensively from a letter Conrad wrote to John Quinn, the American lawyer and collector of manuscripts and first editions, a letter at the Berg, typed, but with holograph additions. While this letter alone does not give us the full play of Conrad's later years—it comes in 1919, on July 31—it does suggest how he was beginning to touch on everything in his thirty years of fiction writing. He writes:

> As to figures [for payment from Doubleday] you and I know very well that their positive value is just—nil. They are worth rather less than the paper they are written upon unless one is convinced of the perfect integrity of the man who has written them down. I am perfectly convinced of Mr. Doubleday's integrity. But I can't say that I am pleased at Mr. Doubleday complaining of my attitude and asking for assistance as though I were an impossible person. [This is of course in connection with a planned Collected Edition of Conrad's works.] For that is what it amounts to. A man is entitled to a certain amount of privacy in his affairs. Mr. Doubleday also talks and even writes about his partners' "discouragement." This looks like, diplomatically speaking, "apply pressure" (to make me mend my ways, I suppose), or in plain Anglo-Saxon, "uttering a threat." If it does not mean that, then what does it mean? That sort of thing will end up by making me feel not "discouraged" but dissatisfied—profoundly so.

With the fullest acknowledgment of your kind offer I don't think this is a case for a buffer. A buffer is inserted between inimical forces to prevent damage. But my feelings towards Mr. Doubleday (the Man and the Firm) are very much the reverse of inimical. Doubleday thought fit to approach me in his own time, and I made no secret of it that I was pleased. On the other hand I was no obscure beginner then. I had made for myself a reputation of the most solid sort, because founded on the recognition of distinguished minds here and elsewhere. My position in English letters was unquestionable; my material position was so far from being unsatisfactory that had I been alone in the world I would have been content with it. For these results I owed no gratitude to any publisher, either in the way of material help or moral support in the past. (That never failed me—but it came from another quarter). I don't see any reason why I should not have perfect liberty to argue on any point, or object to any stipulation in any scheme or plan suggested by my publisher without giving offense. The exercise of a simple right does not imply antagonism (which would be stupid in this case) and does not call for a buffer.

With all deference to Mr. D's opinion I do not like the idea of a special set of "Sea"-books. How would poor Thackeray have liked a set labeled "Mr. Thack's Society Novels"? He lived in society ("The Newcomes" could be described in a sense as a "High-Life" novel). But it would be absurd to brand him as a "Society" writer. The sea is not my subject. Mankind is my subject and "imaginative rendering" of truth is my aim. The *Mirror* certainly is a book of prose inspired directly by the sea. The *Nigger* is a study of a group of seamen with particular attention to their psychology—not to their adventures. *Youth* has been recognized for what it is too long for me to speak about it. *Typhoon*, it is generally admitted now, conveys much more than mere sea-effects. These are the only works where the sea is in the foreground. It is often seen

> in the background of my other books just as "society" (and especially London society) is inevitably present in the foreground or in the background of Thackeray's novels—without making him a "Society" novelist. To be labeled insistently as a sea writer will repel as many or more readers than it will attract, I fancy. That's why I am not enthusiastic about that scheme.
>
> Pardon the long screed. The necessity was not of my making. The worst is that I haven't left myself time to speak adequately of your interesting suggestion of dramatizing *The Arrow.* I am certain that Quinn's dramatization of Conrad would be a great success of curiosity at the very least. Unluckily I am entangled in a negotiation about dramatic rights which prevents me returning you a definite answer at once. Personally I think *The Arrow*, which consists not of action but of shades of intimate emotions, not fit for the stage—less fit for the stage than any other of my books even. It is anything but dramatic in the "Stage" sense. I am afraid you would find it a weary task after a little while.
>
> But it is certainly an exciting suggestion. What does your friend mean by "melodramatic"? That word is used so loosely! A melodrama is a play where the motives lack verisimilitude or else are not strong enough to justify a certain violence of action which thus becomes a mere fatuous display of false emotions. Violent action in itself does not make melodrama. [Farewell greetings and signed Joseph Conrad]

In several respects, this letter—and it is by no means unique among the thousand or so he wrote in his last ten years—is revelatory: Conrad reading his career intertextually. We find not only an abundance of projects such as current writings, dramatizations, a planned Collected Edition, translations into at least French and Polish, but also a reinvention of the self. Along these lines, Conrad is moving back and forth between his earlier career and his later one, imposing meaning on works, reliving them, reenergizing them when necessary, so as to reinvent what he could no longer do. In one area alone, we find a curious circling around, where paper—yes, paper—becomes Conrad's way of retrieving the past, of reseeking his origins.

As a source of income, he had for several years sold manuscripts of novels and stories to John Quinn, who paid usually precisely what Conrad requested. As he told Quinn when he began to sell material at much higher prices to Thomas Wise, a collector, "You [Quinn] are now the possessor of every line of my pen and ink first drafts." Quinn has apparently complained that Conrad has moved on to Wise, and Conrad keeps reassuring him that Quinn's items are all "pen-and-ink Conrad and *all* prewar Conrad." In that, Quinn has no rival. The emphasis on "prewar Conrad" suggests that the writer was measuring his earlier and later career; and the further implication was that Wise—and later Clement Shorter, with pamphlets—was getting lesser goods and at higher prices to boot. Conrad stresses that Quinn's collection has "completeness and unity of period" and, therefore, remains superior, incomparable.

But this is only the beginning where Conrad is feeling his way to a new sense of his self. For as he continues playing off Quinn, Wise, and Shorter against each other, so to speak, he begins to manufacture paper that he can sell. Every scrap now becomes a source of income, and we observe him creating typed versions with holograph corrections which can drive up the price. Even as he tells Quinn that the latter's collection is complete, Conrad offers an additional foty-five pages of manuscript, one the political note on Poland, the other the still unpublished Admiralty paper. Still further, as a sop to Quinn—who sold, in 1923, his Conrad collection at some of the highest prices ever paid for manuscripts—Conrad offers him a heavily revised but typed version of *Falk*—and without seeking payment. The gift is clearly to keep Quinn quiet on the reservation, convince him of Conrad's integrity in this manner, and permit the writer to continue selling to Wise at much higher prices.

The episode, which stretched out over several of the later years, fits well into any attempt to see Conrad reading himself intertextually. It, of course, returns him to his earlier work, the prewar product; it gives him a sense of renewal, in that he has become someone collectors might fight over; it enables him to continue to pour out work, even as his energy is depleted and his depression over the war and his son's dangerous role in it deepens; it works well with other aspects of his career going ahead and rounding out at the same time—translations, dramatizations, limited editions, numbered pamphlets (through Clement Shorter).

Bits and pieces of manuscript continue to turn up, so that Conrad can hold Quinn off. But now he, Conrad, had a modus operandi which allowed enormous expansion of self. In a parallel movement, the relationship with André Gide over the translation of Conrad's entire body of work into French was perhaps even more compelling. For with Gide's supervision of the translation, Conrad had gained the European recognition he sought; and with the movement of his books into French, he was able to relive his greatest productions, *Lord Jim*, especially, but also, in his eyes, *Victory*. And as part of this reliving of his earlier career, we observe Conrad swinging back to duplicate some of this work. His own earlier work influenced his later novels. The influence was partially his way of shaping a scene, but even more so as characters, tropes, perceptions. And yet, even as he was energized by this intertextual reading of himself, he could not ignore that his powers had been depleted, that the early works were not to be duplicated, only cloned.

The correspondence with Gide, which began in 1911 and continued to Conrad's death in 1924, formed the bulk of the relationship. The two met only twice. But whatever the fewness of the visits, they established a strange affinity for fin de siècle imagery, themes, and tropes. So different as men, they became literary secret sharers of sorts. The isolated individual who must come to terms with himself unsupported by social conveniences is something they shared, besides tropes of exhaustion, dissolution, and veils and mists. Incidentally, we should not neglect, in speaking of how Gide allowed Conrad to read himself intertextually, that through *Lord Jim*, among others, Conrad entered French literature, tending beyond Gide to Malraux, Céline, Camus. To complete the circle we can demonstrate that Gide was himself absorbing Conrad to his own work, a point we see specifically when he speculates in his journal on a plan for his own novel while he was reading *Under Western Eyes* and correcting the French proofs of "The End of the Tether." In this regard, intertextuality was working in Gide almost as much as in Conrad.

The question of narrative method must enter into any discussion of Conrad and Gide as "secret sharers." In Gide's work of this period, as in all of his fiction, he was a comparable conspirator in narrating his novel, at times using a semi-objective narrator (like the old language teacher in *Under Western Eyes* or Marlow in *Lord Jim*), a participatory narrator (Marlow in "Heart of Darkness"), journals, diaries, letters (Decoud's long letter in *Nostromo,* Razumov's diary-journal in *Under Western Eyes*), several distanced narrators (as in *Chance*), a convoluted time sequence carried by a combination of variously distanced narrators (as in *Under Western Eyes, Chance, Lord Jim*), and so on. Gide's experimentation with such forms reached its apotheosis somewhat later in the one fiction he called a novel, *Les Faux-Monnayeurs* (*The Counterfeiters*, 1918–1926).

In connection with Gide's fictional practices both before and during the time of his correspondence with Conrad, we should perhaps digress to a comment he made in *Un Esprit non prévenu* (1929). There he distinguished between two kinds of novels, or two kinds of thinking in regard to the novel. Gide wrote:

> The one [novel] exterior and commonly called "objective," which visualizes first of all the other person's gestures, the event, then explains and interprets it.
>
> The other, which seizes first of all emotions and thoughts, then creates the events and characters most fitted to bring these out and runs the risk of being powerless to depict anything that the author has not first felt himself. His

> inner riches, his complexity, the antagonism of his too diverse possibilities, will allow the greatest diversity in his creations. But everything comes out of him. He is the only guarantee of the truth he reveals, the only judge. The hell and heaven of his characters is in him. It is not himself that he depicts, but what he depicts he could have become if he had not become precisely himself. (Paris: Editions Simon Kra, 1929, p. 14)

The latter definition is comparable to Flaubert's "Madame Bovary, c'est moi" and fits the declarations of a long line of Cartesian Frenchmen. What interests us is that Conrad, because of his basic attachment to this tradition, made virtually the same kind of impressionistic, psychological statement in his Preface to *The Nigger of the "Narcissus"* and in his early letters.

Ten years before the "Esprit" declaration, when he was beginning *Les Faux-Monnayeurs,* Gide attempted to work out these ideas, which he noted in his *Journal des Faux Monnayeurs.* Focusing on the "post of observation" and the narrator's role, his comments recall Conrad's utilization of Marlow as narrator, observer, or active participant. Gide wonders whether Lafcadio (a central figure in *Les Caves du Vatican*) should serve as narrator or observer in *Les Faux-Monnayeurs*: ". . . it would be a narrative of gradually revealed events [What Conrad and Hueffer in 1900 had called "progression d'effet"] in which he would act as an observer, an idler, a perverter. I do not think this would necessarily restrict the scope of the book, but it would prevent me from approaching certain subjects, entering certain circles, influencing certain characters" (June 17, 1919). Gide remarks that he is afraid he may be trying to cram too much material into one book, that no form can accommodate so much substance.

Earlier, Ménalque's advice in *L'Immoraliste* (1902) parallels, uncannily, one side of Kurtz and Jim, even young Lingard:

> "If only the people we know could persuade themselves of the truth of this [to live naturally]! But most of them

> believe that it is only by constraint they can get any good out of themselves, and so they live in a state of psychological distortion. It is his own self that each of them is most afraid of resembling. Each of them sets up a pattern and imitates it; he doesn't even choose the pattern he imitates; he accepts a pattern that has been chosen for him. . . . The part in each of us that we feel is different from other people is just the part that is rare, the part that makes our special value—and that is the very thing people try to suppress. They go on imitation." (New York: Knopf, 1920, pp.126–27)

There is a good deal of looping here, and in this regard, for Conrad, we can cite a well-known passage from Roland Barthes, extending Barthes words to Conrad's presence in his later texts as a result of his renewal of self in his earlier ones. Barthes:

> Every text is an intertext; other texts are present in it, at variable levels in more or less recognizable forms: the texts of the previous culture and those of the surrounding culture; every text is a new fabric woven out of bygone quotations. Scraps of codes, formulas, rhythmic patterns, fragments of social idioms, etc. are absorbed into the text and redistributed in it, for there is always language prior to the text and language around it. A prerequisite for any text, intertextuality cannot be reduced to a problem of sources and influences; it is a general field of anonymous formulas whose origin is seldom identifiable, of unconscious or automatic quotations given without quotation marks.

The voice we hear in a later Conrad work—and which gives his final fictions the sense of completeness—is not only the distinctive voice we associate with a given writer's own work, but a voice which has been rerouted through another—in this instance, through Gide's interposition—back into the writer.

How much, for example, does the arrow of gold owe to the silver of the mine? Or M. George to Jim of *Lord Jim*? Or *The Rover* to "Youth"? Or *The Rescue* (both an earlier and a later work, an intertextual battleground, as it were) to *Victory*? Or the unfinished *Suspense* to *The Secret Agent* or *Under Western Eyes*? We cite only some of the works being "returned" to Conrad through Gide.

We can be more specific. We cite the following novel outline:

> X. indulges in a tremendous effort of ingenuity, scheming, and duplicity to succeed in an undertaking that he knows to be reprehensible. He is urged on by his temperament, which has its exigencies, then by the rule of conduct he has built in order to satisfy them. It takes an extreme and hourly application; he expends more resolve, energy, and patience in this than would be needed to succeed in the best. And when eventually the event is prepared to such a point that he has only to let it take its course, the let-down he experiences allows him to reflect; he then realizes that he has ceased to desire greatly that felicity on which he had counted too much. But it is now too late to back out; he is caught in the mechanism he has built and set in motion and, willy-nilly, he must now follow its impetus to its conclusion. The event that he no longer dominates carries him along and it is almost passively that he witnesses his perdition. Unless he suddenly gets out of it by a sort of cowardice; for there are some who lack the courage to pursue their acts to their conclusion, without moreover being any more virtuous for this reason. On the contrary they come out diminished, and with less self-esteem. This is why, everything considered, X. will persevere, but without any further desire, without joy and rather through *fidelity*.

This long paragraph, by Gide, not Conrad, demonstrates how completely the French writer has moved subconsciously within Conrad's *Under Western Eyes* and has, in his way, provided a way of glossing that novel. But more than that, we see how Gide was providing the grounding for Conrad to bounce off him, going intertextually from his own novel, to Gide's remaking of it—what would become *Lafcadio's Adventures* in 1914—and then rebounding from Gide's remaking of Conrad's novel so as to produce his own version in *The Shadow-Line* and in parts of *The Arrow of Gold*, or even in the revision of *The Rescue*.

When Conrad wrote Gide about *Nostromo*, on June 21, 1912, he depreciated the novel, calling it a "dismal failure" and saying that there is something which obstructs or impedes it. Yet Conrad did not really believe this, but was making the remark to indicate what he thought Gide thought, that the novel was "badly made" so as to distinguish it from sleeker, more formalistic French fiction. As for Gide, he wrote in his Journals, although not to Conrad, that he found it too boring to continue.

We recognize how Gide's desire for purity of expression is related to his insistent need to shade meanings and secure muted lights and darks. Like Conrad, he is a novelist of shadows. In *L'Immoraliste* the narrator Michel relates his own story to a fixed audience (summoned for that purpose); but, even more, it is a story, as we are told in a kind of preface, which has passed through the "I" of the novel, just as Marlow's story has passed through the "I" of "Heart of Darkness." Thus, as reader or audience, we are involved in several elements: in the "I" who is in possession of Michel's story, in the audience itself (two childhood friends, Denis and Daniel), then finally, in Michel's first person narrative framed by the external narrative device. And all of it is caught in an even more extended frame, for the "I" of the external story is telling it in a letter to his brother. The similarity to "Heart of Darkness" is uncanny, although there is, so far as I can determine, no way in which Gide could have been familiar with Conrad's novella at this time. "Heart of Darkness" did not appear in book form until 1902, and it is unlikely that Gide read the story in *Blackwood's Magazine* in 1899. If we reject all notions of a direct influence, we must recognize that even as their psychological needs converged, Conrad and Gide were reaching certain common technical assumptions about the novel.

When the correspondence and ensuing friendship begin, we see that the younger man somehow recognized a kindred spirit in the older writer, which would explain Gide's two visits, in 1911 and in 1912, to Conrad's home in Kent. None of the above crosscurrents, however, is in any way conclusive proof that Gide was imitating Conrad. Certainly what we know of Gide through his journals and letters indicates no further involvement than a deepening interest in Conrad's work, with special attention to the *Lord Jim* period. Nevertheless, on the eve of the correspondence, we find two writers who, while seeking self-expression, are also struggling toward some definition of fiction as a way of containing that expression, and finding such a definition in curiously parallel ways. Despite their personal need to break out and confess all, they hid behind narrators, perhaps because they felt that life and art must somehow be separated. Even when their letters begin to move back and forth in a regular pattern, we find some of the same hiding, some of the same distancing of themselves from their real personal concerns.

Gide saw in *Lord Jim* the pinnacle of Conrad's art, at the very time when Conrad was writing a reductive version of *Jim*. We are not certain when Gide read the novel—the French version was not published until 1924, but Gide could read English, obviously; he called it "my preferred book." He saw in its sense of dualities and opposites the material of his own fiction; and it was his steady praise of *Jim* which, this article claims, induced Conrad to try variations on it in his later fiction. Although this return to *Jim* through Gide was only one aspect of Conrad's recycling of his career, as well as its completion, it was a major consideration.

While Gide deemed *Under Western Eyes* masterly, he did consider it overworked, "overconscientious," a little too much without ease. Gide saw an interrelationship between *Jim* and *Under Western Eyes*, for both contained what the French writer called "that irresponsibility of the hero, to redeem which his whole life is subsequently engaged." Gide found some of the same in *The Rescue*, later, and we can reason that Conrad picked up this novel after so many years as the result of his feeling Gide would approve of it, based on *Jim*. Meanwhile, Gide was himself trying to translate *Typhoon*—Conrad insisted afterward that it simply did not translate into French—and was deeply worried about Conrad's objection to Isabelle Rivière's translation of *Victory*.

By the time Conrad completed *Victory*, the translations were in place; and we observe Conrad—when the time for *that* translation came—hovering over *Victory*, as part of a world which would include *The Arrow*, *The Rescue*, *The Rover*, at least. Here the seemingly inadequate translation by Isabelle Rivière created a rift with Gide only a short time after they had cemented what seemed a friendship and kinship. *Victory* appeared, to Conrad, we can speculate, as a kind of pivotal point in his career; after that, he moved toward a rounding off, a return, a completion; but when he was presented to the French public, he wanted a masculine-driven translation, as if to fortify his position as a manly writer.

Here we enter psychological thickets. What we discover in Conrad's later work, given its less intense substance, is a psychological counterpart to loss of personal control: located in certain sexual ambiguities in his later texts, in a personal malaise which went beyond the war years and worry over son Borys's fortunes at the front. Not only was there illness and pain from old ailments, there was the emotional crisis created by or reinforced by Gide's translations, and perhaps also by the beginnings of translation into Polish of his earlier work.

The Conrad of the final three volumes of the letters, then, is not a simple man in decline, but a very complex writer who has found himself moving in several directions, even as he senses his powers waning. Gide's expectations and deference set a mark; Gide's translations set that mark even higher; for the introduction into European literature by way of Gide meant a tremendous boost even as it signaled waning powers. Conrad wrote to Macdonald Hastings, the adaptor of *Victory* for the stage, that his fear is that for twenty years he has been "performing on a tight rope (without net) and I am still at it, and I am 58 last birthday." He says morbidly that he would like to see a brighter prospect, "if only on the brink of the grave."

Then shortly afterward, on December 30, 1917, Conrad measures himself against Gide, the older writer against the insurgent. Gide has just been highly praised in the *Times Literary Supplement*, while he, Conrad, presents himself as not even working, while he, Conrad, had even stopped thinking of work. He does not even have anything to say to his friends; he is alone and forgotten. The phrasing is clear: Gide is basking in praise, whereas Conrad is struggling, immersed in self-doubt, immobile, fearful of even holding a pen. The subsequent Conrad letters to Gide suggest numbness, a tamping down of all meaningful feeling, a withdrawal, his letters merely a way of keeping in touch.

Yet Conrad was being disingenuous, for even as he played down his ability to work, he was about halfway through *The Arrow of Gold*; but the personal nature of the material—and his return to a *Jim*-like text which he could not maintain—may have convinced him he was simply treading water. Work on the *Arrow* rather than heartening him seemed to send him further into depression, and for that we must, at least in part, thank Gide and his efforts.

By 1919, the correspondence was rapid and intense as Gide began his work on *The Counterfeiters*, his last creative work of length and the one book of his he called a novel. In some curious parallel, it was a final effort which we can equate to Conrad's work on *Victory*, however one views that novel. In *Victory*, we have the meeting point of Conrad's powers and then his own sense of decline; with Gide, *The Counterfeiters*, published in 1926, was perhaps the acme of his fiction even as *his* decline was to begin. Here we find some reason for Gide's immersion in the Conrad translations: a compensation in Conrad's strong early work for his own waning creative ability, a kind of psychological sharing in which the French writer could connect himself to something significant and highly literary even as he sensed his own powers diminishing.

But as the two men sought common ground, the peace was broken by Conrad's outburst over the translation of *The Arrow of Gold*, recalling a similar incident with *Victory*, this time in a letter dated November 4, 1919, unpublished, at the Doucet in Paris. Once again, we must emphasize that Conrad's anger here is linked intertextually to his juxtaposition of *The Arrow* and his earlier work, especially *Jim*. He felt there was negligence in the translation of *Arrow*, and from that he extrapolates that he, Joseph Conrad, is not being taken seriously; that, in fact, some conspiracy has taken place to make him look foolish. He says that a woman has "seized upon" his book, and the image is one of harpies and amazons readying themselves to destroy him, or even raping him and stealing his novel. Flashing before him is his entire career, somehow traduced and betrayed by female translators; and he repeats the verb, "s'emparer," in letters to his friend, Jean-Aubry.

To the latter, he vows to protest Gide's choice of Madame Maus (an unfortunate name). Conrad indicates that Gide ignores his suggestion that the translation be given to Jean-Aubry. There is disconnection at every point now, an irrational element, as Conrad sours, Gide attempts to retrieve a worsening situation, and Jean-Aubry, ever loyal, is caught in the middle.

Gide responded that he found the contretemps astonishing, having read Conrad's protest "with stupor." But he agrees that the translation must go to Jean-Aubry, despite the fact that Madame Maus is well into the work. He tries to grapple with Conrad's insistence that he desires a "masculine translation"—apparently missing entirely that for Conrad—as earlier with *Victory*—it was a matter of reaching back along the line of his best work which he wanted to be manifest in the translation. Somehow, an impossible position on the part of an aging writer finds its origins in the kind of work he can no longer produce, but which he wants to be revealed in a translation. Amusingly, when the dust settles, Conrad thanks Gide and misspells Aubry as Aubrey.

The correspondence was now more balanced, with praise going back and forth. Incidentally, when Conrad's *Collected Edition* appeared, he gave away only three sets, one of them to Gide, the others to Edward Garnett and to Jessie Conrad's surgeon, Sir Robert Jones. By the end of 1920, Gide was reading *The Rescue* and arranging for a translation—finally, a translation of *Lord Jim*—while working on *The Counterfeiters*, which had a central intelligence such as Marlow. Gide extravagantly praises *The Rescue*, surely a strategy for maintaining peace with Conrad. The intermingling was now complete: with Gide's translation of *Typhoon*, his dedication to Conrad in his *Voyage to the Congo* (in 1927) and his heavy leaning on *Heart of Darkness* in that book, preceded by Conrad's attempt to see Gide at Cuverville in Normandy in 1923, the settling of the *Victory* and *Arrow* translations—all this provided Conrad with a mirror image of his earlier work, which both strengthened and dismayed him.

Gide's Conrad was the exotic seafaring writer who returned from strange lands with tales few had ever told so well—Henry James fixed Conrad in much the same way. It was this fixation on early Conrad that perhaps made Gide become an admirer of *The Rescue*, whose Lingard suffered like so many Conrad protagonists from what Gide called "moral anguish" or "moral distress." Yet even as Conrad disliked being labeled a sea writer, as we saw, he tried to recreate that "moral anguish" or "moral distress" in his later work.

For Conrad, the final ten years or so are a curious time, full of projects and ideas even as he can't quite make any of them work out. The situation with Gide was a kind of metonymy: as he sank even deeper into depression and anxiety over the war, over failing powers, over Borys's dangerous posting at the front, he had paraded before him what had, in effect, made him Joseph Conrad. The subtext of this was that Gide's kindness only deepened Conrad's conviction that he had to return to an earlier time, all abetted by the translations into Polish, the appearance of a Collected Edition, the sudden value of his "paper," even typescript with a few holograph revisions—a curving around that deeply affected his later work, as he labored to catch earlier tones, attitudes, positioning. To this we might add Conrad's interest in having his works dramatized: at one time or another, he was following up on *Victory, The Arrow of Gold,* and *The Secret Agent* from his most productive period, and even *Nostromo.* Quinn suggests that he himself dramatize *The Arrow of Gold,* but tempting as this sounds, Conrad has misgivings; for he fears that Quinn might turn it into melodrama. But even these peculiar feelers—here from a lawyer and collector—bring Conrad to life and keep returning him to earlier times. The suggestion from Quinn came when Conrad was working on *The Rescue.*

What is the meaning of it all? These remarks only scratch the surface of Conrad's complicated later years. Intertextuality, rounding off, a sense of completion, Conrad reading Conrad, Conrad reading Gide and seeing in him Conrad, and all the possible variations suggest that any simple "decline" theory is insufficient. There were no more *Lord Jim*'s or *Nostromo*'s or *Secret Agent*'s or even *Victory*'s, that is true, but these works reappeared in Conrad's final work. As the letters from 1917 to the end tell us, he never gave up being Conrad.

FAULKNER

I wrote the Conrad biography out of my sympathy with a good deal of Conrad's fiction and my abiding interest in Middle and Eastern Europe. At that time, in 1979, I did not consider myself a biographer simply because I had written a biography. I followed the Conrad with a long book on postwar American fiction and the aforesaid *Modern and Modernism.* My book on American fiction brought me to William Faulkner, whom I had been teaching to both graduate and undergraduate students; but the one book that stuck in my mind as a supreme masterpiece, *Absalom, Absalom!* drew me in to discover more about the man who wrote it. In fact, my entire enterprise in *William Faulkner: American Writer* (1989) was an attempt to discover how that man could have written that book, which I considered the finest long fiction since the great period of Henry James at the turn of the century.

In my research, I experienced little personal connection to Faulkner's life—although I spent a fruitful semester as visiting professor at the University of Mississippi in Faulkner's hometown of Oxford—but I felt an enormous admiration for his achievement, for the above novel but also for *The Sound and the Fury, As I Lay Dying, Light in August,* fifteen or twenty of the short stories, and the collection of pieces in *Go Down, Moses,* plus parts of his other books. I was struck by the fact that in a period of about twelve years, from 1928 to1940, Faulkner was able to turn out one magnificent book after another while dogged by money problems, a bad marriage, and the need to spend time writing scripts in Hollywood. My attachment to the fiction was such that it sustained me for 1,200 pages (still about 800 pages short of Joseph Blotner's two-volume life); and when I was finished I felt even greater respect for Faulkner the writer.

Biography and Narrative

Faulkner's *Absalom, Absalom!*

William Faulkner destroys the objectivity of the text, and this creates enormous problems for the biographer. The latter finds himself or herself forced into numerous possibilities of narrative discourse, not only in Faulkner himself but in all major writers of "telling" and "retelling," such as Proust, Conrad, Woolf, James, Ford, and even in lesser writers who establish several levels of narrative. The question of what Gérard Genette calls "subjective coloration"—whereby narrative, which seems objective, passes over into discourse, which is subjective—embodies one of the major problems in literary biography. The "how to" of the biographical struggles problematically against the "what is" of the subject's own work.

Although my examples will come from Faulkner and Conrad, the choices created for the biographer are discovered, as noted above, in several kinds of subjects. Of course, the simple chronological or narrated life does not reveal these problems; nor does the life told as a chronicle—as in Najder's *Conrad* or Blotner's *Faulkner* where accumulated details *become* the life. As soon as the biographer, however, attempts to use the subject's writing as biographical data, then the dimensions of the situation become complicated. In Faulkner's five or six major fictions, he had mastered the ways in which his narrators both express and conceal the self. *Absalom, Absalom!* becomes the greatest instance of this method of working. As readers—apart from our role as biographers—we have to deal with Faulkner's mastery of this and then decide *what* it is we want to believe. I do not mean that we utilize the work in any direct, confrontational way, but the subject's method itself has biographical implications of disguises, veils, shields, arcane selves, withdrawal and retreat, alternate selves, qualities of transformation. We are caught between discourse and history, between rhetoric and what might be "truth." In Faulkner's major novels, his method becomes what scientists call the field of force, but which for the biographer winds back to questions of narrative, ultimately to how we choose to read and how we use that reading as biographical data.

We catch a glimpse of an approach in Stephen Heath's remarks on *Finnegans Wake*—remarks, I feel, that can be applied as well to some of Faulkner and Conrad. The dilemma for us as biographers, and as readers, is what subjective data we can derive from a book like *Finnegans Wake*. Here we have moved away to the very edge of what biography can glean from an author's work, with the further dilemma of what can be accepted as "truth" against what is discourse. For Joyce has subverted the objectivity of the text at every turn, especially since the novel is itself a dreamwork and responsive, accordingly, to the distortions implicit in dreams. Stephen Heath's point—and it is, I think, a narrative point—is that the "violent ambivalence" of a text must not be translated into another language in order to become "readable"; instead, the problems created by the text are themselves the theme or idea. They are not questions to be solved, but are the very uses of writing. To put it another way: the signifier is not the vehicle through which we derive meaning, but an element in its own right; and the way the signifier is packed with potentialities or used as a center for clustered meaning is *meaning* itself. For Joyce, in Heath's description, communication in language is replaced by an examination of how far language can be extended while still maintaining some level of interaction. Stated still another way: Joyce sets out to test the limits of language so that he can show the boundaries beyond which language may go without losing its function as language.

To relate Faulkner to this, in narrative terms, in a novel like *Absalom, Absalom!* he does not create a signifier in Quentin Compson, who points toward meaning, but makes Quentin himself the test of what can be communicated. The problem for Quentin, and for Faulkner behind him, is the extent to which a narrative can be established when all narrative is embedded in personal histories which lack objectivity. If all is subjective, how does one retell it? And if one decides a story cannot be told, then how does one retell it? And does repeated retelling create a more accurate story or does it remove us still further from what may have occurred? What story, then, can Faulkner tell if his main character in that telling does not himself know what story he is relating? Whether, in fact, he is telling the story of Thomas Sutpen, or of himself, or the story of the South, or a perverted version of the South? And how can his Harvard roommate, Shreve, receive this story when the teller is himself so uncertain about what he is communicating?

Yet for the biographer, these narrative problems which are so problematic for the writer must be resolved. Biography thrives on certainties. Whatever its final arrangements, it seeks chronological order, or some sequencing from birth to death of the subject. Its very premises are those of an orderly procedure. Facts must make their appearance: birth, early growth, marriages, children, books published, career turns, death, and other aspects are all part of the database of biography. These are elements of certainty. We know these things occurred and must include them, however we may slight or highlight them individually. Yet as soon as we try to draw on the subject's novels, stories, or plays in literary biography, we find a very different sequencing; and this sequencing is particularly acute in writers like Faulkner and Conrad.

The problem, thus far, is several-fold. Faulkner and Conrad use narrative strategies whereby they can subvert the very element they are creating. This means they have placed whatever they say in uncertainties, in the seams, as it were, between data. In writing about their work, whether critically or biographically, one must become aware of their levels of narrative, and in particular their use of verbs—about which more later. What they have done is to create a way in which discourse arranges the story, or presents it to us. The events in the story are in one verb frame; the means of getting the story told, or to the reader, is in another verb frame, perhaps in more than one. By subverting narrative, these novelists actually expand it, creating multi-leveled internal activity, reliance on pastness, recapturing of memory, a probe into inner worlds dependent on verbs.

For the biographer, there are other dimensions of no less complication. For he or she, as suggested above, must somehow connect those works to those writers, and find in the work the means by which inner lives can be brought to the surface. To use an analogy, the works serve as a kind of palimpsest, *in the hope that the author will himself, or herself, be revealed.* In writing of the Proustian palimpsest, Genette touches on the problems of narrative, the distinction between manifest and latent narrative, or the counterpointing which the biographer provides with his subject. "The relationship between the work and the system that engenders it," Genette writes, "is therefore ambiguous: the Proustian ideology is not a 'superstructure,' a useless excrescence that one could quickly dismiss in order to approach Proust's work independent of it and in a 'healthier' spirit; on the contrary, it represents an inevitable reference and even, in a sense, the only possible reference for the reading and understanding of the work. But at the same time the positive meaning that it is intended to give to the work is, if not betrayed, reversed and finally *absorbed* by a counterpoint of contrary movements: that which carries a message in plain language and that which accomplishes this message to the point that it becomes obscure and gives way to the question that has no answer" (*Figures of Literary Discourse*, trans. Alan Sheridan. New York: Columbia University Press, 1982, pp. 225-26). Or the palimpsest can be viewed another way: that if we keep peering at the author, we will find, through him or her, ever-deeper levels of the meaning in the work, until, eventually, it will stand forth as the final text, the text buried beneath all the other matter. But even as we push ahead with this quest, the author has laid his land mines in the form of narrative strategies which are destined to subvert our very efforts. In *Absalom, Absalom!* Faulkner has located most of the significant information, chronologies, and narrative strategies in areas of speculation. Except for a few basic facts which have been externally established, nearly everything that Quentin Compson tells Shreve in their room at Harvard is "created"; that is, it is put into a verb tense which has meaning only to Quentin as he tells the story. By "verb tense" here, I mean he has appropriated the material for his own use, transferring it into what he sees or can see, and has given it its own verbs. The true verbs, so to speak, cannot be determined because Quentin has insisted on his; and we must, to read the book, accept some version of *his* arrangement and emphasis even as we recognize it is unreliable subjective discourse.

The biographer, then, if he wishes to use *Absalom, Absalom!* as a primary text in understanding Faulkner, must fight through all of Faulkner's narrative strategies, via Quentin, in order to sort out what can be useful, what is speculative and imagined, and what must be discarded. And yet despite these difficulties, *Absalom* as the highest point of Faulkner's creativity cannot be ignored as a source of biographical information; we cannot merely fit it chronologically into his life and leave it at that. On the contrary: the book in its telling and retelling, in its speculation, imagined events, created data, in all of this, is a means of understanding Faulkner himself, if we can only find how to enter the book and return with something we are certain of. But, as suggested, even as we attempt that, Faulkner is covering his tracks by the very method used in *Absalom* to prevent us from finding him out.

There are still other ways to see the problem. One of them is to use the critic Gerald Prince's concept of the "narratee," which raises the question of whom the narrator addresses. In other words, who is the recipient of words spoken by the narrator? If we ask this question in connection with *Absalom*, we stare into the mouth of the cannon. In the novel, Shreve is ostensibly the narratee; but we can argue that Quentin is also, for he becomes the morbid recipient of the information, such as it is, which he passes on to Shreve. Even as Quentin wants Shreve to try to understand the mind of the South, the ultimate purpose is for Quentin himself to understand. The novel pivots, really, on his ability to comprehend the past, and if this is so, then can we argue cogently that he is the recipient, even while he is the chief narrator?

But that is only part of a complicated equation; for if Quentin is both narrator and narratee, and Shreve is also a narratee, where does that leave the reader of the book? Surely the reader is a narratee of sorts, but he is excluded from the process by a series of strategies which keep him on the outside. The reader, accordingly, is a narratee who is only incidental to the process going on in the book. The book is not being written, as it were, to reach the reader, but to reach Quentin: to shape in Quentin's mind something of history and pastness and memory, so that, as narratee, he can function. Quentin lives on the edge, between the memory and pastness of Sutpen and the beginnings of a new South; he is himself a representative of that new South, since instead of going to Ole Miss he attends Harvard. As someone on the edge, he must comprehend what he hears, or else he will sink, as he does in *The Sound and the Fury*, where he is a suicide by water.

The reader of *Absalom*, no less the biographer of Faulkner, does not wish to sink. As receiver, he must try to modulate the entire question of whom Faulkner is addressing; and he cannot finally settle for some obvious conclusion that Faulkner is working through a process or procedure which is itself the book, although that response is not entirely wrong. What the biographer must try to determine, going at the problem from this end, is what the text is, to whom it is addressed, to what extent it is a biographical construct when it seems more like a labyrinth to entrap the reader, as it entraps Quentin, the ostensible primary narrator and receiver. As becomes obvious, questions of narrative cannot be disengaged from questions of audience. The more questions we ask, the thicker the complications become for the biographer.

If we use *Absalom* as our immediate example, then perhaps by defining qualities of "order," a narrative term also suggested by Gérard Genette, we can find an entrance for the biographer. Drawing once again on Proust's use of Marcel, Genette sees "order" as the story's own chronology working against the way in which discourse arranges the story, or presents it to us. This is, as we examine it, basically one of the problems in biography: the biographer's discourse works against the order of the subject's own life and becomes further complicated when it tries to introduce the subject's works—with their own order—into this discourse. The events in the subject's life are in one verb frame; the means of getting the subject's life told is in another. By this, we mean historical contexts have changed from subject's to biographer's time; but more than that, grammar is itself at issue. Even in something as simple as tense, we find difficulties; for while the subject of the biographical study is moving along in his or her present tense, the biographer has shifted to the past. The subject is alive and doing this or that, whereas the biographer—even with a living subject—has made him dead by locating him in the past tense. Furthermore, mood may play a part. The mood of the verb for the subject of the biography may shift from indicative to imperative to subjunctive, especially the first and last, whereas the biographer has relocated all modalities into the indicative. Narrative strategies of the biographer call for the indicative mood as the mood of telling; the modals for the subject living his life range much further.

Another element that can easily be lost occurs when the biographer attempts to capture simultaneity: there are the simultaneous events going on in the subject's life which the biographer must arrange chronologically, thus disrupting the verb tense of the very elements he is trying to describe. Still further, the simultaneity in a given work in which events are layered cannot be quite assimilated into biographical discourse. For example, if one looks at Conrad's *Heart of Darkness* as a piece of narration, apart from its other significance, we see that it might afford several insights into Conrad biographically if only we could grapple adequately with the narrative strategies. The levels of text are of several kinds, all of them occurring in different tenses, and yet in writing of this work in a life of Conrad, the biographer flattens everything out to create a chronological and coherent sequence. The "what" of the text and the "how" of the biographer's need inevitably clash. In *Heart of Darkness*, several levels of temporal sequencing are apparent. We have the A-text, in which the novelist, Conrad, is in complete control of all the words. Then we have the B-text, in which the novelist has relinquished control of the narrative to the "I" person on board the *Nellie*, a surrender of narrative that occurs very rapidly. The "I" person, in turn, gives up narrative control—although not completely—to Marlow, what we may call the C-text. Yet this is only the beginning. There is a D-text, which includes those elements that are implicit in Marlow's narrative, but which he has not first hand knowledge of—Kurtz's "unspeakable rites," for example. The E-text contains those elements Marlow comments upon, but whose validity may be unreliable, such as his report of the significance of Kurtz's "The horror. The horror." The F-text contains those elements which fall into the seams—Kurtz's relationship to the native woman, for one, or the methods he used to extract the ivory, or the transformation which took place in him as he went from missionary to plunderer. We can also predicate a G-text, if we wish, which exists like the tree falling in the forest which no one hears. We can move toward an H-text, if we assume that a good deal of what Marlow saw, or failed to see, cannot be captured in language; that Marlow's effort to convince his comfortable, bourgeois audience of the horrors out there are inevitably defeated for lack of language; that, like the Ancient Mariner, he has told his tale previously, in the hope that by retelling he may find the words which suit the experience. Or else, conversely, he must repeat his tale with the full knowledge that only repetition will do because his experience cannot find the accommodating vocabulary or rhetoric to capture it.

If we are ingenious, we can perhaps continue with further texts, through the alphabet. Yet while all this is an interesting critical procedure, we may wonder what it means biographically. Yet here is the biographer's dilemma, as he or she observes the texts proliferate. Surely there is biographical data lying in Conrad's narrative scheme. It is not sufficient for the biographer merely to relate Conrad's own trip to the Congo in 1890 and then his reshaping of it in fictional terms, such as we see in most biography. By so doing, the biographer has eliminated the very qualities of the novella which reveal the way in which Conrad reshaped his experience to create the fictional work. That is a biographical question. And here we enter thickets of speculation, but it is this very area that the biographer must transfer into the strategies which inform his biography. Here, it seems to me, we have the nub of the very problem which narrative modes provide for the biographer who wishes to employ critical skills as well as biographical ones. History or historical procedures now give way to other means, in which sequencing and chronology become submerged by other issues. Psychological questions are perhaps not distant; but, primarily, what we have in hand are questions in which narrative overlaps or crisscrosses with biographical needs.

In Conrad, is it enough to point out the difficulties here? Or is it necessary to find some path through the thickets of these multiple texts as dimensions of biography? One way to "see" the material, to use a favorite Conrad word, is to relate it to qualities of imagination in the author. Perhaps what we can say of his imagination—how it was formed, or what it meant—will help us relate Conrad the narrative juggler to Conrad the biographical subject. We recall that on and off for twenty years Conrad went to sea, before he attempted to set himself up as a professional writer. Only toward the end of his sea career did he attempt fiction, the early pages of *Almayer's Folly*; and that well into his writing career, even past *The Nigger of the "Narcissus,"* he attempted to find a posting as mate or captain.

Those several years at sea, at a time when a voyage could take several months, even a year or more, were formative for Conrad. He learned to stare, to enter into reverie, to peer at the horizon for day after day as he stood watch. With no radar or sonar, ships could avoid wreckage or shoals only through the crew's staring; and inevitably on long voyages, the mate could stare almost endlessly as sea and sky merged with each other. Conrad stared, and stared, for months and years. And his imagination, whatever ultimate shape it might take, was formed by this quality of staring and the inevitable reverie which staring led into. Reverie, then, becomes the key experience here, and reverie it is which takes over in *Heart of Darkness*: simultaneity, distortion and condensation, a kaleidoscope of images, a discontinuity of experience, the losing of temporal boundaries—what we can attribute also to dreams. Reverie becomes the mode of narrative experience, and it becomes one way in for the biographer. It is not precise, it is not a fully rational tool, and yet it enables the biographer to combine Conrad's narrative strategies with something in his life. Long before he came to fictional narrative strategies, he had worked out internal strategies. "Telling," for him, was connected to a dreamlike twenty-year experience; and telling and retelling were his ways of reproducing the way in which he came to "see."

Are there other ways to penetrate Conrad's imagination besides the one indicated above, based on staring and reverie? Very possibly, one could try to enter through silences, through avoidance of the large scene, through indirection which derives from his desire to disguise or hide his intentions. The act of telling or retelling is, in one respect, a means of avoiding large dramatic scenes, because in the telling such scenes have already occurred; they are both historical fact and fictional re-creations. The historical context of the scene has been transformed into a verbal medium, into rhetoric, into forms of communication or discommunication. At stake is the whole complex we associate with verb tenses and moods. We can say, then, that in Conrad the avoidance of the large scene was a way of creating a kind of silence—that silence we can trace, once again, to his sea experiences, when the sole noise for weeks or months would be the slap of wave against hull or wind against sail. Or we can say the avoidance of large scenes—creating that area of silence, the "impenetrable"—was Conrad's secretiveness: the disguises, veils, and mists of a man who had himself emerged from such an unusual background into an English novelist. So much of Conrad remained subsurface in his personality, in his past, in his sense of history and betrayal that he translated that into narrative strategies which both denied the historical event and reproduced it in telling.

In such ways, narrative and its strategies can be introduced into biography. But we must beware. We cannot know how far afield we are moving, how much we are straying, or if we are; and on these elements, no two biographers will ever agree. The "life," whether of Conrad or someone comparable, will shift according to how the biographer related the narrative drives of his subject; whether he even takes into account the narrative or if its disguises in the subject's own works should even enter into biography.

In his theory of the "narratee," already cited, Gerald Prince throws several cautions into the process of reading; and these cautions inevitably carry over to the biographer, who is a special kind of reader. Prince distinguishes among several kinds of reader, an act which relates profoundly to narrative and its devices. The "narratee" of a fiction, as we have seen, is the person for whom the narration is intended, the person whom the narrator addresses. But the narratee is not to be confused with the reader, or at least with one reader. The narratee may be described as having certain qualities or characteristics which are not repeated in the reader—as in *Heart of Darkness*, where the narratees are a director of a company and other professional men. One narratee, the "I," is not identified. Nor should the narratee be confused with the virtual reader, who is a kind of generalized reader making up the author's idea of whom he is writing for. The virtual reader is not at all to be identified with the real reader, who may be anyone. There is still another category, also of significance in delving into narrative strategies, and that is the ideal reader. The ideal reader is the perfect audience for the writer, the person who understands exactly what the author wishes to accomplish, who reads all the fictive codes correctly, who understands the generic and historical issues, who can penetrate the thickets of difficulty that differing levels of text might create, who fits himself or herself into the language or languages of the writer and discovers hidden meanings. This ideal reader may be similar to the narratee, but they are not identical, and any similarities must be attributed to chance or circumstance.

Once we have established all these possible audiences—the narratee, the reader, the virtual reader, and the ideal reader—we must ask the inevitable question of where the biographer fits? What kind of reader is he or she? Is the biographer, in fact, a reader at all, or does he or she fit into another category? Does the biographer perhaps fit into all the categories of audience, the four types of reader? And if so, how does the biographer as reader handle the materials when he writes about a particular work, like *Heart of Darkness*, or *Absalom, Absalom!* or *Mrs. Dalloway*, or Proust's novel, all of which establish problems through narrative strategies. Here the biographer enters undefined areas, and it may be sufficient merely to have defined the biographer as a particular kind of reader without attempting to resolve any of the questions raised. It is tempting to posit the biographer as *all four kinds of reader*, in a way the narratee, the reader, then the virtual reader, finally the ideal reader, because the biographer does enter the codes of languages of the subject with more understanding than virtually anyone else. And yet as we read literary biographies, we recognize that the author of them may not be suited to his or her job; that as a reader, he is neither virtual nor ideal; that even as narratee, he is not being spoken to by his subject.

In at least one respect, the biographer is an ultimate reader, if we can coin still another description. The ultimate reader is one who not only reads the work but reads the life, and then can draw from one or the other the materials needed to interpret and identify what is in the life, what in the work, and how they interact. The biographer becomes, in this regard, a kind of godlike figure; for he makes the arrangements, he establishes the themes, he emphasizes what is significant, what is less important, he sets up the chronologies, and he creates narrative coherence even when little or none seems apparent. Gerald Prince has a term, what he calls "overjustification," for the novelist who overnarrates. The author who explains himself, excuses himself, winds back on himself, all through his narrator—as Faulkner with Quentin—is practicing overjustification. Through the narrator, the author has created a narratee defined by the narrator's overjustification. Through the narrator, the author has created a narratee defined by the narrator's overexplanation of him; and he, the narratee, is created more by what is said about him than what he says about himself.

Here we have the biographer's entree into the process. In this regard, the biographer is the overjustifier. The biographer becomes another part of that explanation which lies in the work itself. He or she reinforces and reexplains what has already been explained; he retrieves history, but an impure one quite removed from what was once "real." Citing Conrad's *Heart of Darkness* again, we explain and justify—overjustify, in fact—Marlow's role in the novella; and in this respect, we serve not only as reader of the narrative, we serve as explicator. The biographer, in fact, takes over as author, by telling and retelling elements of a work which have already been told and retold.

We return to the most complicated biographical text of all, the narrative structure of *Absalom, Absalom!* Once again, Genette offers us some insight into this process, in his use of the terms *diegesis* and *mimesis*: the first, diegesis, refers to narrative, and the second, as we know, to imitation. Diegesis refers to a simple form of narrative in which the author speaks in the person of a character. These are ideal forms, since an author rarely maintains his own voice, and just as rarely can directly imitate what the character says. But if we adapt these terms to *Absalom, Absalom!* we can see Faulkner working in and out of Quentin, speaking in his own voice as author, but disguised; speaking in the voice of the character, but also recognizing the limitations of that procedure. Finally, Faulkner is forced to counterpoint author and character by creating a dualistic Quentin, a Quentin who is as divided as the author. Quentin looks back to Sutpen and that South even as he tries to look ahead to his own South, which recognizes that the days of Sutpen are over. But since Quentin cannot reconcile these two sides, he remains caught in the agony and anguish of love and hate, feelings he expresses not only at the end of the novel but throughout.

Narrative forms which result in the deep division within Quentin do have biographical dimensions. Not only in the simple way of saying that Faulkner—like Quentin—was divided between the old and the new South, but in more complicated ways suggested by counterpointing, by narrative strategies which create divisiveness and voices which cannot be reconciled. Usually, we observe narrative forms as elements which lead to reconciliation or resolution; narrative would in itself seem to be a unifying force for the author. And yet Faulkner's use of narration leads to quite different results, and surely this is of biographical interest.

In another sense, Genette's distinctions among tense, mood, and voice are appealing weapons in this search for meaning. The voice of the narrator, here Quentin, and the mood (the character's perspective, attitudes, outlook) must be distinguished from each other. When we do so, we understand that Quentin's words and voice differ from his outlook, that they must be distinguished so that we can see him as voicing words which run askew from his perspective because he recognizes that the emotions he feels cannot be brought into words. Language, then, fails him, even as the novel revels in language.

As things fall apart, we get glimpses of Faulkner's creative imagination, the deepest reaches of the biographical act. With language problematic, we perceive that the elements language tries to define—race, history, memory, the past, personal feelings—are themselves uncertain elements. In Faulkner biography, we become aware of how he withdrew from defined statements, how he celebrated pastness and memory simply because they could not be relied upon. Faulkner's view of the South—and this is biographically significant—was based on his recognition that southern history or pastness could not be defined by language. If one attempted to "see" what had occurred, one was caught up in intangibles which were as much the history of the region and era as anything which could be called "data."

The counterpointing and irresolution in the narrator and the way in which Quentin becomes both narrator and receiver are forms of perception for the author. Once language breaks down, then everything as a form of focus breaks down; and the language appears to fail, the more dependent he and his narrators become upon it. In a way, *structure devours the substance*, if we include structure in the workings of language. The fact that race and history cannot be defined by language means not that language must be forsaken, but that it must be piled on; in the same way, since structure devours substance, structure increases in significance, to the extent it is the only thing remaining once substance has been marginalized or made problematic. Faulkner is always dealing in such paradoxes; and this, too, is as much biography as it is criticism.

In his problematizing of language and of structural strategies, he turned history and race on their edge. He transformed them from classroom elements into subjective forces which could be recreated only through their denial, a kind of litotes. The largest elements identifying the South could, then, be perceived only in Faulkner's transformation of them. Consciousness—mainly Quentin's—becomes all. In his skewed, personal, subjective sense of history, Faulkner has taken narrative elements and located them as forms of consciousness in Thomas Sutpen, in the past, and in Quentin in the present, making them secret sharers of sorts. In his method, Faulkner clarified some aspects of his own biography; for he demonstrated in moving between Sutpen and Quentin several of the hostilities and antagonisms he himself felt toward the South and toward those close to him. In Sutpen's being turned away from the Great House when a child, Faulkner recreates the drama, in his own life, of being turned away from the Oldham's house when he asked for Estelle Oldham's hand. But the equation is not that definite or clear. Faulkner worked through a whole range of rejections—a few which were real and most which were part of his imaginative processes working on those real ones in order to create an entire order of being around them. All this was part of his need to turn "real matters" into subjective elements: to devour the real into the creative and into the imaginative.

In several respects, *Absalom, Absalom!* is, of course, *The Sound and the Fury*, the earlier book in point of writing, but the later narrative in terms of Quentin's suicide. Yet since *Sound* preceded *Absalom*, it is impossible to "read" the later book without the knowledge of what occurred to Quentin: that he is already dead and has been resurrected in the year before his suicide. What this means is very complicated, since it readjusts historical events, it relocates fictional fact, and it presupposes that the reader will accept for himself a subjective view of events. The narrator and receiver of *Absalom* is, in fact, a dead man. Is this merely a trick on Faulkner's part, this aspect of the palimpsest? Or is it something deeply meaningful in biographical terms? Can the biographer ignore the way in which both historical narrative and probability are being rearranged? If not, what point can the biographer make? Does this assume a consciousness on Faulkner's part that he must reenter his own life and see what was possible before he, figuratively, died? How much of this is personally attributable? Was Faulkner a mental suicide, and how closely did he identify with Quentin? These are all narrative questions.

But the question of palimpsest goes much further than the two Quentins. In the person of Henry, Thomas Sutpen's son, and heir to the Sutpen dynasty, we have a palimpsestic version of Quentin. Quentin's father in *Sound* is a man who has surrendered title to any role as man of the house. He is the opposite of the dynamic, ruthless, brutal, success-oriented Sutpen. Henry and Quentin are two sides of very different fathers: Henry does his father's bidding, while Quentin is paralyzed, unable to come to terms with any destiny. Henry's destiny is to carry on the dynasty while becoming actively involved in destroying it; Quentin perceives destruction, also, but is unable to act on it.

Both are "suicides" of sorts. We can see Henry as part of the palimpsest, the two young men as overlappings. In his remark on Proust, Genette speaks of how confusions of memory create "mysterious transformations" of characters: a dulled Gilberte becomes Odette, or Gilberte blends with Albertine; Swann and Marcel are telescoped. Certain stabilities, he points out, become paradoxical. Faulkner's method is similar: as narrative devours substance, or becomes indistinguishable from it, clear identities give way to mass, to silhouettes, postures, shadowy social strata.

As we become aware of this—and we could extend it to several Faulkner novels—we must return to our premise: that these repeated destructions of objectivity of the text have not only critical but biographical significance. The holes or lacunae in the narrative have obvious linkage to qualities in Faulkner's own temperament, to his silences, withdrawals, his refusal to provide bridges or transitions between his words and himself. We can see lacunae, also, in his handwriting, which was cryptic, secretive, full of personal codes, undecipherable in its minuscule appearance, part of a self which has closed in on itself. An analysis of Faulkner's handwriting discloses his inability to give, his desire to play arcane games, his need to withhold. That aspect alone finds its counterpart in his narrative strategies, in the fact, above all, that much of the important information we need for an understanding of the Sutpen family has fallen into the seams of the narrative, that what is most needed is, so to speak, most lacking.

In terms of race alone, Faulkner comes at the subject by way of metaphors of disguise. Race is part of the secret, an arcane society in which certain codes are understood and need not be verbalized. Race, then, is assimilated into this "hole," into silence; and by withdrawing from its verbalization through narrative strategies, Faulkner has intensified its presence as something which can exist without language, so powerful is its presence. *Absalom* moves toward forbidden and inconclusive areas by methods which disallow divulgation. Race arises out of shadows, labyrinths, caves. The hidden aspect of the South is, then, part of Faulkner's biography. Just as with

Conrad—we had to take into account those long weeks and months of silence and staring at the sea—so with Faulkner we must take into account how the South is, as it were, his own "sea" in which silence and staring and withholding have become the way in which he attempted to survive. Faulkner's method indicates great shame, since the most significant elements of the south now come out of the shadows and retreat into caves or into violent destruction. This particular South is the one Faulkner assimilated, not the South of revenge, pride, chauvinism. If we try to equate this view of the South with Faulkner's own needs—where the region's history crosses with the private urgencies of its chief writer—we discover we cannot speak of Faulkner in any area with certainty.

If we absorb the lessons of the narrative strategies, we recognize that Faulkner was a person who perceived life and himself in terms of units or segments which could not connect, that he was not a man whose life can be described as continuous or as part of a smoothly running chronology. Any effort in the future to rewrite Faulkner's biography—as new material at the still-closed Humanities Research Center archives opens up—cannot turn his life into a coherent sequencing. The fiction cautions us. Even Faulkner's verbal streams—which would seem to be the opposite of withholding—give far less than what we expect from so many words, from such a flow of language. The verbal stream is often a closely monitored temporal stream in which voices are divided into subtexts, the way information is conveyed in an epistolary novel. That division among voices, which appears so endemic to Faulkner's way of thinking, means all significance will lie in secondary texts—those areas falling between voices, not in the voices themselves.

All this is part of Faulkner biography. Chopped-up sequences, aborted characterizations, assimilation of race, pastness, memory, and history into narrative strategies, the devouring of substance by the technique—all are biographical, not merely critical matters. They are not "data" in the formal sense we associate with factual material, such as dates of birth, death, marriage, or career highs and lows. But they are data in a more profound way, and woe to the biographer who fails to see that the very narrative means used by his subject can be perceived in biographical terms.

AN ADDENDUM

A related but more conventional way of approaching narrative problems is through the examination of the subject's letters. Every time the biographer uses letters, he or she sets up an adversarial or counterpuntal position with his subject based on narrative distinctions. The use of letters in biography is one of a biographer's most complicated decisions because of the differing natures of letters and biographical narrative. The two different generic elements do not fit together easily, and the biographer can never be completely at ease when using a letter, for it upsets the sense of "truth" every biography seems to demand. Here is the paradox. Biography is made up of seams—of facts, data, details, and episodes that are stitched together with meaning, interpretation, and commentary, which is another say of saying, with narrative density. Each time one detail confronts another, such a seam occurs: a decision, often a critical one, is made on how those two pieces of information should be stitched together. Yet the biographer's decision is extraneous, as it were, to the subject matter, lying outside and beyond the subject in narrative emphasis and in demands of readability and interpretation that the biographer has already established on his own. In every respect, those seams are part of an external process.

A letter, on the other hand, is deeply internalized, for it belongs, of course, not to the biographer but to the subject, and was written not to fit a life but to describe a situation or express feelings or to reveal a psychological or emotional problem. It may be, as so many of a subject's letters are, concerned with business. Or else they reveal a variety of concerns, not only business, but artistic needs, personal details, financial despair, self-examinations. While extremely important as letters, such missives pose intensely difficult problems for the biographer. Most obviously, they fit no narrative pattern; since the letters involve several types of content, they break out into areas that narrative can hardly contain. But less obviously such letters may, in fact, partially negate the biographer's almost constant task, which is to create some sense of development or "progress" in the subject's life. This progress, and the word is used advisedly, is based on the reader's normal expectation to see a writer advance, develop, and mature. The reader and the biographer carry over from life the desire to see patterning in the subject's life, and a smooth narrative line and a sense of progress or development fit into that expectation.

The problem can be defined in several other ways. Not only is the letter internalized, it forms part of the subject's "history," as the subject sees himself or herself and as a document in itself. It has historical value because it helps place the subject at a particular time and place, with particular concerns, and offers us something of the nature of the recipient, becoming a text in the life. Yet biography has different texts. It has fictional dimensions and, in several ways, not the least narrative, it is closer to fictive form than, possibly, to any other genre. Despite the fact that it is, of course, part history, part psychology or psychoanalysis, and part sociology, its fictive form intrudes. As Hayden White and other commentators have remarked, we view biography as having a novelistic sense. It has the patterned coherence associated with fictive form (or attributed to fiction): a story, even a plot line; a middle, a beginning, and end; several climactic events; drama and conflict. The reader of biography has a fictional expectation, and, consequently, biography seems like fiction even when the biographer strives to maintain a nonfictional sense.

An offshoot of this point is that the biographer is always selecting, shaping, and transforming the subject's historical documents into story or plot, into forms or narrative. Details, facts, data are not for the biographer what they signify or might have signified for the subject. On the contrary, for the biographer, a detail must fit into a very different construct, even a competing one, since in using a letter or other document, he imposes his—not the subject's—point of view on it. It is a truism that the biographer fails to achieve *the truth*, although truth may be his ultimate aim, even his original motivation. He starts with too much subjective baggage, with a theme or scheme that can be imposed on the subject's life, with something he has intuited or wanted to prove about the subject before beginning the biography. The shaping idea, then, might come as readily from the biographer as from the subject. The former works through his own preconceived plan, using details and documents to illustrate what he has in mind. Such shaping or patterning obviously changes from decade to decade, and the biography of a subject in one era differs, often markedly, from what it is in another. This is a way of saying each era demands its own kind of narrative.

What the letter does more than anything else is to throw the biographer into a profoundly uncertain area at the same time it forces the assimilation of the personal material into a welter of other arenas: artistic, most of all, but among other things also political and social. Not the least consideration is the use of language. The letter belongs to the subject's use of language, which frequently differs markedly from the biographer's. But linguistic differences are not mere matters of words; they contain major distinctions in outlook, emphasis, and interpretation, and eventually they wind around to questions of narrative. More precisely, to whom does narrative belong, the subject or the biographer?

The relationship of letters to biography can be seen as fitting into what the Russian critic M. M. Bakhtin has defined as the dialogic process. Although Bakhtin's use of this term is more philosophically and culturally attuned than my usage here, the word nevertheless describes a conflicting, adversarial, yet symbiotic linkage. The letters pose as a biographical mode's enemy and yet at the same time are indispensable to it. The relationship is adversarial yet sympathetic. In another sense, the letter interacts with other aspects of the biographical process while also conditioning those dimensions. Further, it calls into question the very nature of that process, not only as a document, but, as suggested before, in its language. The letter preexists, having emerged in a different era under differing conditions, whereas the biographical language is created for a unique function at a very different time, under quite different social and cultural conditions. Even further, the letter may be in a different language from that of the biography, this engendering another dialogic element as the translated document struggles to find its way in another language altogether. In every instance, whatever combination of elements, the dialogic process ensures not a unitary but a heterogeneous response. What Bakhtin called *heteroglossia* is that condition in which utterances come with a cultural impact that cannot be recapitulated or recaptured. Thus, letters carry cultural significance that creates both centrifugal and centripetal meanings the biographer can only try to duplicate. Once again, narrative forms are trapped between subject and biographer.

ELIOT

By the time I completed the Conrad, Faulkner, and Kafka biographies, I finally considered myself a biographer, and it was time to look around for another subject, a major writer with whom I could live for three or four years. I had always admired the fiction of George Eliot and had taught her novels to hundreds of students in Victorian fiction classes, so when my older daughter suggested that she would be a good topic for a biography, I decided to look into it.

It was now in the early 1990s, and the last full-dress Eliot biography was Gordon Haight's magisterial work in 1968. I did not intend to replace Haight's, but styles of biography had changed, the genre had opened up, and new material which Haight had himself helped to uncover, but was unable to use because of restrictions, had surfaced, particularly Eliot's relationship to Herbert Spencer. I decided that she was a perfect subject for me, especially since I thought that writing about a major woman writer would be a huge challenge.

I planned research trips to England (to examine her manuscripts at the then-called British Museum and to visit her homes), to spend some time in and around Coventry, near where she was born, and to get what help I could from the very cooperative Eliot Fellowship. My start on the biography coincided with my acceptance of an endowed chair at the University of Hawai'i, the Citizens' Chair, and since I had few obligations at the university, I sailed through nearly 1,000 pages of written manuscript in that year. Looking out of my window at palm trees swaying in the breeze, I wrote about Eliot and her anguished personal life and her enormously successful professional career.

Writing George Eliot's Biography

IT IS FITTING that I should write about George Eliot and biography in this most welcome *Festschrift* for George Simson. For it was while I was visiting Citizens' Professor of English at the University of Hawai'i at Mānoa, Professor Simson's home base, that I wrote almost the entire first draft of my Eliot biography (*George Eliot: Voice of a Century*, Norton, 1995). With a quite manageable teaching schedule and with few acquaintances, I found myself with a great deal of free time, most of it in large chunks conducive to steady work. I had already sent on from New York some twenty cartons of books and also found the university library well stocked with Eliot material. Without any major interruptions, I was able to put together almost a thousand pages of my first draft in that year, 1990–91.

My archival research would wait until later, when I could use the British Library, where the manuscripts of all but one of Eliot's books are located. The exception, her first book, *Scenes of Clerical Life*, three novellas, was in the manuscript archive of the Morgan Library in New York City. But I had in hand in Hawai'i nearly everything else that I needed. The most fundamental material was the nine-volume edition of Eliot's letters edited by Gordon Haight. The editing is meticulous, although when I returned home, I checked everything that I used against the manuscripts of the letters at Yale's Beinecke Library. Each day, as I arose in the morning, I planned on writing four or five pages; so that by the time I left in early May I would have an almost complete first draft of 350,000 words. So with palm trees swaying in the distance, I catapulted myself back to Warwickshire and to the English countryside not too distant from Robin Hood's Sherwood Forest.

But before I detail my quest for Eliot, I should point out that I had thought long and hard about a subject for a new biography before settling on her. My oldest daughter, in fact, encouraged me to try Eliot, since the sole full biography extant was the one by Gordon Haight. The Haight biography was considered a monument, something like, at the time of its writing, Gordon Ray's *Thackeray* or Edgar Johnson's *Dickens*, or, later, Richard Ellmann's *Joyce* and Leon Edel's *Henry James*. Haight was a meticulous scholar, and one could trust he had gotten most of the facts right. He, too, depended heavily on Eliot's letters; and he had in fact devoted most of his scholarly energies and his career to work on the writer. If I were to write another biography of Eliot, I would always have Haight in my line of vision, a considerable landmark in biographical studies. I had no quarrel with him and did not wish to challenge or compete with him. Yet from the first, I saw Eliot differently.

Some of the difference was that I was from another generation, and biographical writing itself—as Leon Edel observed in his own one-volume revision of his five-volume James—had altered. Not only had it opened in terms of what could be revealed; it now sent out tentacles in several directions, into psychology, cultural and social studies, history, even politics. Biography also had to take into account that it had been hit hard by the critical theorists, who like Roland Barthes emphasized the texts, not the life—and serious biographers, I felt, should not proceed as if literary criticism did not exist, or as if it had stood still. My aim, as I contemplated the Eliot biography—after having written three others—was not only to write "biography" but to acknowledge what was occurring in other critical discourse. I wanted both to defend biography and also to lead it in new directions. I wondered if this would be possible with a subject seemingly as traditional as Eliot, someone so solidly placed in the pantheon of nineteenth-century novelists.

In all my previous biographies, I had situated my figure—Conrad, Faulkner, Kafka—in a broad and extensive cultural context. I used historical data, cultural events, and related material as much as I did biographical detail. For Conrad, I had to recreate three separate cultures in which he moved: the Poland of his birthplace and adolescence, the France of his later teen years, the England of his growth as a writer and as an Englishman. Such a choice on my part—what I called the "three lives" of Conrad—involved a broad use of historical contextualization, plus a good deal of larger, cultural matters, as Conrad moved fairly smoothly from one language group and society to another.

With Faulkner, my problem was to situate him securely and firmly in the South which so infused all of his work: that is, to make it possible for the non-Southern reader to understand how Faulkner was who he was; and this involved the re-creation of Southern politics, culture, society, religious atmosphere. I dug deeply into some of the most unpleasant episodes in our history; I needed to try to think of the Civil War from a Mississippian's point of view, and race was, of course, paramount in my account. I had to show that while Faulkner was a decent man in racial matters, he was caught up in enormous peer pressure and historical accounting, so that he was torn, and that it was this tearing that gave his fiction so much texture.

Finally, in my biography of Kafka, I had an even more difficult task of recreating the Austro-Hungarian Empire in its dying phase, the very subject matter of so much of Kafka's fiction. This involved historical work of an extensive kind, since the empire was not merely Kafka's Czechoslovakia, but vast parts of Poland, Austria, Hungary, a large segment of what we call Eastern Europe. The social, political, and religious ramifications of the Empire were extraordinary; and in religious terms, I found myself concerned with the extent of Kafka's own ambiguous Judaism. There was also his tortured relationship with his parents, both his mother and father; his tuberculosis, which eventually killed him at forty; his circle of friends in Prague, many of whom like Franz Werfel and, to a lesser degree, Max Brod, also became well known.

For both Conrad and Kafka (but not for Faulkner) their letters proved invaluable. In Conrad's case, I had many years earlier started to collect them for an eight-volume edition which Cambridge University Press was to publish (six volumes have appeared), and so I had a bonanza. For Kafka, I had several volumes, the most valuable proving to be his letters to members of his family (including the never-sent letter to his father) and the large group he wrote to his on-again, off-again fiancée Felice Bauer. The latter are a treasure trove of Kafka lore, inasmuch as he kept her alive at the other end of his letters so that personally he would not have to be with her.

For Eliot, the letter trail proved almost equally significant. When Haight wrote his book in 1968, he could not use fully some of the letters that Eliot had written to Herbert Spencer, the economist, evolutionist, and the man who, at one time, she thought might marry her. This is a batch that was locked up until well into the 1980s, and the reason why is clear: they are plaintive, demeaning, sad, not at all what one might expect from Eliot, almost desperate as she ages and begins to fear she will never attract a husband. All of this occurred before she started to write fiction, and the "affair" with Spencer helps us to understand what Eliot discovered fictionally in disappointment, frustration, and loneliness. But the inaccessible cache of letters, available finally to me but not to Haight for quotation, was also accompanied by thousands of letters in which Eliot revealed her intellectual development as a person and as a writer.

But letters, we know, are devious missives. While we tend to depend on them for data, they all reveal the unreliability of the writer when he or she chronicles a personal or professional life. Letters that might seem more fruitful turn out to be fanciful—in the way Eliot's letters in and around the ones she wrote to Spencer give no sense of what strain and disappointment she suffered. It is difficult to measure tone, attitude, angles in a letter, especially if the biographer uses only the printed version. The manuscript letter may contain more—a wobble, an uncertainty, a blotting, a hesitation, or something that gives that particular letter more meaning than just the face value.

Letters often—perhaps always—are part of the author's fictional output, texts in their own right. Letters must be approached on several levels, as my work with Eliot revealed—and here I departed from Haight, who tended to take the letters as data. For unless we understand Eliot's letters as layered and textured, we cannot enter into her creative or imaginative processes, except in the detailing of hard fact. We may say she read this or that, researched in this or that library, walked the streets in one town or city or another; but we cannot account for how she transformed this material into fictional texts of a very different kind.

We start by agreeing that we, as biographers or as readers, cannot hope to enter into the context of a given letter. There is no way we can relocate ourselves into another era; the new historicism cannot work its magic here. Except for the specific data—events, dates, relocations—the letter must be read as an unreliable narrator. Eliot's letters, which seem so solid and so rooted in reality, are in fact misleading, to the extent that she leaves out her creative or imaginative processes when she is composing her major works. She slides in and around them, emphasizing instead terms of contracts, advances, publication dates, the physical look of the novel; but in the light of what we want to know most—where her creative abilities cross with her life—we must proceed guardedly.

In most instances, we stake out our own narrative and subsume the narrative of the letter. Take for example a letter Eliot wrote to her publisher, John Blackwood, on July 30, 1859, where the subject is apparently the receipt of a pug, a gift from Blackwood. Eliot uses the occasion, the coming of the dog—an expensive thirty guineas—to comment on life.

The pug has come "to fill up the void left by false and narrow-hearted friends. I see that he is without envy, hatred, or malice—that he will betray no secrets, and feel neither pain at my success nor pleasure in my chagrin." The remainder of the letter concerns the dog. But interwoven into her gratitude for such a thoughtful and expensive gift is an entire world of feelings and attitudes. In the near background is what she still considers the perfidy of Spencer; she feels she had been led on, and then dropped. Spencer always said he was drawn only to physically attractive women. More to the point, Eliot's lack of physical attractiveness was not the issue—Spencer was; he remained a bachelor for his entire long life, and probably a virgin. But also in the background are all the people who considered her not much better than a kept woman for having run away with George Henry Lewes, a married family man, although separated from his wife.

Eliot thinks of all those desertions, all that backbiting, all the gossip that trailed her around London, and only ended at the continent. But further than that, she was feeling out her own mixed emotions as she was poised between her first book, *Scenes of Clerical Life*, and her first novel, *Adam Bede*. She was suffering a failure of confidence, as she almost always did when she was completing or contemplating a book; and she wondered if what she wrote was close to what she hoped to achieve. She was unusually divided at this time, as her career as a fiction writer was about to begin, and she was still unknown as Mary Anne Evans, still hiding behind the name George Eliot as a male writer, a cleric, a retiring gentleman—as Lewes presented her image to Blackwood. Rejected by her family because of the relationship with Lewes, pretending to be man of the cloth, unsure of her own abilities in this new medium, and suffering from emotional debilitation because of Spencer's rejection and the consequences of the Lewes attachment, she uses the dog as a way of commenting more on herself than on the pug. If we can maximize one letter this way, the path through thousands of pieces of correspondence will be thorny indeed.

One of the difficulties with Eliot biography was, paradoxically, an excess of material about the details of her life—especially her researches and travels—but too little about how her life and work connected. She was introspective at the level of intellectual life, but not forthcoming at the deepest level of her craft. We rarely catch any glimpses of transformation, of how research and reading became imaginatively conceived. In a novel such as *Romola*, we recognize that the research overwhelmed the fictional element, so eager was Eliot to get the details of the Savonarola period correct. Also, in parts of *Daniel Deronda*, her research into Jewish matters shows, as she parades historical detail at the expense of creative development. But other parts of *Deronda*, as well as *Middlemarch* and *The Mill on the Floss*, to mention only those, involved transformational qualities which Eliot did not put into her letters.

The breadth of detail along with the lack of artistic introspection is only one problematical area in the writing of Eliot's biography. There was, as noted before, the solid presence of the Haight volume, and the fact that the succeeding biographer had to find ways in which Haight either lacked material or else interpreted it according to an earlier, more guarded time. Haight is clearly uncomfortable with sexual matters, and yet it was surely a cornerstone of Eliot's successful relationship with Lewes that it rested on a mutually satisfactory sexual life. The raking, profligate Lewes found an accommodating mate in the seemingly opposite Eliot; we have enough hints here and there and sufficient intimations to female friends from Eliot to make that statement. But other than that, it became necessary to examine Eliot's attraction to her own sex; that while she was clearly heterosexual—and expressed that—she drew to her a number of women who worshipped her and who, apparently, excluded men from their lives. All of this is shrouded and veiled, a gray area, but it bears interpretation as part of Eliot biography—although not perhaps a major element.

In other areas as well, Haight could be found not wanting but hesitant. He did not choose to discuss Eliot's fiction in detail, skipping over the ambiguities which they reveal. His is a "true" biography in the sense of an earlier time, when the work was separated. We recall how in Edgar Johnson's biography of Dickens the fiction was located in chapters disconnected from its place in the life. Once I made a decision that Eliot's body of work was also biographical, as much a part of her life—and perhaps more—as the chronological life itself, then I found numerous problematical areas. It was impossible to blend life and works without a strong psychological strain; old-fashioned American biographers and contemporary English biographers (although not the much-maligned Peter Ackroyd in his splendid *Dickens*) are wary of psychological interpretation and usually skirt the work of their subject. They provide chronological sequencing, which is often not the way the life was at all. I wanted much more, and that involved not only a strong psychological base, but also frequent interruption of narrative flow. If the work was to be integrated into the life, there was simply no way to keep up a sequential narrative flow; prolepsis and other literary strategies were necessary. Chronological sequencing was almost impossible, since works might be incubated at one time in the life, then worked on at another, finally produced at a third time.

But that was only the beginning of the problems. The question arose of what kind of criticism to apply: social? political? broadly cultural? deconstructive, where possible? reader-response? Lacanian? Was a close reading too subjective, even while the method posed as objective? Weren't all critical methods subjective and, therefore, a matter of personal distortion? Did I feel transference or countertransference with my subject? How does one explain Eliot's very ambiguous attitude toward women?—a feminist in her work, not keen about it in her life, and yet unconventional enough to "live in sin."

While not my sole area of critical attack, I decided on an eclectic psychological reading of Eliot's life and work. I did not construe her life as needing analysis in the typical way—no couch, no strict Freudianism, Lacanian, or other discipline, no theoretical paradigm that would squeeze her into this or that meaning. I wanted something open to alternate discourse that liberated rather than constrained Eliot, and allowed me, somehow, to enter both her life and work with a kind of balance. I turned to ideas of transference and countertransference, and here I immediately ran into several choices, none of them really resolvable. There was, of course, the gender difference, and while I dismissed an essentialism based on maleness or femaleness, I nevertheless had difficulty in reimagining what it was like to grow up as a girl and a young woman. In any biography that attempts a psychological approach, such a problem is evident.

Second, there was the obvious disparity between eras—my contemporary America, her pre-Victorian England. Third, there was geography, her country life and its presence in her fiction, my views based mainly on an urban existence. There were, additionally, religious differences, even though by her twenties she had ceased to be a believer; but her early life was infused with religious fervor, whereas I had never felt either fervor or belief. Most of all, and possibly the most difficult problem of difference, was the fact she knew a lot more than I did; she was both intelligent and creative, intellectual and imaginative. She simply read more and knew more than anyone else in the century among fiction writers, and perhaps overall among writers except for John Stuart Mill. She knew foreign languages, seven of them to read, some to speak; she had read deeply in philosophy, theology, literature, history; she was aware of most developments in the hard sciences; she kept up with evolutionary theories and with developments in mathematics. She could understand any idea or text put before her. In these respects, she was a daunting subject, clearly my intellectual superior.

Withal these difficulties, I went ahead with my psychological approach, as something that could reduce the distance between me and Eliot. Speaking generally, all biographers in writing about a significant figure seek some way to lessen the distance between them and their subject. In nearly all cases, the subject is a far greater figure than the biographer. The point is how to bridge this difference, or how to avoid letting it become a visible issue. By using transference and countertransference, I threaded Eliot into my own world, and, conversely, threaded myself into hers; thus erasing the fact that we were so dissimilar, or at least creating the illusion that such differences could be overridden.

We are all familiar with transference, since it is central to biography; and, one might add, to the critical analysis of nearly any text. But less well known is countertransference, whereby an emotional tie between biographer and subject is so intense that it often leads to the former placing a subjective template on the latter. In such instances, whether we use Freudian terms or Erikson's "idealization" and "unconscious identification," the clear danger was that I would seek formative dimensions in my subject's life that validated my own experiences as well as hers. We can illustrate this with Eliot's response to her father, whom she venerated as a young woman and who, it seems, she came to resent later on.

The resentment derived from her own intellectual expansiveness, which enabled her to observe the narrowness and provincialism of her father, especially in religious matters. As she drifted from any formal belief, he insisted on his Church of England bearings, and demanded that as long as she lived at home she must also toe the line. When her father, Robert Evans, fell ill, it was Eliot's job to take care of him, since she was unattached. His illness was, as her letters reveal, a kind of imprisonment for her; her time was taken up with chores in the very years she considered precious. Now moving past her mid-twenties, she was close to middle age for a Victorian woman, still single, still unfulfilled, still aware of huge intellectual potentiality without any avenue of escape.

Here was my problem. If I read her situation along the lines of how I would have felt, I would have found her short-sighted indeed for wasting year after year; but in taking that position, I would have neglected to see how her devotion to her father transcended such anger and created a far greater ambiguity than I would have found for myself. Since I had a father with whom I was not emotionally engaged, and who was a passive, shadowy, almost invisible figure in my life, I could easily have concluded that Mary Anne Evans—who would, after all, become George Eliot—was losing her life. She owed this man only so much; she owed herself much more. My reading of this very important area would be countertransferential, and it could possibly have trapped me in a reading that, on one hand, was valid, but on another was well off the mark.

I determined, in fact, that because of my own feelings I underestimated Eliot's devotion to her father; further, that I was theorizing about father-daughter relationships based more on American ideas of separation of the generations than on the Victorian sense of coming together. I was in danger of misreading on two levels, that of the individual case and that of the more generalized view of familial attachments. Here countertransference, while useful in some aspects of Eliot's life—in my reading of her depressive moods, for instance, or in her desire for reclusiveness—would be overreaching in others.

But my caution in matters of countertransference should not, I felt, subvert my belief that such a psychological relationship with my subject is necessarily a faulty one. Studies with a strong psychobiographical or psychohistorical emphasis have recently been hit hard by critics and reviewers; but a psychological approach need not be exclusive, no more than a deconstructive or hermeneutic one need be. What is emerging increasingly in biography is an eclectic approach, and with this in mind my attempt to put Eliot under a psychological lens was not to narrow responses, but to broaden them. Even in what is usually considered to be a lesser work (by far), *Silas Marner*, I discovered a great deal of compelling matter, not only in the text itself but in ways the text patterned itself after elements in Eliot's life: her feelings of isolation, her sense of herself as a pariah once she had eloped with Lewes, her somewhat contradictory desire for money as a means of power and yet her recognition of its limitations, her age itself when she wrote the novel, an age when she was past childbearing and what that meant to a woman in her time. Finally, we must take into account an interesting piece of transference on her own part, when she became stepmother, as it were, to Lewes's three sons: less than blood mother, not even a legally recognized stepmother, and yet still a mother figure, at a time when she is writing Silas as a "stepmother" to Eppie, a maternal man.

Aspects of Eliot's life—and the way her life rubbed off on her work—turned out to be far more complicated than I had originally considered. Teaching the novels in the classroom and applying critical methods to them is quite a different matter from assimilating the life and work in a biographical study. One need not give up critical tools, but one must range into areas of self-understanding which critical method by itself might ignore—although in some perfect world, we would recognize that criticism is itself a subjective procedure with many of the biases and prejudices we associate with biographical writing. With psychological tools, the probing of a biographical figure reverberates not only into social and political areas, but into the symbiotic relationship of the subject to the biographer, frequently in unforeseen ways. The Eliot I started out with in Hawai'i had deepened and broadened by the time I took her back to New York.

MORE ON JOSEPH CONRAD

Since I am editing Conrad's letters, an ongoing process with five volumes of a contemplated eight having appeared, several of my analyses of the writer combine letters and biographical approaches. For me, the letters are a source of a good deal of what we know, but, at the same time, letters are quite fallible if we rely on them too trustingly. They are, in their way, a different language from the narrative language imposed on a subject in biographical writing. And since they are a different language—a different time, place, and emphasis—they are often unreliable, much as a subject's diary, memoir, or autobiography would be unreliable as to fact but invaluable as to revelations. Put another way, letters are data, but only if they can be supported with other evidence. Conrad often told three and four correspondents in the same day three or four different versions of the same thing, tailoring his remarks to what he thought each correspondent wanted to hear. Thus, to John Galsworthy, he praised his latest play, whereas to others he had various levels of criticism. What did he really think? Even when letters are less deceptive, they can be expressions of the writer acting out, playing a role, framing himself for the recipient of the letter. All these various poses are played out in the following pieces, where letters cross with biography, and the biographer crosses his fingers.

Conrad's Letters and Biography

SEVERAL GROUPS OF letters Joseph Conrad wrote become, in their way, not only commentaries on his work, but guides to his creative life and, thus, to his biography. I have in mind the immense series to James Brand Pinker, his agent, amounting to over 1,200 items; to John Galsworthy, his close friend, over 200 items; to Ford Maddox Ford, his friend, coauthor, and then alienated colleague, more than 100 items; those batches to Edward Garnett, his devoted first editor; to Richard Curle, a later friend and supporter; to H. G. Wells, who early on spotted a unique talent; to André Gide, a give-and-take correspondence which was Conrad's one undisputed exchange with a major writer; to John Quinn, later, the avid collector and successful lawyer; to Cunninghame Graham, a very personal correspondence, over 80 items; and other, briefer exchanges, especially those with publishers. By consulting the latter groups alone, one can gain a side of Conrad which the fiction does not reveal. One gains a narrative with a creative dimension of its own.

Most of these batches of letters are known only to the most diligent of Conrad scholars; and some of those to Galsworthy, for example, are known only in the imperfect Jean-Aubry transcriptions in *Life and Letters*. The compelling Galsworthy group, after being publicly available at the University of Birmingham Library in England, was folded into the private Forbes collection; but not before a microfilm was made available to this writer. The letters to Gide, to cite another example, have been published, but in esoteric pamphlets, or are only available in part in Jean-Aubry's execrably edited *Lettres françaises*. Even the letters to Garnett, more carefully transcribed, are incomplete in the available American edition and far more reliable in the almost unavailable Nonesuch Press English edition.

The first interest in Conrad's selected letters came with Jean-Aubry's *Joseph Conrad: Life and Letters*, in 1927. Jean-Aubry brought together about 2000 letters and then made a selection for his edition: some letters abbreviated, some in full but poorly transcribed, many with serious deletions of what the editor considered to be delicate matter. Unfortunate about this edition are not only the above flaws, but the fact that after he assembled his choices he did not keep track of those he omitted and, for all, failed to give the source. As a consequence, about 50 of the letters Jean-Aubry returned to their owners have never surfaced; and several others that he did print inadequately have no originals available to compare them with. Moreover, Jean-Aubry, well-meaning but with a different outlook for a different era, culled the letters for even esoteric references that might reflect poorly on Conrad or his correspondents. For those letters which lack originals, we have no way of knowing what Jean-Aubry cut, or even if there were ellipses, since his editing was so haphazard.

After this publication—which despite its deficiencies was a very significant step in Conrad studies—several other volumes of letters appeared: those to Richard Curle, Edward Garnett, then Marguerite Poradowska, as well as earlier in what purported to be Conrad's "French letters," also edited by Jean-Aubry in which he muddled together English and French punctuation, misread his own language (French), and omitted without even ellipses entire chunks of letters. Equally damaging, he did not indicate that his "collection" did not include many letters which were available, such as those to Poradowska, André Gide, and himself. Since some of these letters are among the most important in Conrad studies, especially those to Poradowska, which cover the early years when Conrad was shaping his writing career, their haphazard editing and selection is particularly disturbing. Poradowska's letters were, finally, themselves well-edited and presented in translation in 1940 by Gee and Sturm, although they made many errors which a later French edition corrected. Conrad's Polish letters appeared much later in an English edition, although several of the originals were not available or had been destroyed, and the texts had to be reconstituted from copies or published letters. The real breakthrough in editions of Conrad letters to single correspondents came in 1958 with William Blackburn's *Joseph Conrad: Letters to William Blackwood and David S. Meldrum* and C. T. Watts's *Joseph Conrad's Letters to R. B. Cunninghame Graham*, in 1969.

In the main, however, much of the active, but inadequate, collecting of Conrad's letters occurred in the fifteen-year period after his death, in the late 1920s through 1940. In terms of early Conrad biography and criticism, the lack of an authentic letter file resulted in several poor efforts, Jean-Aubry's own work in 1927, his second effort in 1957, also Jocelyn Baines's in 1960. Critically, the problem was much the same: efforts were made to understand and "read" Conrad's fiction and life without the context of a broad and accurate letter file. For several decades, critical books piled up without the authors being aware of the 1,200-plus items in the Conrad-Pinker archive at the Berg Collection of the New York Public Library; and, astonishingly, one still finds work on Conrad appearing, both articles and books, which rely on Jean-Aubry's faulty 1927 transcriptions.

This is, however, only the beginning. In textual terms, in editions of Conrad's fiction, little or no effort *until quite recently* has gone to determine the order of composition, the twists and turns of narrative or plot strategy, the numerous revisions tried out or rejected, all of these, as revealed in Conrad's correspondence. This has been especially true of those who have condemned *Victory*, Conrad's final prewar novel, without understanding how thickly textured the novel was, how carefully it was shaped and crafted, how meticulously Conrad prepared his final version, much of which could be determined only by the Conrad-Pinker archive. The tens of thousands of words Conrad wrote to Pinker during the composition of that novel help us to recognize not that his powers were failing but that his powers were at their height, however one considers the final product of his labors. One needs the details *before* judgment.

In more specific biographical and critical terms, we see how someone like Najder in his documentary-like study can use the letters not as literary documents, not as themselves complicated biographical data, not as psychological signposts, but primarily as valorized expression. Such studies imply that Conrad "knew" what he was writing in his letters, as though subjective factors did not transform the letter into an uncertain document as much as the fictions were themselves products of uncertainties. For once we have established a letter file—accurate transcriptions, complete texts, authoritative editing—then we must see the letters as part of a very complex biographical-critical problem. Conrad's letters in particular provoke reader dilemma, in that the writer was secretive in his fiction and, therefore, we must assume, secretive in his letters; but further, that while he was a solid letter writer in many stages of his career, he was not the kind of correspondent whose letters stand as literature apart from his fictional endeavors. With some exceptions, his letters should be read as part of the fiction, as interwoven with it, as a function of the same psychological context.

Nothing in Conrad, for example, compares with Franz Kafka's 600 pages of letters to his fiancée Felice Bauer, a collection with qualities of a fictional effort, as Kafka plays one role after another. Conrad's comparable collections to Pinker, or Galsworthy, or his early friends the Sandersons and Edward Garnett, or later to the American lawyer and collector John Quinn, are strong, even powerful; but they signify to the degree they point to other factors in Conrad's life, mainly his creative life. The later letters, in fact, are keyed in to the novelist's desire to expand his income by selling manuscript and typescript pages, not the desire to role-play or act out.

One group of letters, the 110 to Marguerite Poradowska, whom Conrad referred to as "Aunt," but who was not a blood relation, underscores how carefully we must "read" such letters. This batch comes closest to Kafka's with Felice Bauer, in that each man is moving in and out of conflicting feelings and trying both to reveal and conceal his uncertainties. Psychologically, it may be tempting to see Conrad as acting immaturely in his dealings with his "Aunt," flirting, then retreating, possibly fearful of consequences. Yet there is much more to it, and an analysis of the correspondence, heavy in the early 1890s, a difficult time for him, reveals how letters must be contextualized with other factors. Any attempt to privilege immaturity cannot neglect a myriad of other details feeding into Conrad's life at this period, not least his early efforts at fiction writing.

"Writing," then, becomes the area of context, whereby letters and fiction interweave and link. Flirtation and even marriage with Poradowska was not necessarily a sign of immaturity, but an effort on Conrad's part to nourish his literary career. In the 1890s, he was not simply a gauche young man. He was also working through, imaginatively, enormous inner conflicts, in which sexual stirrings (Poradowska was a handsome woman), a declining sea career (suitable berths were unobtainable), and the glimpse of another kind of life were all telescoped. Further, in more general cultural terms, he was caught among several unresolved elements: his Polish background, but also French and English culture in which Poles found themselves. At over thirty, Conrad may have shown awkwardness in his dealings with a sophisticated woman, but in other areas, intellectually and imaginatively, he was harboring great things. The letters, then, are not isolated elements revealing an awkward Conrad, but connections to a far more complex man entering critical years.

The point here is both biographical and critical; and the further point is that what we see with Conrad-Poradowska can be paralleled with Conrad-Galsworthy, Conrad-Garnett,

Conrad-Crane (to a somewhat lesser degree), later Conrad-Pinker. Each linkage created complex contexts, although the crossover point was always writing. With Poradowska, he went from Konrad Korzeniowski to Joseph Conrad; with Garnett and also Galsworthy, he emphasized both his Polishness and his Englishness; and with Pinker, he became wedded, author to agent, then author to friend, then author to the one reliable figure in his later professional life. We must assume that Conrad could not speak to his wife Jessie in serious intellectual or creative terms; in many respects, she was an excellent wife for someone as volatile as he, but hardly a sounding board for ideas. Letters served that function.

Another large factor is the distinctive contextualization of each correspondence. While Conrad's personal letters to Poradowska, with their heavy overlay of Polish and French references, was diminishing, his professional correspondence with Ford Maddox Ford was becoming most active. The large group to Ford was necessarily more attuned to creative work; but they also reveal how much Conrad leaned on the younger (and as yet untried) man when his own written English was shaky. The Ford correspondence came at a fortunate time, when Conrad was entering his most fully fashioned work, from *Heart of Darkness* and *Lord Jim* to *Nostromo*, and the letters must be read not only for what they say but for what they imply. For what they don't quite say is that the novelist needed support, in the way an explorer heading out into unknown territory depends on guides. Venturing out into areas of English usage he was unsure of, as well as into ever more experimental fictional areas, Conrad had, as it were, Ford at his elbow for reinforcement.

In a similar way, still another overlapping, but different, correspondence with Edward Garnett, his editor and "discoverer," enabled him to continue on what became a very personal and difficult quest for a fictional voice. By the early 1900s, as we know, Conrad had become unique in English fiction, its most prestigious (although almost unrecognized) practitioner; and the burden of trying out the new was personally lightened by those who believed in him, that small circle of correspondents. His letters at this critical time, with Garnett and Ford, lessening with Poradowska, coming sporadically with Stephen Crane and H. G. Wells, just beginning with Pinker, picking up with Galsworthy, are all part of the context in which the fiction was written.

Other more personal correspondences started up: one thinks of the extensive file (growing to seventy-three letters) with Mr. and Mrs. Edward Lancelot Sanderson. Most of these came at Conrad's most anxiety-ridden period, from 1895 to 1900, precisely when we want to know more about him as he moved from seaman to man of letters. While these particular letters are not too revealing of the creative side, they do demonstrate the life of a literary man in his ordinary routine; that is, in his relationships to people neither writers at the time nor especially interested in writing. Further, the correspondence, unlike later personal ones, reflects a warmth and generosity on Conrad's part for a relationship uncomplicated by economic or other peripheral consideration.

Once we look beyond this simple need for friendship with bright, appealing young people—Sanderson would go on to become a schoolmaster, Helen Sanderson a strong but minor writer—we find several aspects of Conrad's character opening up through the correspondence. Ted Sanderson was, in several respects, the English boy Conrad had wanted to be: the epitome, in the novelist's eyes, of courage, manliness, and determination to do right. Ted fitted, so to speak, into the Marlow side of Conrad—and we must emphasize this was only one side of the writer. When the correspondence began on August 24, 1895, Conrad saw himself as almost a father figure, the age difference being almost fifteen years. Many of the writer's comments are guileless, as befitting someone toward whom he felt affectionate and who was not a threat. Conrad reveals that he is working, as ever, with difficulty, that days pass when he feels himself incapable of putting a sentence together, long periods when he says he is unable to invent anything. He was now working on *An Outcast of the Islands*, an important work in his development in the Malay group. He admits he is becoming day by day more uncertain, as though his choice of a new career was in jeopardy. He is conscious, he says, of his unworthiness because of his desire for perfection—surely part of the Conrad who had already begun to measure himself against H. G. Wells and Henry James.

By following his comments to the Sandersons, we can track Conrad's career as he moves from *An Outcast* to *The Nigger of the "Narcissus."* A seemingly off the cuff correspondence proves revealing. Particularly revelatory in the light of attacks on Conrad's inability to deal with his fictional women is his straightforward, admiring, candid commentary to Helen Sanderson: never condescending, never less than honest in his remarks on her early efforts at writing, or on his own. In 1897, as he was poised on the brink, uncertain about his future, still seeking a sea command but with two novels behind him, he was feeling his way toward new territory, toward a novel even Henry James would praise. This was also the time when he wrote his Preface to *The Nigger*, a manifesto of what he hoped to do as a novelist, at least as he saw himself developing now that he was forty and more or less committed to the pen. He tells the Sandersons that his life is now "all stories"; that in his effort to express something about life's essence, he is preoccupied with illusions and shadows. Still in 1897, he tells Ted that the future is as mysterious as it ever was and that every additional happiness is simply another terror added on to life. He senses he may be following a trail that leads to destruction, a chimaera at best. This letter coincides almost precisely with Conrad's suggestion to Ford Maddox Ford (then Hueffer) that they collaborate, a suggestion which resulted in an extended correspondence but a fairly fruitless joint effort. While Conrad may have needed Ford's fluency in English, he also sought friendship, once again with a man almost young enough to be his son.

The complexities increase when we recognize that Conrad's career was moving along, at different speeds, on at least three different fronts, all three of them caught up in correspondences with very different people. At one level, Conrad moving toward collaboration with Ford, especially on *Romance*, their most ambitious project; on another, he was struggling to write *The Rescue*, which proved intractable and which took him twenty-three years to complete (1896 to 1919): on the third, he was moving toward his own distinctive voice, with *Heart of Darkness* and *Lord Jim* at the turn of the century. To reflect these complications, Conrad's correspondence, besides that with the Sandersons, included a give-and-take with H. G. Wells, whose own aesthetic views differed essentially from his own; a sporadic interchange with Henry James, to whom Conrad deferred and at whose artistic goals he aimed; Ford himself, over the collaboration but ranging more broadly into a friendship so intense that Jessie Conrad could not abide the messy, inconsiderate Ford; Garnett, a long-standing professional and sometimes abrasive relationship; Galsworthy, more friendly than professional, although now and then Conrad revealed artistic fears to his well-placed friend.

By isolating just this crucial period in Conrad's development, we see how letters provide contexts for his sense of himself as an artist. He needed location, reshaping, and reinforcement. On the professional front, the proliferation of letters with James Brand Pinker begins in 1899, but these early letters, while revealing and even poignant, are more often business missives than creative. Yet those to other writers not only help us chart Conrad's progress on particular books, but give us insight into the fictional and imaginative premises of his early forays. Only barely mentioned, but perhaps one of the most significant correspondents, was R. B. Cunninghame Graham, the radical Scotsman who captured Conrad's imagination despite their apparent political and social differences. As noted, C. T. Watts, in 1969, edited Conrad's letters to Graham, in what was one of the first meticulously edited collections of Conrad letters to a single person, equal in care to René Rapin's *Lettres de Joseph Conrad à Marguerite Poradowska*, in 1966.

The letters to Graham, professionally, are as significant as anything in Conrad's epistolary history. They are rich and abundant in just that early period when we want to know everything, although later they appeared only sporadically as Conrad went his own way. Graham proved nearly everything to Conrad: sounding board for creative ideas, personally supportive, politically challenging. The landowner from Scotland and the son of Polish gentry found common ground, even to the exotic areas of the world they both found creatively fascinating. The letters to Graham, which add up to some 81, are among the few in which Conrad felt he could write to an intellectual equal. To the Scotsman, he emphasized the hallucinatory element of writing, his fears that his work fell below expectation, his effort to define his own brand of modernism.

WHAT OTHER LETTER groups are of note? All through we have Conrad's extensive correspondence with publishers: Unwin, Blackwood and Meldrum, Methuen, Heinemann, Doubleday, Dent, Knopf (then at Doubleday). A diverse variety of other exchanges took place: with Stephen Crane, letters early on when Crane was more formed literarily than Conrad; Stephen Reynolds, a seaman and writer—a series of 28 from Conrad; the 80-odd batch to William Rothenstein, painter and friend; 50 to Norman Douglas, who for a time became a close friend; the 41 to Wells, already mentioned; a sizable group to Hugh Walpole and to Jean-Aubry; several dozen to Thomas Wise, the collector and forger; over 50 to John Quinn; the 150 to Richard Curle. At one time, individual collections of these letters would have proven valuable, as would have the 1,200 items in the Conrad-Pinker archive. But with the publication of Conrad's *Collected Letters*, coedited by this writer and Laurence Davies, such editions are no longer needed. As this latter edition moves past its fifth volume and into its final three volumes, the full range of Conrad's over 4,000 letters can finally be assessed.

To what use should they be made? While the earlier batches provide contexts for Conrad's fifteen-year burst of creativity, later ones—to Galsworthy, Curle, Quinn, Walpole, Pinker (in particular), Jean-Aubry, and others—chart how his literary work began to take on uncertainties. His plaints during and after the war are many, even as he achieved greater popular success and his financial position was eased. To Pinker, who had now been transformed from agent into confidant, Conrad poured out fears, which spill over into personal books such as *The Shadow-Line*, *The Arrow of Gold*, and the impossibly intractable *The Rescue*. His worries about his son Borys obviously preoccupied him, as Borys fought at or close to the front in France in some of the most dangerous actions of the war. But other worries entered, not the least that for the first time he was making money and in a position to subvert his earlier aesthetic ideals by addressing a more commercialized market. With John Quinn prepared to buy all the Conrad paper he could, the writer produced paper: versions of one piece after another, revised copy, galleys, rewritten proofs, each item now marketable.

How this affected him creatively we cannot pinpoint, but it did preoccupy him with the commercial side of a writer whose very paper had suddenly become valuable. There were other worries. His plaints about Jessie's crippled condition—especially in the letters to Pinker—her need for knee surgery, their frequent trips to London and elsewhere for operations, the fact she might need an amputation, all created in him an unsettling which made it difficult for him to concentrate on what were very personal books. Then he sensed that his powers were failing, that his own disabilities—while not yet of a fatal kind—were bringing him down. Letters to Galsworthy, Walpole, Curle, and Pinker sound like communiqués from a hospital. Gout, neuralgia, bouts of bronchitis, were proliferating; and beyond that, the degree of personal material in these later novels suggests he had depleted his imagination and was now forced to draw ever more closely on elements related to him. If we add all these factors together—and nowhere more than in the Pinker letters are they reflected—they reveal a Conrad dependent on correspondence for support, definition, the working through of uncertainties about himself and his career. Whereas once his letters defined goals or artistic aims, now they focused, even obsessively, on his worries.

Apart from individual batches of letters, even the forty-odd with the illustrious André Gide, broader questions arise of how letters should be read or used in conjunction with a major creative figure. Letters are usually considered deeply subjective, while a literary work has within it more objective reality, a reshaping of the personal, as it were. In critical terms, each is the product of a different kind of narrative. Letters may be disorderly, unfocused, or else particularized; the literary work is shaped, defined, goal-oriented, pruned and polished. Yet, paradoxically, when the writer produces subjective materials (letters, journals, diaries, personal notebooks, jottings), they become "objects" to us when we take up critical or biographical positions. We say that personal documents such as letters give us a direct line into a writer's mind. But especially with a writer like Conrad, caught so closely in the merging of several kinds of life—seaman, Pole, and English novelist—the letter is in a different time frame, a different narrative. Some writers, like George Eliot, serve better as subjects for the blending of letters and fiction writing; Conrad, however, creates a distinct difficulty, since past and present in his imagination were so skewed they squeezed out the specificity of any given letter. In its way, the letter becomes as uncertain as any part of Conrad's fictional self. This is possibly true of most major creative forces, but in Conrad's case it is more emphatic and more intense because of his various reshapings of himself; each reshaping carries with it a different story.

Other problems with letters accrue, particularly when we "read" them as Conrad's efforts to explain himself. We can, as ourselves readers, never more than approximate what that letter meant at that time, since the letter fits into a different order of temporal being from the work being done at that moment. This is not to claim that letters tell us nothing. Early on, Conrad informed Ted Sanderson (October 12, 1899) that he felt "menace" both within and without, but more so from within, as danger, weakness, failure to meet expectations. He writes of fear, which translates into an unreality that penetrates into his very bones, to the degree one becomes "the slave of Hallucination" and can respond only to shadowy substances. The letter appears to create a level of passivity or even ennui in Conrad which would negate the chance of serious work, and it probably reflects his impotence on *The Rescue* manuscript, his fears of marriage and fatherhood, his terror at not being capable of supporting a family, and the anxieties and traumas of the past piling up to haunt him.

Yet while the letter is revealing, and we want to objectify it as a document, it does not tell the truth of Conrad's imaginative processes; for even as he rued inabilities, he was revving up for the most important years of his career, with *Heart of Darkness*, *Lord Jim*, and most of the work on *Nostromo*. Which "truth" do we accept, and how do we read the letter, when the life seems to contradict its message?

We must, in fact, view both the personal words to Sanderson and the inner creative life as extensions of each other. However contradictory, the passivity and ennui seem the very agents which activated Conrad's imagination, so that he struck bottom, as it were, in order to emerge. Letters here, even to someone as neutral artistically as Sanderson, are critical, yet they remain to be read not as they are, but as they fit into a critical/biographical context. Their interpretation depends on what narrative we put them into, on what worlds of Conrad's we choose to define at that moment. The subjective or personal nature of the letter, then, achieves a kind of objectivity mainly because the letter *cannot* be read as it was written. The time frame is off, the historical era differs, the creative element cannot be located. As a consequence, we transform the letter into a document which, like all documents, must be interpreted in several ways. And after that, it still remains uncertain, unfocused, ambiguous. We have lost its narrative and have staked out our own.

Conrad's letters, it becomes clear, must be engaged on several levels. Since he was such a complicated writer and person, we perforce move warily. Collecting the letters and editing them as meticulously as possible is, of course, a high priority. Except in the few instances cited above, this has been a mixed effort; and, in fact, even with the Collected Edition entering its sixth volume and with two more to come, much remains to be done. Each year, letters turn up at auction from private collections and then disappear into other private collections. Or else letters remain completely undisclosed, in someone's attic or cellar. Beyond that lies the need to work with the letters themselves once the texts and possible variants have been assembled. But most of all, we must deal with Conrad's own Proustian sensibility, in which his creative mind did not function chronologically or in chronicle fashion, but like a mosaic, in which some pieces were novels and stories and others were these large blocks of correspondence. Perhaps more than most creative artists, he possessed an inner life with few linear dimensions; and into this we must fit his letters, not only the blocks but even smaller groups, even individual letters which go beyond mundane business matters.

As a final example, we can cite the exchange between Conrad and Gide, extending from 1911 to 1924. For several reasons already cited, this was a trying period for Conrad, as he began to move to a more popular audience with *Chance*; as he struggled with *Victory*, perhaps his most controversial novel; as he suffered the anxieties of the war; as he finally had to confront *The Rescue*, which looped back to the very beginning of his career. The correspondence with Gide—which involved a good deal of bowing and scraping on both sides—reveals how Conrad's career curved back on itself as the consequence of Gide's supervision of the French translations of the former's work. Gide's interest in Conrad's career, as manifest in the correspondence and an occasional visit, came just as Conrad was undergoing uncertainties about his progress in the postwar years; and in translation, Gide, somewhat ironically, brought back before Conrad his earliest and strongest works when he was distinctive and unique, the period of *Jim*.

Yet, further, we find in the correspondence often heated exchanges over the quality of the Isabelle Rivière translation of *Victory*, with Conrad insisting on complete, idiomatic accuracy. Even as that novel receded into the past, he hung onto it, as if recognizing it represented his last major achievement. With the writer being returned to his more powerful early work, we, as readers of all this, find past and present in Conrad blending with each other on one level, but struggling against each other in another. If we read the correspondence well beyond the flattering words Gide extended to Conrad, we observe how the French writer's letters threw Conrad into a further quandary, even as they purported to support him. As a further point, Gide's seriousness about the *Victory* translation reinforced Conrad's own strong view of that novel, which was no longer duplicable.

Just this single correspondence brings us into the recesses of Conrad's imaginative processes, well out of sight of routine critical or biographical data. We enter areas that possibly Conrad was not himself fully conscious of, and we discover both a cornucopia and a desert. Very little externally is occurring—Gide purred and genuflected—but within, the exchange was a maelstrom. *The Arrow of Gold* and *The Rescue*, the two works directly affected by Conrad's return to the past, were possibly impeded or reinforced by the correspondence and the translations, especially since Conrad expressed to Gide how much he valued *The Arrow*. With that novel so full of phantom material—fact as fiction, fiction as fact—Conrad was doubly protective of it. In many ways, it preserved the myth or legend of Joseph Conrad, the Polish youth turned English mariner and novelist. Yet parallel to this was Conrad's appreciation that his younger self was being presented to a French audience, that a new generation would come to know his work in one of his adopted languages. He was caught in Proustian tropes of past and present, and whatever we say of him must take this correspondence, as we must at other periods of his life take all letters, into account before we can speak critically and biographically. Beware the reader who confuses the differing narratives.

The Biographical Dimensions of Conrad's Literary Theory

DESPITE THE GREAT interest shown early on in Joseph Conrad's fiction, there has appeared comparatively little comment relating the ideas on literary technique expressed by Ford Madox Ford in his several chapters on Conrad to the latter's own remarks in his letters, essays, and notes to his first *Collected Edition*. These remarks, when brought together and evaluated, go far to provide a basis for Conrad's literary intentions and suggest criteria by which to judge his early artistic successes as well as his later generally less successful work. They demonstrate almost conclusively that when Conrad forsook the theories he worked out with Ford and those expressed in his early letters and essays, especially in the now famous Preface to *The Nigger of the "Narcissus,"* his work became thin and uninteresting, losing the range and texture of his best fiction. They demonstrate further that when he wrote his Author's Notes, from which several critics have been tempted to derive his aesthetic, he was already shucking off many of the early ideas in favor of the very practices he had once repudiated. Conrad's notes were almost frivolous for a major novelist intent on the seriousness of his craft, and they were obviously conceived more to establish rapport with his newly won popular audience than as a guide to his artistic intentions. If we want insight into the major Conrad, we must return to the critical comments thrown out when he was an apprentice writer still excited by the ideas he and Ford had agreed upon, a time almost twenty years before the debility set in which marked his last years of creative work and which carried over into the notes written during the same period.

It should be mentioned that although this paper will make passing references to Conrad's development as a creative artist, such remarks will always be secondary to the main intention: to examine in detail his literary theory as part of his biography to determine upon what base he built his major works. Consequently, in this paper, I employ Conrad's novels merely to provide concrete examples for various aspects of his theory; a close application of these ideas to the parallel development of his fiction, including the direct relationship between his shallow Author's Notes and later novels, must, for reasons of space, be relegated to another paper.

Ezra Pound said that what Flaubert had done to change French prose, Conrad and Ford did to transform English prose, and he, Pound, was trying to do in order to reshape English poetry. Conrad's use of *phanopoeia*—the piling up of imagistic details which replaced, in part at least, a direct narrative—was, said Pound, the way of the Imagists. The breakup of the conventional novel's narrative into small scenes makes the scene function as an image in poetry, in a way like the images in Pound's own early poetry.

As Pound astutely remarked, Conrad and Ford had arrived at some general principles, a kind of unwritten manifesto of the "New Novel," which in practice profoundly influenced the course of the genre in English. Method in the novel, according to the two experimenters, was as important as in poetry; technique was congruent with style. Technique, says Mark Schorer in an essay that clearly echoes Conrad and Ford, is what Eliot means by convention: that is, "any selection, structure, or distortion, any form of rhythm imposed upon the world of action: by means of which . . . our apprehension of the world of action is enriched or renewed. In this sense, everything is technique which is not the lump of experience itself (in "Technique As Discovery")." Schorer continues: "Under the immense artistic preoccupations of James and Conrad and Joyce, the form of the novel changed, and with the technical change, analogous changes took place in substance, in point of view, in the whole conception of fiction."

The object of Ford and Conrad was, through appropriate technique, to create a semblance of actual experience. Conrad himself had said earlier in his Preface to *The Nigger*, perhaps with Pater's words in mind, that the novel must "strenuously aspire to the plasticity of sculpture, to the color of painting, and to the magic suggestiveness of music—which is the art of arts." He added that it is "only through complete, unswerving devotion to the perfect blending of form and substance . . . that an approach can be made to plasticity." Robert Penn Warren, among others, remarked this blending in *Nostromo* when he noted that the rhythms of that novel seem to suggest the very process of creation. Conrad achieved this, Warren continues, through his use of vista, landscape, time sequences, historical process, anecdote, and language itself.

Ford and Conrad, in their numerous sessions together, worked out their idea of the "planned novel," in which each step in the novel points toward a predetermined effect and leaves nothing to chance. Every word and every action, they said, must carry the story forward—what they called a novelistic *progression d'effet*—wherein the intensity increases as the story develops. This attempt to convey increasing urgency and intensity in the story would involve, said the authors, an assiduous study of all factors relevant to the pace of the novel. One idea, however, always predominated: to unsettle the conventional narrative sequences which had hitherto prevailed in the novel, and by so doing to create new interest in what the two authors feared was now a faded genre. This method meant slow and calculating work, paying unflagging attention to the effect of each scene and character, and maintaining always strict control. Conrad, with his enthusiasm for the French novel and possessing the French penchant for experimentation and analysis, was especially fitted for this role.

The first step was their mutual agreement that a poem was not what was written in verse by anything, "either prose or verse, that had constructive beauty." The emphasis both placed on the interdependent parts of the novel demonstrated that they considered its form like the form of an edifice in which beauty and solidity are interrelated elements. In the construction of the novel, the basic rhythm has to be suggested, they said, in the opening paragraph. The opening part, in fact, should prefigure the entire work. *Romance* (1903), their second and lengthiest collaboration, begins *in medias res*, the (chronological) opening scene not appearing in full context until page 76. But *Romance*, despite its elaborate trappings, is only a simple adventure story, and all the high-minded theories applied to its development do not disguise this fact. The true test of their theories did not come in the collaboration, but in Conrad's individual works; and it is to understand them better than I shall examine some of the conclusions reached by the two experimenters.

As Ford remarked, the opening scene, although disconnected from its true context, should plunge in and suggest dramatically the substance of the work to come. This use of a disjointed initial scene influenced Conrad's later refraction of chronological time sequences, especially those in *Nostromo* and *Chance*, whereby he enters with suggestions and fills out the scene only after roving back and forth into anterior and future time. Replacing a direct narrative with fragmentary scenes is like the poet's use of images, particularly the way the nineteenth-century French poets proceeded. Poems like Rimbaud's "Le Bateau ivre," Mallarmé's "Hérodiade," "Cantique de Saint Jean," and "L'Après-midi," as well as Baudelaire's "Le Voyage," "Les Petites Vieilles," "Le Cygne," and others, are, in many ways, sequences of brilliant and startling images whose juxtaposition often replaces a conventional narrative. This method of poetic breakup applies not only to the narrative structure of the novel but also to the presentation of character. If the trouble with the English novel, according to Ford and Conrad, was that it always went forward, then the obvious thing was to go forward and backward so that once a character has been introduced strongly enough to be remembered, his past is to be caught up with *while* his present and future are being projected. Axel Heyst's past (in *Victory*) is filled in only after his present activities have been set into motion, and Nostromo's activities are picked up almost solely by fragmentary comments for nearly two hundred pages. Similarly, Flora de Barral in *Chance* is the center of a number of concentric circles, and before we can reach her, we must pass through numerous protective layers of commentators.

What was achieved with narrative structure and character development, the collaborators realized, could also be effectively accomplished with speech. Conrad and Ford, perhaps influenced by Flaubert's experiments with interrupted speech, decided that to avoid boredom, long speeches must be broken down, interspersed with narrative, and bolstered by little "jumps" in the pace of the novel. These "jumps" would provide, they said, a "constant succession of tiny, unobservable surprises" which would alleviate the monotony of incessant speech. But Conrad, as an admirer of James, was unable to eliminate altogether the lengthy dialogue. The best he could do on occasion was, like Flaubert in *Madame Bovary*, to temper a lengthy conversation with the bustle of the passing scene as, for instance, in *Chance* when Marlow and Flora talk amidst jostling people and passing carriages in front of Captain Anthony's hotel, or in *Lord Jim* when Marlow first meets Jim in the center of confusion at the court inquiry. Despite these specific instances, however, Conrad frequently broke away from this self-imposed limitation and piled conversation upon conversation, often losing all sense of pace—more than 150 pages of *Under Western Eyes*, for example, consists of lengthy dialogues, most of them consecutive, between Razumov and the various revolutionaries or between Razumov and the Haldins.

The object of all these efforts at control, as far as Conrad was concerned, was to lend an air of inevitability to his scenes and characters so that what does happen must seem to be the only thing that could possibly have happened. Conrad, with his close attention to character development, always had in mind the intricate interactions of the minor personalities as complements to his major figures. Like Browning in *The Ring and the Book*, Conrad believed that a minor character might in the course of things affect the psychology of major characters and thus create a chain of external or internal events of some importance. In *Victory*, the villainous Ricardo, an essentially minor figure who is allied psychologically to Lena, sets off a series of events which result in the destruction of both Lena and Heyst. In *Lord Jim*, the brief scenes with Brierly, with the French naval officer, and with Stein are all of great significance for their relationship to certain elements in Jim's psychology. This theory of interaction maintains that everything that has gone before has some importance in the making and subsequent development of situation. Conrad, therefore, had to be especially careful to "prepare" the facts surrounding every new character and every change of pace, for in this sensitive arrangement of personalities, narrative, and speech, everything is of importance and nothing can be neglected. To get beyond the particular, Conrad realized, is to gain entrance into the total complex of forces acting in and beyond the novel. For beyond what the novelist explicitly states is a blurred mystery that can be reached only through new means. We call this blurred mystery "rich," "various," "like life itself," and it is toward this manifoldness of meaning that Conrad was striving.

Even by the time of the Preface to *The Nigger* (1897), now too well known to need more than a brief summary, Conrad had spoken of the artist "snatching in a moment of courage . . . a passing phase of life" and bringing to bear upon it an imagination bathed in tenderness and faith; the artist, he said, must show life's "vibration, its colour, its form; and through its movement, its form, and its colour, reveal the substance of its truth—disclose its inspiring secret: the stress and passion within the core of each convincing moment" (Kent Edition, p. xiv). Whoever holds to these convictions, Conrad continued, cannot be faithful to any one of the temporary formulas of his craft. All the gods of realism, romanticism, naturalism, and sentimentalism must abandon the artist on the threshold of his struggle with his own conscience. At that moment the convenient categories are left behind, and only the individual intelligence remains: "In that uneasy solitude," Conrad claimed, "the supreme cry of Art for Art itself loses the exciting ring of its apparent immorality. It sounds far off. It has ceased to be a cry, and is heard only as a whisper, often incomprehensible, but at times and faintly encouraging" (p. xv).

Conrad echoed James and Flaubert on the necessity of artistic awareness: he indicated that to show intelligence at every moment and to search out the fundamental, the essential, and the enduring are the work of the artist. The artist appeals to what is in us a gift and not an acquisition. All art appeals emotionally, primarily to the senses—to our senses of pity and beauty and pain and mystery. And how, Conrad asked, can art—particularly fiction—catch this air of sensory reality? How, in short, does "it penetrate to the colours of life's complexities"? Art must, he continued, aspire to the perfect blending of form and substance and through a "magic suggestiveness" bring life into commonplace and overused words (p. xiii).

Conrad, repeating James's dictum that the artist should "produce the illusion of life," then made his famous declaration of intention: "My task which I am trying to achieve is, by the power of the written word to make you hear, to make you feel—it is, before all, to make you *see*" (p. xiv). It is to catch in stasis each passing moment and to reproduce that moment so that it arrests the interest of men; that function, he said, is the aim "reserved only for a very few to achieve." At that moment, the artistic aims of the creator assume a moral importance, achieving a sense of grandeur and of something fully *done* which captures the moral significance of the moment. Thus Conrad realized James's words in which the latter had exhorted the young novelist "to be as complete as possible—to make as perfect a work. [To] be generous and delicate and pursue the prize."

Conrad and James both were careful to distinguish between journalism and literature when they deplored the "fatal futility of fact" alone and opposed it to the forces of imagination. Fact is fidelity to reality, but truth, said James, suggests a world that gives the semblance of reality, and includes *more*. To work toward this "more" is a mark of literary devotion; to succeed in reaching it, they agreed, is the mark of the artist.

In his essay on James, Conrad made the Aristotelian distinction between poetry (fiction) and history; documentary history is based, he said, on second-hand impressions, whereas fiction, or human history, is based on the reality of forms and the observation of social phenomena. Fiction, therefore, is nearer the truth, and the novelist is an historian of human experience. James, as a writer of fiction, as the "historian of fine consciences," becomes something of a moral hero to Conrad for his heroic struggles with his materials, for his ability to record them "with a fearless and insistent fidelity to the *péripéties* of the contest, and the feeling of the combatants" (*Notes on Life and Letters*, p. 15). Fiction, Conrad suggested, can penetrate into the suprareal; history must record the mundane. Fiction gives a semblance of truth in all its variety; history, the facts alone.

"Final meanings," both novelists noted, must be left to the individual writer's power of creativity, for, as Conrad observed, artistic truth lies only in the presentation, and the artist's attention to veracity of expression "is the only morality of *art* apart from *subject*." By claiming this, Conrad joined with James in harking back to their common master, Flaubert, who had once spoken of himself as alone in a crowd, "wrapped in [his] bear skin," while he searched his imagination for the right phrase.

In this connection, Ford commented that Conrad was always in search of new ways of infusing energy and new ideas into the novel. Conrad was, he said, "seeking most of all a new form for the novel, and I a limpidity of expression. . . ." Both authors worked tirelessly on ideas, style, language, the reporting of conversation, the color and texture of prose, toward what Rimbaud a few decades before had prophetically called an all-unifying fiction. Conrad himself prophesied that imaginative prose work would be in a new form, but "a form for which we are not ripe as yet."

Accordingly, Conrad conceived of the novel as history, psychology, sociology, fiction, and poetry cast into one structure and informed by the power of the imagination. Of course, this Wagnerian emphasis on inclusiveness meant that the novel had to become the receptacle of a large vision of human experience. Ford wrote that he and Conrad had agreed "that the novel is absolutely the only vehicle for the thought of our day. With the novel you can do anything; you can inquire into every department of life, you can explore every department of the world of thought" (*Joseph Conrad*, p. 222). In making his characters themselves narrate the story, and thus, so to speak, create the novel, Conrad was moving toward a representation of history in the making. *Chance* and *Nostromo*, with their various points of view which carry the narrative backward and forward, are a sort of literary history in which the "facts" of the story are fictitious while their arrangement aims at historical and social truth.

As his letters amply testify, Conrad was skeptical of the accuracy of any single action. But by presenting several actions and points of view in conjunction with each other, he could weld them to the matter of the novel by building fugue-like scenes; so that the overlapping of characters—as, for example, in *Under Western Eyes* and *The Secret Agent*—ramifies their personal problems into universally felt situations. It is his insistence on inclusion which places Conrad in the line of major novelists of all time with their marked tendency toward comprehensiveness. The twentieth-century quest, in particular, for technical improvisation is perhaps part of the necessity to include as much as possible; certainly *Finnegans Wake* is the most inclusive of novels. New knowledge in every age is absorbed by the novel, and this knowledge could be caught, as Yeats once remarked, only by new rhythms and new forms.

It is perhaps paradoxical that the novel, which exists as a protean and amorphous form for material that cannot be fitted into any other category, should have received such attentive formal treatment. Nevertheless, recognizing that a concern with prose fiction meant a concern with form, Conrad proceeded to attack the problem of structure with a bias that extended poetic techniques to certain aspects of the novel. When Conrad, like Flaubert before him, stated the action of the plot in terms of situation and scene and not from the point of view of the author, he was of course bringing to bear a poetic device upon the novel. Similarly, when Conrad, like James, strove for the creation of pictures—especially those tableau settings that we find in Conrad's early Malayan works—he was using, so to speak, plastic images to "narrate" story and suggest themes. This mixture of the different arts was surely part of Conrad's effort to give form to so formless a medium as the novel.

In this connection, one of Conrad's letters to his friend Mme. Poradowska is instructive, a letter in which, while confiding to her his difficulties in writing English, he especially underscored his trouble in trying to put what he called the "ideas of the novel" into definite form. He wrote: "I prefer to dream a novel rather than to write it. For the dream of the work is always much more beautiful than the reality of the printed thing." Conrad came to realize that a clear-cut and well-defined form for the novel was an impossible attainment and that his frequent use, for example, of the Chinese-box like narration was an indication of his arbitrary procedures. No *single* procedure could be satisfactory. In the "dream of the novel," Conrad implied, the form is protean, and in contrast with reality, the dream has an attractive shiftiness. Form, he recognized, can be only the semblance of experience, but in artistic hands the semblance is often of greater intensity than the real. Conrad had always maintained that his "unconventional groupings and perspective" were purely temperamental, that they existed to give a shifting and fluid sense of effects, and that his entire art rested upon this fact. He particularly emphasized the plasticity of his character and scenic arrangements which he felt were essential to his literary technique.

In *Chance,* for instance, the Chinese box, with its story inside further stories, is at its furthest development in a Conrad novel;

Flora's tale is frequently thrice removed from the reader, and the quotes within quotes appear doggedly on every page. But *Chance* is a radical example of involved scenic arrangements, and in no other book did Conrad indulge his inclination for author withdrawal to this extent. In his other narratives, whether with Marlow or not, impersonality is obtained at a single or double remove. What, however, on a superficial look, may seem extraneous or a mere exercise in virtuosity becomes, on closer view, a matter of importance. The involved method of seeing the material, then, is another way of expressing what Robert Penn Warren called "the urgency of experience," the trademark of the philosophical novelist or poet who is always striving to "rise to the level of generalization. . . ."

One sure way of proceeding from particular to general Conrad revealed late in life in a letter to Hugh Walpole. In considering Flaubert's influence upon him, he protested that his only legacy from his French predecessor was the latter's rendering of concrete images and visual impressions. In the same letter, Conrad remarked that he did not think he had really learned anything from Flaubert. But of course Conrad's entire theory of surface objectivity—the particular image, scene, or extended visual impression suggesting circumstances beyond—is in a direct line from *Madame Bovary* and *La Tentation de Sainte Antoine*.

In matters of tone, a quality or condition in which carefully selected language and images suggest subsurface rhythms, Conrad was an experienced practitioner from *Almayer's Folly*, his first novel. In that book, his reliance on figurative language and simile operated to give a tone beyond that of surface realism. The spirit of generalization was already at work. By tying images to a sense of recall, like Proust in his great work, Conrad was able to create a matrix of images and thus shape a work of considerable density. The image, with its reference to things in memory, becomes evocative, abundant, and charged with associational material. We find Conrad again and again using images which, as they reappear in new contexts with new clusters of meaning, become relevant symbols. So we have the jungle and river of the early novels, the silver of *Nostromo*, the city images of *The Secret Agent* and *Under Western Eyes*, and the island setting of *Victory*. Similarly, the major themes receive some of their substance from a succession of concrete images which at first may seem extraneous. *Heart of Darkness* and "Il Conde," for instance, acquire their structural weight through a series of significant background images, and correspondingly all the major novels are heavily dependent on sequences of imagistic detail for their psychological import. The reiterative imagery increasingly qualifies the bare verbal narrative until the story or novel in question becomes like a dramatic poem in its execution. These recurring imagistic patterns work closely with larger structural units—with time shifts and recurring characters and situations—to give a tactile quality to Conrad's subject matter.

Nevertheless, despite his continual psychological probing toward the center of his subject, Conrad as a novelist worked essentially from the outside. Through the accumulation of concrete imagistic details from as many sides as possible, he created, as it were, a stream of consciousness from the outside. His rich material, he somehow realized, called for a device as psychologically creative as the stream-of-consciousness technique; but without being able to take that step, Conrad, with his proven ability to rove back and forth into memory and into different time sequences through recurring images, developed (without originating) a method that is almost equivalent to the stream itself. If we agree that the stream works through psychologically conceived images which relate to the outside world, then we can see that Conrad's method was similar, although his procedure was to commence not with internal facts but with surface images. In his hands, psychological associations are conveyed through outside detail, an impersonal process in which physical images bore in toward the subject while carefully defining and particularizing their effects.

Commensurate with Conrad's attempt to suggest psychological depth through a surface of multiple images was his desire for precision, a move away from abstractions and unwanted connotations toward what we may call a realism of the word. Part of Conrad's endless dissatisfaction with the English language stemmed from its manifold connotations. He admired French for its clean edges and limpidity. As an example, he mentioned the word "oaken," which in its French equivalent signifies "of oak," while in English it has a variety of possible significations. Conrad desired surface clarity; he did not want his extensions of meaning to stem from verbal confusion but rather to be projections from his sense of scene and human psychology. Too often, he complained, the English word, full of potential ambiguity as it was, would cloud and not extend his meaning. Verbal clarity was essential for exactitude, and surely his inability to write rapidly derived from his need to convey the precise meaning and the precise connotation he wanted. That almost exclusive feeling for the exact word and exact image was part and parcel of his attempt to view his material objectively, however difficult that might be when the subject matter was deeply felt.

In his nervous concern with choosing the exact word—the word free from secondary meanings and undesirable connotations—Conrad was reflecting his background of French reading. In his essay on Maupassant, Conrad commended the French writer's sense of exactness, remarking that actualities rendered are the stuff of the novelist who deals with the concrete in order to glean realities from a "universe of vain appearances." Conrad further praised Maupassant's diligence in polishing his work to obtain "the vision of its true shape and detail," for seeking its inscape, which can be only one true form from an infinity of possibilities; Maupassant's aim, like Conrad's, was that the subject be adequately seen.

Conrad carried this emphasis on detail to his reading tastes. His mixed reaction to Dickens was caused by the latter's "sloppy technique" and moralizing tone. At the same time, he recognized Dickens's great power. And Melville's *Moby-Dick*, Conrad thought, was full of "portentous mysticism," perhaps because of its lack of surface concreteness. He was enthusiastic, though, about *Omoo*, *Typee*, and the South Sea stories, which, probably, he could accept as unpretentious romances. But in Stephen Crane, Conrad found an approximation of the ideal: Crane was a man inspired, "a seer who saw the significant on the surface of things." Crane worked from the concrete to the unstated and could suggest a scene by an odd simile. Notwithstanding Crane's ability to reach into life's truths, within appearances and forms, it is, said Conrad, as if "he had gripped you with greased fingers. His grip is strong but while you feel the pressure on your flesh you slip out from his hand" (To Garnett, Dec. 5, 1897).

Crane's ability, however, to see beyond the surface was also the virtue of the French, particularly, as mentioned, Maupassant and Flaubert. Maupassant himself meant many things to Conrad: his steadfastness during the long years of apprenticeship to the writing craft; the slow development of skills and the never-forgotten goal of excellence; the lack of compromise with style and subject matter; the patience in finding the *mot juste* without flaunting a verbal facility—"a tranquil excellence," Conrad called it; the courage to face mankind with compassion and still maintain detachment while not qualifying his view of reality; the trusting of "his senses for information and his instinct for deductions"; and most of all, that "exact knowledge of the means and that absolute devotion to the aim of creating a true effect—which is art" (*Notes on Life and Letters*, p. 31).

Everything Conrad says about Maupassant also applies to Flaubert, whom the young seaman had read and reread "with respectful admiration" by 1892. Although he wrote no essay on Flaubert, Conrad's letters are peppered with allusions to the French writer's major novels. As early as 1914, Richard Curle compared Conrad with Flaubert, and in a later critical study Edward Crankshaw (*Joseph Conrad: Some Aspects of the Art of the Novel*) pointed out psychological similarities between Conrad's first novel, *Almayer's Folly*, and *Madame Bovary*. It was, however, not Flaubert the realist nor Flaubert the symbolist who attracted the young Conrad, but the Flaubert who in "his unworldly, almost ascetic, devotion to his art" was "a sort of literary, saintlike hermit." In Flaubert's combination of surface detail and constant suggestion through concrete images, Conrad found the Hellenic balance which he recognized as the imaginative faculty, that balance perfectly maintained by Turgenev and Maupassant as well as Flaubert. Conrad's neurotic compulsion toward writing itself was partly based on his fear of losing this delicate balance of imagination, what he at various times called manner or style. He referred to style when he remarked in *A Personal Record* (p. xxi) that in "this matter of life and art it is not the Why that matters so much to our happiness as the How. As the Frenchman said, '*Il y a toujours la manière.*'" Conrad constantly felt an almost Coleridgean dejection at the frailty of his own imagination. In his early letters to Garnett, he wrote of his difficulty in dragging ideas out of himself, for his impressions, he said, are now faded and like "romantic ruins pervaded by rats." He complained that he is continuously haunted by the necessity of style, that his fortitude is being shaken by doubts that are monstrous and have begun to devour him. Each day he found less substance in his work, each day it became more difficult to write and conceive.

Any prolonged study of style or imagination as part of biography must, of course, eventually return to Flaubert, whose letters reflect a spirit almost identical with Conrad's. In both writers, the awareness of style and its possible stagnation became part of their creative processes and helped to mold their aesthetic. Conrad, in a frantic letter to Garnett, lamented that while other writers can lean on dialect or tradition or even the fad of the hour, he had only his personal uncertainties, his "impressions and sensations," to draw upon. In Flaubert, the development of a style likewise signified the relinquishment of props, personal and societal; and this artist, isolated and "wrapped in [his] bear skin," while exploiting personal doubts, must "stand to his work as God to his creation, invisible and all powerful; he must be everywhere felt but nowhere seen."

Both Conrad and Flaubert stressed the impersonality of the creator as a way of preserving the uncertainty, the "half-knowledge," necessary to all points of view. Flaubert wrote to George Sand that "high Art is scientific and impersonal" and that by an effort of the imagination, one must transfer oneself into one's characters. Similarly, Conrad advised Galsworthy to be more skeptical, more impersonal, and to preserve an attitude of perfect indifference toward his characters. Conrad had also warned Arnold Bennett that the latter stopped just short of being absolutely real because he was too faithful to his dogma of realism: "Now realism in art," Conrad said, "will never approach reality." Conrad's writing was based on the variability of human nature and human action. A work of art, he said in a letter to Barrett Clark, "is very seldom limited to one exclusive meaning and not necessarily tending to a definite conclusion."

This staunch belief in incertitudes placed Conrad under personal as well as professional apprehension. His early letters to Edward Garnett, to Richard Curle, and to Mme. Poradowska are sufficient evidence of the power of uncertainties and doubts to pervade both the man and the writer. On September 16, 1899, he wrote to Garnett: all is illusion—"the words written, the mind at which they are aimed, the truth they are intended to express, the hands that will hold the paper, the eyes that will glance at the lines. Every image floats vaguely in a sea of doubt—and the doubt itself is lost in an unexplored universe of incertitudes." For Conrad, as for Flaubert, the pledge to artistic creation was too serious to allow for relaxation or humor; both their public and artistic lives were directed toward creating a personal aesthetic.

In those early letters and essays cited above, Conrad emphasized the qualities of suggestion in his major work and deemphasized its literal significance. He saw fictional art as the manifestation of a fluid and ever-shifting world responsive to immediate intuition but inaccessible to the intellect. His refraction of time, for example, and his frequent use of durational or psychological time were just two ways of defying surface reality. In his essay on James, he spoke of all creative art "as magic, [as] evocation of the unseen in forms, persuasive, enlightening, familiar and surprising. . . ." Conrad maintained that the writer can only educe, that he must leave "final meanings" to imagination, that no word is adequate to convey every nuance he intends, that "the *whole* truth lies in the presentation," and that this attention to veracity of expression, as stated above, "is the only morality of *art* apart from *subject*." Conrad insisted on visualization, on suggestion, on forms, colors, shadows, on the senses as opposed to intellect, on the aesthetic faculty, on man as a symbol-making and not a rational animal.

Accordingly, as he entered his fruitful middle period, from *Nostromo* (1904) to *Victory* (1915), he integrated and objectified his use of images; image gradually became symbol in its suggestivity, and fancy was transmuted into imagination. Conrad learned to conceptualize his material even while recognizing that subjectivity, *qua subjectivity*, did not necessarily preclude effective fiction. But he did realize, as Mrs. Langer (*Feeling and Form*) states it, that "It is usually with the advance of conceptual competence that an artist becomes able to find material outside his own situation, because he becomes more and more apt to see all things, possibilities as well as actualities, self-wrought already into expressive forms in terms of his own art." In his letters, Conrad indicated that the kinds of subjectivity that fail to project emotive knowledge into objective forms, that fail to transmute mere discourse into the illusion of moral illumination, that fail to recognize the variability of experience—all these kinds of subjectivity, he realized, are the province of journalism and not of art.

This ability to conceptualize, which Conrad demonstrates in his major works, sets off the essential illusion from the surrounding world of actuality and articulates its form so that it coincides unmistakably with forms of real life and real feeling. The artist, thus, creates semblances and articulates vital form. From Flaubert and Turgenev to James and Conrad, we find this stress on the transformation of personal material into impersonal masks, to use Yeats's phrase, achieving what has since been called "aesthetic distance."

Central to Conrad's conceptualization of his material was the emphasis he and Ford placed on the sense of the incongruous, which, they said, should be based on the use of contrasts and comparisons. The incongruous situation could, through overlapping and repetition, dramatize combining or contrasting characters and themes, and at the same time keep the author at an objective distance from his material. *Lord Jim*, for example, is full of characters whose personalities are symbols of segments of Jim himself. Likewise, in *Nostromo* and *Victory*, we find characters and situations that hold the novel in balance through their interaction with previous characters or situations. Further, Heyst and Jones (*Victory*) complement each other like Jim and Brown (*Lord Jim*) and in some ways like Decoud and Nostromo. In *The Secret Agent*, the idiot boy Stevie, who draws circles of perfection when disturbed, is an ironic contrast with the "normal" anarchists who want to destroy while he wants to create.

This is how Conrad attained objectivity, imaginatively and not discursively, precisely without being journalistic, clearly without being obvious. When Conrad wrote to Hugh Clifford that no single word or method is adequate—that the "imagination of the reader should be left free to arouse his feeling"—he was of course suggesting that really big themes come through the novelist's awareness of all the potentialities of his subject matter.

In trying to travel the rocky literary path between an 1890s' "code" of artistic anarchy and a Victorian code of professed didacticism, Conrad took refuge, as did Flaubert and James, in that devotion to craft wherein art and morality meet in commitment, responsibility, and lawfulness. By creating the semblance of events lived and felt so that their organization constitutes a completely experienced reality, what Mrs. Langer calls "a piece of virtual life," the artist fulfills his duty to himself and to society. It is only through projection, through dramatization, that the totality of feeling can be communicated. Only artistic projection could bring forth works like *Nostromo* and *Victory*, which are based on the frailest of personal experiences.

When Conrad, in the Preface to *The Nigger* and in his letters, inveighed against the naturalists, the realists, and the romanticists, he was opposing the categorization of art, art that he later said can be only "a wondrous power of vision" which reaches into "life's appearances and forms, the very spirit of life's truth." He said that the scientist and thinker appeal to our common sense and intelligence, always to our credulity, but that it is otherwise with the artist. The artist, Conrad continued, appeals to that "part of our being which is not dependent on wisdom . . . and [is], therefore, more permanently enduring."

The other side of the coin is the position of H. G. Wells, who in his famous statement of self-indictment disdained playing the artist and put himself solidly on the side of the journalists. Wells equated education with rationality and chided Conrad for never admitting that "a boat could ever be just a boat." The impressionist, he felt, was uneducated and, even worse, somewhat ridiculous for forsaking surface reality. Conrad, Wells said, was "always trying to penetrate below my foundations, discover my imaginative obsessions and see what I was really up to." Writing to James, Wells remarked: "When you say 'it is art that *makes* life, makes interest, makes importance,' I can only read sense into it by assuming that you are using 'art' for every conscious human activity. I use the word for a research and attainment that is technical and special. . . ."

Wells, of course, was making fidelity to fact and fidelity to truth one and the same, for as a journalist he was able to make them identical. But not until Conrad's later Author's Notes do we find him blurring, like Wells, the distinction between journalism and literature. Accordingly, when we turn to these notes that Conrad wrote for his first Collected Edition, we notice a remarkable wavering in his aesthetic position, which, significantly, paralleled his loss of creative power in the last ten years of his life. *Victory*, written from 1911 to 1914, was in intention and execution his last major full-length work. Of the remaining ten volumes he published before his death in 1924, only *The Shadow-Line* can command our interest, and even then as something of a farewell to former power. Moreover, it is important to remark that these Author's Notes are *a posteriori*; Conrad was looking back and defining himself to his newly acquired reading public, and not trying to establish a *modus vivendi* for the young Joseph Conrad. Therefore, we should not expect the thrust of youth or the excitement of exploration found in the earlier letters and essays. The reader's disappointment, then, does not lie here, but in the lack of wisdom and insight that should have come with maturity and ripening. Conrad indeed displays little of this advancement; instead, his creative and critical powers seem to have run their course.

As Conrad's ability to imagine his material began to wane, he relied increasingly upon stabilizing props of reality. These Author's Notes abound in attempts to root the story in reality: to provide real people as his models, to substantiate the geographical location of his fiction, to underplay the suggestiveness of his work while emphasizing factual and tangible details. Characteristically, in the note to *Lord Jim*, Conrad spoke of its theme as simply "the acute consciousness of lost honour." In a further remark on the novel, Conrad's emphatic denial of the book's morbidity is a virtual denial of its very power; for in its finer moments the book offers a view of life which is nothing if not morbid. For the biographer, Conrad's morbidity becomes celebratory.

If we judge by these notes alone, Conrad is surely most disappointing among major authors as self-critics. As we sift the notes to the key novels and stories, we find an almost total lack of that "aesthetic feel" running through the Preface to *The Nigger* and the early essays and letters, many of which coincide with his work with Ford. A spirit of weariness is ever present, the same sense of exhaustion that seeped into his fiction of this period. That desire to return to peace and quiet and rest, typified by the rover Peyrol returning home to die, may have signified a general intellectual lassitude in Conrad's later years. The memories were running out, and the remaining props of personal experience were far in the past; the initial energy had been expended, and pressures of nervous attacks were frequent. Furthermore, popular praise was greater than ever before, with the resultant rise in sales.

If, therefore, we want to seek the working aesthetic, that individual approach to the novel which resulted in the best of Conrad's work, we must go back fifteen or twenty years. Just as the amateur seaman had become the professional seaman, so the amateur writer had become the professional novelist, but with professionalism came a decline in power and a loss of the adventure of experiment. In 1912, Conrad triumphantly spoke of those early years as full "of devoted practice, with the accumulated anguish of its doubts, imperfections and falterings in my heart. . . ." But, later, in looking back on his abandonment of *The Rescue* in 1897, Conrad speaks of having then lost for the moment "the sense of the proper formula of expression, the only formula that would suit." It was during a similar loss of conceptual power that he created his later fiction and wrote the docile Author's Notes, rooted as they are in fact and not imagination.

Despite personal inconsistencies, Conrad, however, rarely wavered in his belief in the high seriousness of art, and his literary ideas were catholic enough to include many authors not necessarily sympathetic to his own mind. The high points of fiction were, in his eyes, the sea novels of Marryat and Cooper, the work of Flaubert, Turgenev, James, Chekhov, Maupassant, and Proust, and a mixed appreciation for his contemporaries W. H. Hudson, Cunninghame Graham, and Edward Garnett, an admiration no doubt heightened by his close personal rapport with these men.

The incongruity of these tastes—placing James and Turgenev with Cooper and Marryat, for example—demonstrates that his respect for these writers struck as deeply into their motives as into their results. He had to find not only a sense of responsibility but also a formed and ordered surface. Part of Conrad's distaste for Dostoyevsky, apart from his antipathy to the latter's Pan-Slavism and Czarist politics, came from his recognition of the Russian's formlessness and his "confusion and insanity," the same qualities which had also limited his enthusiasm for Dickens and Melville.

For Conrad, if art and beauty were to unite as moral factions, then there would have to be virility as well as verbal skill, sincerity as well as devotion, responsibility as well as sensitivity, and integrity as well as involvement. Conrad was harsh to those he thought pseudoartists, those who went through the motions without the substance, the fire, the restraint, and the detachment that could transform everyday facts into an artistic vision and the particular into the universal. If the imagination were to bear fruit, it must be an imagination rooted in responsibility, a conception of the world in moral terms that is presented indirectly through a nondidactic surface that derives every nuance and possibility from the arrangement of the material.

MUTANTS/HYBRIDS

It is now clear that many memoirs, autobiographies, and biographies no longer fit into separate categories—such categories were always suspect—but in a postmodern sense overlap each other. They are what I call mutant or hybrid forms of biographical writing. The best single example is Harold Brodkey's *The Runaway Soul*, which while purportedly a novel, is as much a biography of the writer intermixed with what we expect in autobiography. In its utilization of elements from different forms of writing, it becomes a perfect example of a postmodernist work, in this instance a hybrid of forms, something that, rightfully, defies definition.

Following the same lines, I have included an article-review in which there are several mutant/hybrid biographies, of Crane, Wharton, among others. These are successful ventures, but cautionary in that they can be done poorly when the biographer loses a sense of balance and argues forcefully for a thesis that excludes rather than includes. Then we have a tunneled dissertation rather than a meaningful piece of biographical writing. Most of the books under review here are tasteful and insightful and do not make exorbitant claims for their particular angle of vision. The point is that the mixture of genres can result in an exciting and revelatory kind of biographical writing, one that breaks with traditional chronological, sequential biography with its false inevitability and forced continuity.

A Mutant

Biography/Autobiography/Fiction

EVERY NOW AND then a remarkable literary mutation comes along which is so mauled and misunderstood by reviewers and critics that the book for the time gets lost. This occurred with William Gaddis's *The Recognitions* in 1955, now with Harold Brodkey's *The Runaway Soul*. The latter is of particular interest to us since it is a fiction in the (auto) biographical mode, in fact a kind of mutant form of biography and autobiography, or else an autobiographical memoir transformed into a fictional mode. Inasmuch as it opens up many possibilities for biography, even while fictionalizing autobiographical experiences, it seems to fit into a volume dedicated to quest for biography.

The Runaway Soul (1992) is a true MegaNovel, an immensity without inevitable closure, an exploration more than a definition. Its sequence of voices, as in biography, seems to derive from both within and without, from a middle area between conscious and unconsciousness. A monster of self, this book helps define an enormous range of emotional and private life. It is, in one respect, the ultimate in the life of the individual consciousness, and, apparently, it cannot be everyone's cup of tea. Most clearly, it is not for daily reviewers, nor even for those with a weekly deadline. Those comfortable with Updike, Oates, or Bellow, or other quality writers like them, apparently cannot handle long, convoluted, difficult novels not only by Brodkey, but by Gaddis, Pynchon, McElroy, to name only four. These books require another dimension of reading, a sympathy with innovative, often opaque narrative strategies, an ability to enter into difficult contexts, an openness to the fictional process in all its mutational abundance, and the tolerance, in several instances, to withstand longueurs, and missteps. (An exception is Robert M. Adams in the *New York Review of Books*, Nov. 21, 1996.)

When we take all considerations into play, the Brodkey novel is a pioneering piece of work, a testing out. Rather than letting down his audience from his previous collections of stories—several of which are incorporated here—Brodkey made *The Runaway Soul* into the apex of the short story writer's craft. The man who wrote the stories has matured into a many-leveled writer. Unfortunately for many critics, the book appears to disregard its audience, becoming an introspective journey of such proportions that the reader becomes lost in byways and labyrinths; so private in places that one follows only with peril; and, overall, so full of private hatred, anger, hostility, and reactive energy that the emotional life within is always near disintegration:

> The reality of being empty [Brodkey writes], of being defiled by grown-up life—by love among other things—the distillation and concentration of love is the heart of long-term fucking, perhaps too of the efforts on one's part to rule one's life. To understand one's choices, even that one has made choices and the connections and parallels, the threads and gimmicks of the foreseen: all that happens in a certain somewhat literary, French tone, in emptiness. She, Ora [his Harvard lover], *fights* to see that we love, that I do . . . I really don't know why: I know it is a human and not an absolute thing. It scares me . . . makes me uneasy . . . makes me ironic and superior. . . . (p. 198)

The emptiness goes well beyond the hole that the narrator, Wiley Silenowicz— adopted at two by the Silenowiczs—feels as an adoptee. It moves well beyond accommodating difficult adoptive parents (while his blood father is still alive and able to send support checks) who fight constantly and try to destroy each other in the boy's presence. It, the hole, goes well beyond the sexual imagery which underlies nearly every aspect of the book, mainly heterosexual, but also homosexual, as Wiley teeters on one edge or another. It goes beyond Wiley's own comprehension of his precarious situation, as he confronts the abyss of his own existence and recognizes how fragile his sanity is. The emptiness goes into the very metaphysical condition of life as Brodkey forms it—in the tradition of Kafka and the French literary elements frequently alluded to. Emptiness, however, is not merely negative, but a force to be reckoned with, containing an energy of its own. Brodkey turns emptiness, *his* black hole, into a weapon, part of his sensitivity to the nuances of his responses; and part of his sexual makeup. To confront and struggle against emptiness, he must mount a mighty offense; and it is that offense which compels Brodkey to keep coming at his material. Emptiness becomes the great equalizer as well as the great obstacle. It gives Brodkey, and Wiley, a handle on life, as it were. It takes on spiritual significance, although outside any conventional sense; and it does create a kind of sacred condition which allows Wiley to "float," when he might otherwise sink. It shapes the fictional equivalent of the biographer's search for the source or origin of his or her subject's creativity, the imagination or epiphany which makes the subject unique.

Emptiness shapes the meaning for Wiley's life; and Brodkey, as biographer of Wiley Silenowicz, must discover the many ways of this black hole. One way in is through chronology. The narrative is based on interruption, from infancy to adulthood, with numerous side trips, including those as brief as twenty minutes. Time loops shape the labyrinth and valorize the emptiness. Wiley is born in 1930, in a single page, then removed to 1944 (for four brief episodes, when his adoptive father,

S. L., died), then moved back to 1932, when he is two years old, forward to 1956, for a episode with his Harvard friend Ora, returned to 1932, at two, then forwarded again to 1956 only twenty minutes later. At other stages in the novel, Wiley returns to the times when he was thirteen, fourteen, fifteen, for extended episodes with Cousin Daniel, Leonie, and Remsen, one heterosexual relationship, two homosexual. There seems no apparent reason for this division, except that Wiley's blood mother dies when he is two (1932); but 1956 seems arbitrary. The twenty-minute break in 1956 is not developed as a temporal idea; and the return to teenage sexual experimentation could have come chronologically as well as through interruption. Meaning must lie elsewhere.

These cuts back and forth, some in long, swooping episodes, themselves full of time loops, make no overwhelming statement in themselves. Little in the novel "adds up" conventionally. Like an adventurous biography or autobiographer, the novelist works more on association, which the accommodating reader comes to accept. The associations describe Wiley's inner workings, both early and later, his sexual adventures, his relationship with parental figures, most of all with his extraordinary creation, his adoptive mother, Lila, not to mention his adoptive sister, Nonie. The grounding must be not the "why" but the "how," an element often missing even in serious biography.

As we know from "A Story in an Almost Classical Mode" (and the volume containing it), Brodkey is splendid on mothers and sons, his specialty, one might say. That story is more than a shadow piece for the novel. The relationship the son has with his mother is the emblem of a broad journey Brodkey encodes for the reader. The key word is journey. The language serves as a sucking-in force, so that once the reader is engaged, it is not narrative that captures him, but the pull of words which create their own kind of labyrinth. The journey takes several turns and operates on several performance stages: the inner journey of the protagonist Wiley, which is dominant, extensive, and exhaustive; the journey toward knowledge—sexual, psychological, familial, intimate; the journey we associate with the transcendence of the individual, toward some process of self-re-creation and transformation; finally, the journey toward spiritual awareness of our place in the world or universe. The latter is not in any traditional sense a religious quest, but a metaphysical grappling with the nature of our existence, which Brodkey hopes to achieve through language. The young boy is a reader, but reading alone is limited; he must discover the words which approximate *his* thoughts, reaching back past his conscious mind into some region of the unconscious. The blurring of narrative, the confusion of realms, the privatizing of emotions, the convolutions of Wiley's story, all, are part of Brodkey's quest for the way in which that "unconscious realm" can be penetrated.

Yet his aim is not to resolve the forces which may lie in the unconscious. To penetrate to the shadows does not mean he can bring matters to the surface or claim special archeological powers. Quite the contrary. To penetrate close to the kingdom of the unconscious is to discover the process by which the unconscious functions. If he can bare Wiley's deepest thoughts, going well beyond the traditional therapist's goals, then Brodkey can probe not the matter of the unconscious—which is unknowable—but possible ways in which it works. Process, not results, is all. The neo-Lacanian implications of this for biography and autobiography are immense, not the least in terms of narrative and psychological probing of the creative mind. Brodkey seeks epiphanies, just as the biographer seeks those moments in the subject's life which provide transcendence.

To express his quest for penetration, for his ability to transcend, he describes numerous passages of "reaching," some of them quite convoluted. These are passages which soar from earth to heaven and back again, part of that openness in which the writer yearns for ultimate freedom from traditional restraints. "The Talmudists," Wiley meditates, "who proposed a contraction of God—called *zimzum* (I think)—to allow in the abandoned space the world to exist with its inhabitants condemned after Eden, to moral choice—separately from the omniscience of Omnipresent god—also proposed never listening to women. Or rarely. What my mother hinted at was her sense that thought was the track or wake of the truth but wasn't the whole truth but was as strange, as ambiguous, as subject to interpretation as Biblical text was for the Jews—and for others" (p. 225). The thought here is both simple and very complicated. It intertwines zones. After the Fall, Jews were allowed a space of their own, without God's omnipresent interference; and this Wiley extends to the exclusion of women, a misogynist idea not out of keeping with the Old Testament. Yet from this, what he extrapolates further is Lila's assumption that truths lie beyond thought, as much as the biblical text allowed for freedom of movement beyond God.

In a related passage which also suggests transcendence, Wiley notes that Lila lets him "peek at reality. . . . she lied about reality—both about the crimes there, the pains, the assertions of will, the blindness and the rest of it, and about the limits that the crimes perhaps do not go past. She lied about the degree to which we [Wiley and Nonie, his older troubled stepsister] were not in Eden and the degree of absolute innocence she, and we, had." But that is not all. "But, you see, then, Nonie and I, S. L., too, we were in Eden part-time, when she allowed it. And, sometimes, we were sent out by assassins from a castle to deal with reality" (p. 226). Her commands were always ambiguous, for Wiley could not know if they derived from her desire to permit him into Eden or were part of her expulsion of him from the Garden.

The language of a sacred place of course links several aspects of Brodkey's thought here; where the family, a "holy family," is traduced by the reality lying outside; where the children are offered a sacred resting place, only to be expelled by a remark, a domestic argument, a discontinuity, a reckless bit of behavior. The sacred place would seem, at first, to be the area God has allowed them, safe from evil committed in the Garden; but then that is vanquished with words or with a sleight of hand. Whimsy controls more than rules. Brodkey must struggle to maintain Wiley's persona against Lila's attack, in much the way the biographer must entangle and then disentangle himself or herself from the subject.

As a presence, Lila is both an archangel and the devil incarnate; her alternate roles right up to her death are necessary fixtures in Wiley's mind. Even Nonie, his wild, unfocussed, difficult, half-mad stepsister, is often an extension of the wild and half-mad Lila. The latter is a gray eminence, someone who dogs Wiley into his eighteenth year, even as her words nudge him toward some transcendence.

On her death bed, Lila sends for Wiley, now a freshman at Harvard—in order to set the record straight, if we assume anything she says is reliable. As a narrator, she may be no more credible than the biographer. Many of the scenes at which Wiley was not present or was too young to understand are now filled in—she is witness, once again with her reliability in question. In a curious reversal of roles, she now becomes Wiley's biographer, and in her way she subverts Wiley's efforts to write her life. The subtext of all of Lila's assertions is that she must rationalize and defend herself, that while we may think of her as candid, she may really be deceptive and incapable of containing her venom. Wiley refers to her: "she meant to be remembered—to have earned her way. She was a fatal, mortal Scheherazade, a Morgan Le What's-it, *fatale* to the end—innocent by virtue of death, virtuous chiefly as a come-on—how startling she was for me" (p. 597). His assessment of her, in this critical segment called "Love Story," reveals sexual machinations Wiley was not privy to earlier. His sister and Casey, an older female relative, were having a covert affair; Wiley's blood mother was in love with her maid; and more. Lila's intent, superficially, is to educate Wiley in the ways of the world, but nothing is quite that simple. We move deeply into biographical matters, especially those questions of reliability, of validating information, of choosing points of view.

We have to reckon with several factors which reach deeply into this mutant form. Like a biographer, Wiley is himself the funnel for information for the reader, via the dying Lila. Her motives are not clear, and, therefore, her narrative of events is clouded by mixed motives and her dying state. Wiley is himself grappling not only with what happened, but with how those events—those true, those perhaps imagined, those in the shadows—have molded him into what he is. As any narrator, he is himself not a reliable witness, even though he is reclaiming his own experiences. The autobiographer is no more grounded in truth than the biographer. He is unreliable not because Brodkey wishes to deceive us, but because Wiley has become so subjective that everything has been transformed by inner need, and ego. In his compulsive need to know, and to transmit that knowledge to the reader, he, Wiley, has placed a pattern on experience and events which are themselves open to question. Indeterminacy is key. The result may be numbing, soporific, or exciting, as the case may be, but the narrative unfolding has, in fact, almost infinite possibilities; thus the great length which usually characterizes this mutational form. Mutation may be the generic label, but discontinuity and disconnection are the catalysts.

Even as Lila narrates her "stories," even while Wiley questions her veracity, he suspects her of deception and argues she cannot be trusted; nevertheless, she becomes, for him, the link between past and present—as if she were the biographer shaping his life. Part of the adoptive process, he feels, is that pastness has been discontinued from present. His blood mother died when he was two; his blood father continues to send support money, and his adoptive parents are the ones he relates to, even when he feels they are more cousins than parents. As for his "sister," Nonie, she is of course not related by blood, but is part of a blood group from which he is excluded. That exclusion in Brodkey's hands is like the expulsion from the Garden; somehow, in the boy's and adult's mind, the linkage by blood to parents is an aspect of the Garden from which he has been excluded by the circumstances of his adoption. He also feels cut off from what he was, since his "stories" are not experienced in a natural setting, but in an unnatural one. As he moves around with various relatives, he is both included and excluded: part of that edginess which makes him want to accommodate the stories of the dying Lila. To carry our analogy to the next stage, it is as though Wiley suddenly found himself in a biographical study and had to grope his way to familiar coordinates against the biographer's own shaping.

THE MOTIF OF this huge, sprawling text is caught in the evocative title, the story of Wiley/Brodkey as "a runaway soul." The author tries to capture it in a few words, although the title resonates throughout. "The *runaway soul* goes groping—and plunging—flying and lying—and trying—and dying. . . ." The runaway soul evokes the spatiality of adolescence and young adulthood in America, the spatiality which, while offering so much, is also an entrapment; the sense of escape linked to the where to? of the run. But the phrase also involves other dimensions: to run away from oneself, into unknowns—here chiefly sexual and social; to run away from familial relationships, here two sets of mothers and fathers, a sister who is less than sister but more than cousin; cousins with whom homoerotic games are played. The runaway soul, also, must grapple with stabilities, which turn out quite otherwise, volatile and unpredictable.

Most of all, the runaway soul is a wild, primitive thing, itself so volatile it can hardly be contained. Much of its wildness comes from almost ungovernable sexual urges, but not all; some from the need to find anchors when one's background has proven so mixed, strange, uneven, even destructive. The "soul" must run away from Lila and Nonie, from the influence of half-crazed women, into a world of maleness, which itself does not prove satisfactory. Self-discovery is at the core of the runaway soul, but it is never resolved, never finalized. The "soul" forbids closure.

The 1980s lent themselves to a whole spate of mutational autobiographical/biographical/fictional memoirs, although pointed more toward memoir than Brodkey's work. We can list just some: Richard Rhodes's *A Hole in the World* (1990), Paul Auster's *The Invention of Solitude* (1982), John Edgar

Wideman's *Brothers and Keepers* (1984), Tobias Wolff's *This Boy's Life* (1989), Susan Cheever's *Home Before Dark* (1984), Edward Rivera's *Family Installments* (1982), Carl Bernstein's *Loyalties* (1989), Edmund White's *A Boy's Own Story* (1982); in 1979, Geoffrey Wolff's *The Duke of Deception*. In these memoirs, it is apparent that the time, the 80s, and place, America, have come together to give birth to a particular kind of book. As with Brodkey's sense of adoption, discontinuity and disconnection are the battleground for 1980s memoirists. Their wounds—some of them severe—are part of the psychological wounding of the country: the failure of institutions to help desperately needy children; the lack of concern for family care and values; the lack of emotional maturity in parents; the economic deprivation of families living without support systems; the absence of adequate health care for those just outside systems; and beyond that—particularly in the Brodkey book—the general feeling that anarchy is out there, an absurd sequence of skewed adult lives and random incidents simply waiting to devour victims, chiefly the young. Families are, quite clearly, no longer families. The basic theme is the disharmony between the child growing up and his or her immediate society, and then, in the next stage, between disparate elements in the child.

Growing up in these memoirs is a large military campaign, with skirmishes, maneuvers, strategies, delaying tactics, losses, gains, advances, retreats. The big news is not that these memoirs constitute a new subgenre, but that they are so clustered in one decade: they suggest, among other things, rebellion, revolt, insurrection against the holiest of institutions, the family, and beyond that the state or government. The primary trope is the "hole," characteristic of the memoirs and of the Brodkey novel, the hole outside and within. The question is how to fill it. It devours, engorges, consumes, in some primitive peristaltic way. The "hole" is linked to Wiley's inability to define his own story. "It is genetically *weird* to be adopted. From deep inside yourself, what you are is stuff that is visiting, not entirely, not even all-in-all, but enough that you feel like an intruder even in grief, even when it's your own grief" (p. 32).

What creates the emptiness in the runaway soul is the feeling nothing is real; "he" is not my real father, Wiley says, and he extends that to virtually every aspect of his existence. The dual parents dwindle to none, or else the dualism is balanced out by the nothingness. He speaks of the hole, which creates a doubling action, to fill it or to evade it. "I want to avoid my [adoptive] mother and sister . . . I don't want to be part of their dealing with their father's and their husband's death" (p. 32). Even though he came to the Silenowiczes at two, they represent the hole, not the filling of it. He enters their weirdness, becomes a supplement to it, serves as a crutch for them, but can never be part of the family. Their story and his can never coincide. Two young sons died, both in the care of Nonie, and she is suspected of having done in one, possibly both, although nothing could be proved. Wiley is the replacement, and Nonie treats him with both contempt and flirtatious interest. While she is adamant, half mad, ungiving, a would-be Medea, Wiley develops as fragile, uncertain, sexually confused, undirected for the most part. The desire to run away is of course to achieve self-discovery, but also to validate himself as a person; unfocussed in his identity and direction, the adoptee hopes to seek the Garden outside the home, possibly in himself.

In several respects, then, the Brodkey novel is a Growing-Up fiction, but a mutation that, as it were, devours all genres. Very late in this novel, about 400,000 words along, a passage encapsulates what the runaway soul must confront both inside and outside itself. The context for the passage is compelling. It comes in a section called "Leonie's Fiancé," in a long chapter-like segment titled "Leonie or The History of a Kiss," a segment that also includes "On Almost Getting Laid." The hundred pages plus of this interlude are among the most Proustian of the Brodkey chapters, with the "kiss" the rough equivalent of Proust's tea and madeleine. The kiss here is supposedly the prelude to "getting laid," but it proves to be something else entirely, since the enormously long episode ends with masturbation. The kiss functions as a means of centering different kinds of information, including speculation on the entire range of one's sexual activity, male as well as female.

The following passage allows Wiley/Brodkey to spin out intermediary ranges of experience, areas close to reverie and fantasy, recoverable only through a kind of personal therapy which blindly seeks out words. Brodkey targets nothing less than an innerness impenetrable by language.

> The evening is a pimp. The finality of the sexual terrain is terror-cum-outcry in the scandal of being male, not as a preliminary, as in my experience so far, but at being given a huge white world, whitelit, brief, briefly comprehensible, in regard to others' destiny—a gambler's intrusion on further time—and on life . . . Romantic distances are not real distances—not like time or like going out into a river. Romantic distances ache with their breakability. . . . The childish part of me, the leftover blondness of what I am, is a dirtiable, naughty sunlight warmingly touching her. She was supple—some girls I'd fooled around with had collapsed after a while into woodenness and fluster into being rooted and heaving twigs and leaves in a wind, sexually. The clumsy intimations of how anarchic and ungeneral the power is in love in each person—love in regard to one's own self, which is all one can know from immediate experience—one's own powers and defenselessness in regard to that interfere with one's perceptions: the sickening and deliciously sticky sense of guilt and innocence fixes one's eyes, inward and outward—not everyone can bear this stuff. (p. 739)

The play of reverie here is carried on chiefly with women, Lila, Nonie, and Leonie, with later interludes with Ora, when Wiley is a Harvard student; although some homoerotic episodes exist as well, with Daniel, his cousin, and then Remsen, plus other minor figures. But the chief line of reverie derives from women, not only as sexual creatures but as femaleness itself. Brodkey is trying, among many adventures, to discover the very significance of what it is to be female, what it takes to be male. He does not accept received information. Here autobiography merges into biography, the subject as narrator of his own condition, and then fictionalized, so that biography and autobiography become submerged in the creative "I."

Much of Wiley's sexual experimentation—some episodes running on at great length—is concerned not with sexual fulfillment, certainly not with reciprocity, but with the way in which mechanics (kissing, foreplay, even forms of penetration) and feeling can possibly become linked, or else fail to connect. By way of sex, he is seeking another dimension in life, and thus the episodes of seemingly endless speculation and, yes, kissing. In kissing, he senses the ways of the world. "One of the things you feel in a kiss is the degree of susceptibility and resistance of the other person to being ruled and how nice (and submissive) you are each being now or not. I could feel in her that she was a death-or-freedom girl. . . . No one to joke with" (p. 736). This is with Leonie. But Nonie, too—she nuzzles and tempts, half seduces her stepbrother.

Sex is not a completed act—there is little enough of that in the 835 pages of the novel. Like autobiography itself, it remains "open." But sex is prevalent almost to an obsession. The way in which one is aroused, or led along, the way in which one comes together with another, all, are far more significant than orgasm or even satisfaction in the act. The point of view is male, but Brodkey goes further than any contemporary American male author in trying to understand the femaleness of the female. The biography of a woman, chiefly Nonie, is as strong as the (auto)biography of Wiley. Brodkey spends a hundred or more pages trying to penetrate into Nonie as an individual, as a woman, as a daughter responding madly to an almost mad family. Wiley speaks of Nonie—whom he hates through most of the novel—as having "a lasting tact about some of the pragmatic realities of childhood" (p. 828). She has fought off madness, perhaps she's been mad, perhaps, even, has committed the unspeakable act of smothering one or two of her brothers. Although uncharged, Nonie grows up with Lila believing her daughter has killed one or two of the small boys, and that is a factor in the shaping of the relationship—as it also rubs off on Wiley. The latter comments: "But that tact [about the pragmatic realities of childhood] turns outward and is clearly part of a case of Nonie's being the center of decency in her system, the central repository of civilization; she is a young girl of suffering semi-equilibrium now, a consciousness stretched taut over certain inadequacies of consciousness" (p. 828). Wiley is writing this after Nonie has burned to death in her house, married, mother of five sons, all of them "black-mooded, difficult, detestable" (p. 819), unsuccessful, from Wiley's point of view. But now as the writer of Nonie's story, he has to come to understand her terrible fight to win her personal way: "We're all trash but in different ways" (p. 819). By attempting to understand her, Wiley hopes to understand how he is like her, suffering comparable pain.

As the "writer" of all these stories and also as the subject, Wiley is both narrator and participant in a panorama of pain. We know from several of the longer stories in *Stories in a Classical Mode* that agony cannot be evaded. Brodkey is a master of ceremonies at a spectacle in which pain is played out in three rings. He controls the circus, with each act in it as a form of pain—to the extent that it is a defining moment, a test, so to speak, a time when one can assert oneself as a human being. He derives from Kafka in this respect: the moment of pain is not negative, but a testing ground; and without pain, the individual slumps into otiosity. Since pain is the subject, the motif, the spine of the novel, the sensation can be prolonged indefinitely: the more episodes of pain—familial, sexual, growing up—the more the book can be extended. Not unusually, the first segment of *The Runaway Soul* is titled "Life on the Mississippi," indicating the journey Wiley must take.

If pain defines the moment and, in its way, defines the person, then Wiley must struggle to come through. He can never settle for less than the struggle within himself, and he catches this in a Kafkan and Proustian image. "If it is like being locked in a coffin, rather than a cell, then it follows that it is sensible for the senses to bulk up so in one's consciousness that every fragment of color and bit of smell registers and not nostalgically but as a blur of clarity of something largely not to be explored here, merely experienced and to be thought about later and known then if it is to be known" (p. 504).

Narcissistic though *The Runaway Soul* is, it goes beyond narcissism and defines how one can look at oneself. With Wiley as analysand, we can perceive the entire novel as a sequence of therapeutic sessions, with time leaps, chronological convolutions, and vast deserts. Without regard for any censoring device, the novel is the process of a consciousness unfolding. The consciousness will be as candid as it can ever be, although we know that the narrative given to the analyst in therapy is not the original or "Ur" narrative, but one molded and shaped, even as the biographer molds and shapes his or her narrative for the reader. We know this, but even so, we see in Brodkey's exploration the possibilities of the "ultimate self": not as a pleasant boastful thing—unlike the Mailer mode—but as a weak, deplorable, often repellent element. Brodkey is not attempting to prove how great he is, but to display how, despite all his weaknesses, he has at least the strength to come through. He is not vaunting himself, as many did in the 1980s, but seeking the roots of consciousness, as a man of the 1960s, when the project began to take shape. While a writer like Mailer wants power, control, the Napoleonic energy to command and triumph, Brodkey eschews the larger world, seeking the energies which will enable him to burrow in and turn his pain into writing.

In a curious twist, personal, religious, and political intertwine. Despite playing with religious imagery—in his "affair" with Ora, for example, her name suggesting oratory, a religious service, prayer—Brodkey eventually folds the religious into the political in its broadest sense. The religious element recurs in the desire for transcendence, which never occurs; in the desire to turn words and language into forms of transformational or sacred worship; in the pursuit of spiritual imagery, as in the moth image that comes with Ora, a "giant, fluttering moth," which may be a personal image for some spiritual or divine experience. Repeatedly, Brodkey searches for ways in which religious imagery and personal, private sacred images can suggest and define human experiences; and, repeatedly, he comes away empty-handed.

The consequence is that the religious and spiritual must be given over to the political, by which we mean something territorial. Wiley is constantly seeking the ground on which he can win, although we must emphasize that he rarely "wins," more that he avoids losing. In his repeated teenage sexual affairs, he plays with power and control: at thirteen, with his cousin Daniel, whose homosexuality he perceives; a year later with Leonie, who is ten years older and engaged; then at fifteen, with Remsen, also older by two and a half years. These "affairs," such as they are, do not end in sexual satisfaction; rather, they are staging areas or arenas where power games can be played out. But the control and power gained from the sexual games are not expansive or cumulative; they do not make Wiley into a powerful person. Unlike Mailer's CIA operator in *Harlot's Ghost*, they do not give him any prolonged sense of his increased strength. The events with the older men and women are merely stages, without any accumulation of wisdom accruing from them.

The political elements, accordingly, reinforce the acquisition of knowledge which helps Wiley to become a writer. By the time he has the affair with Ora at Harvard—Ora, who cannot come to orgasm—Wiley has published some stories and is on his way to becoming Harold Brodkey. The auto(biographer) has become the fiction writer. He has not become more resolved or settled as a person, but now he accommodates knowledge that may become part of the process he calls writing. As suggested above, Brodkey is searching for some "truth," however invalid that search may be when the subject is one's own consciousness. But he is not to be distracted: he seeks fiction, not biography. "If everything is possible to belief," he writes, "then one might throw oneself from the porch in the conviction that one might fly. We have only small laboratories of time and limited abilities and we have large wonders and great horrors to deal with; and often a vastly unconquerable unhappiness stands in our way—so we had better be limited—limited in terms of knowing anything—limited in terms of fidelity to abstract truth since, then, lying has special importance. Because then the truth is testified to by the lie, by its, the truth's, not being what the lie is. It exists then" (p. 510).

Prototypical Brodkey, the prose takes us to the edge of an idea, that since we have only "small laboratories of time and limited abilities," we must be limited in our aims; that is, in our desire to get at the truth. But the swoop of prose encompasses more, for Brodkey then can move to his real point as he enters the interstices between fiction and biography: that truth is not some abstract principle, as he has implied, but an element which is tested by a lie, so that truth remains after the lie has been leached out. But even that is not certain, inasmuch as we are dealing with "truth"; and what remains after the lie is gone may not be truth at all. All we count on is possibility, an "immediacy." Brodkey follows this with a typical symbolic passage about sleep as a journey carrying one into "a merciless transience of light that proposes itself as stillness and absolute meaning and as theater. . . ." (p. 510). The echoes of Baudelaire, Mallarmé, and other French symbolist poets are not by chance. Brodkey wants to note that sleep as a journey is not unlike our movement in our waking life, where reverie and fantasy are themselves a kind of theatre. In the center of that theatre is a stillness, which is a form of life-in-death or death-in-life. This is the ambience the individual moves around in, and the soul running is the way in which that somewhat transcendent movement can be captured.

The life Brodkey charts for Wiley is a kind of opera (opera sets are rarely far from the novel's imagery), which can be a fearful experience for a boy growing up. If pain is the center, and the ability to withstand it the process, the fear of isolation from normal events and activities can be intense. Wiley speaks of his fear of "having no mind except a specialized one . . . I didn't think I was smart; I thought I had very limited possibilities. . . . I didn't see how to exert will without doing damage" (p. 526). One salient fear is that his isolation will condemn life, that he will become a prisoner of his own imagination. The perception is revealing, in that his recognition that the very internality which gives him the material for his reveries and fantasies may well entrap him; he becomes a prisoner, unable "to escape from those postures" (p. 526).

The Brodkey journey, twisting this way and that, forward and backward, all as part of some timeless, unconscious process, leads to an amusingly titled chapter called "David Coppermeadow," caustically modeled on Dickens's Copperfield. As an adopted child, Wiley feels he has been both wanted and rejected, feelings which are intensified when he visits uncle and cousins. They are rich, he is an upper-middle-class pretender, and he senses how they move to different time schemes from his. He is, once again, the odd fellow out, unwanted, an adoptee; and as in his other ventures, he must be accommodating in order not "to have worse memories about oneself" (p. 330). Words, even expressions of feeling, cannot mitigate being an adoptee. It is a state of being, an unconditional situation. "You are not perhaps a person quite. . . ." (p. 330). He is a pet and an enemy, an intruder in the family of three, "an outsider—a distraction—a possible ally. . . ." (p. 330). He becomes a reclamation project for Lila, an unknowable commodity for S. L. He is not sure who likes him, or if their tie to him is simply a matter of duty. His own father, after all, is alive, so that the death of his mother when he was two does not mean that Wiley had to be put out for adoption. But all drop away: his father then dies, as does S. L., as does Nonie much later, and also Lila, in between, of cancer—that terrible cancer as we know from "A Story in an Almost Classical Mode."

Implicit in Wiley's survival is the subtext of violence. Not only is Nonie suspected of having killed one or two of her brothers, she is involved in other instances of both physical and emotional violence. The contradictory nature of her parents during her childhood leads her to a barely subdued public character which disguises a personality based on anger, hostility, and violence. That she dies in a blaze is not happenstance; she is herself part of fire, mephitic in her undertones of distress, deceptions, desire to shape her femaleness, her frustrations and inability to control elements despite a dictatorial nature. That subtext of violence lies everywhere: in Wiley's adoptive father's rages against marriage, family, household; in Lila's overwhelming need to break out of what she has herself created for herself; in the cousins, with their labyrinthine tastes, disguises, anguish; in Nonie, as stated above; and in Wiley, whose gentleness of manner cannot hide a need to get under the skin, to make life difficult or unbearable for others. He refuses any easy commitment to romance, nostalgia, certainly not to love, not even to affection. He bends and melts and reshapes himself in relationships, until all that remains is that unformed self, like an octopus in its many reaches.

The Runaway Soul resists categorization and classification. It is a screed, but then it is also the biography of a family. Ostensibly, it is about a search for love, or self, or definition, or all three. But it goes much further than those sentimentalized quests; it aims for the divinity in human life that is not basically religious or spiritual. Brodkey, in other words, is seeking what can never be recovered: the sacredness of self when all the siren calls are secular; the divinity within the individual who fears, most of all, his separateness from the main body; the spirituality of human aspirations when spirit and God and church are themselves commodities. *The Runaway Soul* is a plea for letting all the unreason in the individual and in the world around him (or her) have its rope, for unleashing the forbidden, the inhibited, the unspeakable, and seeing what is there. Brodkey reaches for an epiphany. But once that is attempted, as this mutant reveals, no matter how much is opened up and spilled out, we sense that at least as much still remains. Brodkey is not finished at what remains. Like all biography/autobiography, it is incomplete; the narrator is not up to the narrative. Or conversely, the narrator is too much for the narrative. The auto (biographer) has met his/her subject; one must lose.

Some American Biography

While more conventional or traditional forms of biography are still alive and well, there have recently been several instances of mutant or hybrid kinds of the genre. Such mutant forms—I have in mind Christopher Benfey's life of Stephen Crane and Gloria Erlich's biographical studies of Edith Wharton and Nathaniel Hawthorne—do raise questions for conventional biographers; but more than that, they extend the genre into areas of cultural studies, linguistic analysis, psychological probing, and social issues. They make use of several contemporary determinants: the more recent findings in psychology and literary criticism—especially Lacan and forms of poststructuralist deconstruction, the new historicism, reader-response, as well as sociological and anthropological research. Overall, there is a recognition that a broad cultural history underlies all biographical subjects.

In Erlich's *The Sexual Education of Edith Wharton* (1992), psychological, social, and literary analysis brings together the life and the work, seamlessly. The biographer explores Wharton's erotic development even as she uses writing to explore possibilities and potentialities in that development.

The study is about continuities between Wharton's life and work—something that in more conventional studies is always difficult to achieve. In traditional studies, the reader is often left with the feeling that the life and the work of the subject—even when that work is heavily autobiographical—are moving on parallel tracks. Linking the two, so that we can understand how that writer wrote those books, is so difficult because, obviously, the life operates on one kind of data, the work on another. The life consists of certain givens (facts, dates, chronologies, events), whereas the work is infinite, lacking closure, often unresponsive to objective analysis. Two different psychological contexts, also, are involved: the life with all its attendant anxieties; the work with an effort to resolve or at least reflect those anxieties and circumstances creatively, or to contain them.

In her study of Hawthorne and now here in Wharton, Erlich has tried to come to terms with these biographical dilemmas. As she says in her Preface: "Indeed, the book studies this writer's [Wharton's] use of fiction to rework her maternal imagery, to imagine scripts for future development, and to integrate alienated aspects of her self. This reciprocal method allows us to see not only the autobiographical elements in Edith Wharton's fiction, but the psychic work fiction performed in the construction of the author's selfhood at various stages of the life cycle" (p. xi). The language indicates that Erik Erikson's work lies in the shadows, and this is as it should be, since Erikson was concerned with integration, unification, even closure. Erlich uses quasi-Eriksonian schemes to link several apparently disparate domains: "family constellation, cognitive style, sexual development, and literary themes" (p. xi).

Dominating all, it would appear, is Wharton's relationship to her parents: a kindly but loser father, a domineering, not too kindly mother who relegated her not-too-pretty daughter to a kind of personal hell. Beginning with Wharton's upbringing in what is called a "nanny culture," Erlich demonstrates her subject's divisive loyalties, her ambivalence toward her mother, her lack of sexual development in her long marriage, her release in her affair with Morton Fullerton, and then her personal depression even as she emerged as one of America's most complex writers. As Erlich gives it context, it is a compelling story: the money and social position Wharton was born into, magnified by her personal success as a writer, with the friendship of many famous people, among them Henry James—all of this underscored by a personal unhappiness that derives from the emotional inadequacy of her parents. The overtones of incest in several of her fictions, as Erlich points out, can only be explained by how she configured her own father in her imagination. Once Erlich establishes the theoretical basis for this, and the probabilities in Wharton's early life of incestuous yearnings, she can then weave her way through the fiction. Her readings of several works—*The Age of Innocence, The Reef, The House of Mirth,* and others—demonstrates how Wharton grappled with her basic themes. Not the least is Erlich's use of sexual denial as part of her social analysis; so that she does not emphasize a society of manners so much as she reveals the ways in which sexual sacrifice both appeases the mother and also hobbles the daughter.

Erlich is excellent in getting into the interstices of the Wharton phenomenon, a quality often lacking in more conventionally styled biographies. Her subject's neurasthenia in the ten or twelve years following her marriage, at twenty-three, was so acute she required psychiatric care. Erlich rightly connects at least part of Wharton's depression, nausea, and other ailments to her lack of sexual knowledge, her inability to gain sexual pleasure in her marriage, and her emotional blockage that resulted from sexual ignorance. The strongest statement of incestuous yearnings emerged in the "Beatrice Palmato" fragment, which Wharton assumed would remain unpublished. In this fragment, sexual pleasure lies in "hands," manual stimulation, until the actual consummation of a father-daughter relationship.

Erlich further shows how Wharton displaces her own unacceptable sexual desires, or her repressed desires, onto a marginal, minority figure like Simon Rosedale, a Jew, in *The House of Mirth.* Although his behavior is frequently more admirable than that of his Christian brethren, he is disdained as vulgar and crude, as somehow beneath the other mountebanks and deceivers Lily Bart moves amongst. The Jew, then, is the taboo object, not because he *is*, but because he becomes one of the ways Wharton can displace her own sexual conflicts.

While such tabooing of the Jew is not by any means the whole story, Erlich is able to show through this and other theoretical constructs how Wharton worked. The advantage of this kind of biographical study is evident, since it provides a means of encompassment, without going through endless details. It is not "pure biography," nor is it strictly literary criticism or a psychoanalytic reading in any deterministic way. By emphasizing gender roles, by way of the parents and Wharton's own confused journey into sex, Erlich gives us a way into the fiction; and then by way of the fiction, a kind of countertransference, she can find ways to probe Wharton. As we shall see with several of the other biographies under discussion here, noteworthy as many are, they often do not bridge the obvious gaps and schisms which arise in biographical writing. Frequently, the life and the work are interrelated only because they fall on the same page or in the same chapter.

Erlich writes that "the social constraints that lead to almost tragic destinies for Wharton's protagonists, that destroy Lily Bart and limit Newland Archer, are externalizations of psychic inhibitions, rationalizations for giving up the fullness of life" (p. 49). Caught as Wharton was between her driving appetite for experience and the bonds (maternal, broadly familial, social) she imposed on her desires, she grapples with the conflicts which drove her work. Lily Bart consistently thwarts her chances for marriage, even as she decides, now that she is nearing thirty, that marriage can be her sole salvation. Erlich probes the Wharton sense of the tragic: that while some flaws lie in a society which dooms Lily, the major flaw rests in Lily herself—she establishes the conditions whereby the very things she wishes to pursue are sabotaged. None of this denies the social aspects of the novel; clearly, some of Lily's actions and choices are driven by external factors. She views herself in a kind of Lacanian mirror image, through the eyes of others and, thereby, makes herself into a striking ornament to be admired, even worshiped. Here, too, Erlich has an explanation, for Wharton's mother played the ornamental role and made herself and her daughter miserable by way of the very ways she presented herself. Implied in Lily's own ornamental view of herself is a narcissism, a hubris, and an inability to judge herself realistically. Inevitably, she heads for a rendezvous with doom.

This is biography of one type, and a type that seems to be more and more credible. We see it in John Maynard's "sexual life" of Charlotte Brontë, in part in Ian Watt's first volume of his Joseph Conrad "biography" (more cultural contexts than pure biography). It is perhaps one way to go now that major figures are being done and redone—more Hemingway, more Fitzgerald, more Conrad, more Hawthorne, more Emerson, to name only a few.

In *The Double Life of Stephen Crane* (1992), Christopher Benfey sees Crane as driving his life as based on his work: that the work energized the life, rather than the life energizing the work. His statement of purpose: "We mistake when, in trying to understand an author's career, we take the 'real life' for granted, and look for its imprint in the 'imaginary life' of the subject's writings. For surely this is the wrong way around; what solidity, and givenness, there is in a writer's life exists first in the writings. The problem is to see how the work of art shaped the writer's life" (pp. 5–6).

This could alter how we write biography, but there are, inevitably, problems. The scheme fails to account for anything unconscious in the writer and his work; it makes all such matters conscious: choices and artistic decisions at a rational level. Or nearly so. In a more psychological reading, one would see the writer as interacting with his life and work at a level he or she does not fully comprehend. At that level, the writer "uses" his life, but even before he writes his works, he is living them through, or experiencing them, in his life. In one respect, his early life is not driving him toward these works, but he is already interacting with them. They are implicitly within him, not some later representation made out of career choices. Such later representations can be muffled or baffled by extreme conditions—disasters, starvation, extreme family problems, a series of accidents—but lacking those, the artist or writer has intermixed his life and work from his earliest years. We do not say that the life drove the work, or the work drove the life, but that each is implicit in the other in ways even the writer cannot rationally understand. Once this is said, Benfey's thesis must be qualified, although by no means dismissed.

The advantage of the Benfey point is that it makes us reinsert an author's work into the interstices of his/her life. Too many traditional biographers fail to see that the work is as much of the life as is the life itself. Benfey acts as a corrective, especially when he demonstrates that Crane's "obsessive attempt to shape his life to the patterns and plots of his own stories" (p. 102) can be viewed in his experience of war. Once he had written *The Red Badge of Courage*, he attempted to create warlike situations for himself as a war correspondent in Cuba and then in Greece. Having never seen war when he wrote his novel, he risked his life later in order to validate what he had already written. Some of the same can be said of Hemingway, who tried in the Spanish Civil War to validate some of his experiences in World War I. That doubling back of life and work is often lacking in more conventional biographies of the writer.

Yet Benfey, despite the compelling aspect of his theory, does not always make an airtight case. In many places, he does precisely what he says he will not do: he lets the life drive the work. Often, he allows his biography to follow traditional lines of a sequential, even chronological, telling. Also, in another area—the difference in length between the manuscript of *Red Badge* and the published version, which is about two thousand words longer—Benfey is too dismissive of what the manuscript tells us. The first version of the book is more cynical, more corrosive, especially in its handling of Fleming's illusions; this was somewhat smoothed out for the book. We wonder: what was there in Crane's life which led to the shorter, more ironic version of his most significant work? Here we seek some attempt at explanation.

Benfey's method works when it works; and in other important areas it becomes conventional. He is quite convincing when he shows that Crane's *The Third Violet*, like his earlier fictions, will help predict the author's future, especially his erotic life. But Benfey does not demonstrate how that is any different from nearly all major creative figures, whose early works (poems, books, paintings, musical compositions) are foreshadowings of the life, if we can just bring a psychological perspective to the process. After all, with a dead subject, we know what has occurred as well as we know what is coming. It is quite easy to foresee into the future what has already become the past. We could also argue that *The Red Badge* is an imaginative text, with all the attendant problematicals a text creates, not a blueprint for the author's future. To justify his point, Benfey should have argued out his position; as it is, it tantalizes without fully convincing.

AMONG MORE CONVENTIONAL biographies, there are, of course, different degrees of effectiveness; and, furthermore, not all conventional lives are fully conventional. Several involve some alteration, for example, of sequentiality or chronology, although all, in varying degrees, rely ultimately on a straightforward narrative. The results are mixed. One of the least successful is Jeffrey Meyers's *Scott Fitzgerald: A Biography* (1994). Even the title—what the narratologist Gérard Genette would consider part of the "paracritical" apparatus and a narrative function—by not preparing us for any defined point of view lets us down.

The smooth and easy writing hides most of the difficulties in F. Scott Fitzgerald's life and work. As a professional biographer, Meyers keeps the narrative going at a rapid clip; but he slides over some of the most important questions we might have about the author of *The Great Gatsby*, generally agreed upon as one of the most masterly American novels of the century. In its brief narrative, *Gatsby* catches a sense of America which we find in few other novels—perhaps Dreiser's

An American Tragedy, surely Faulkner's *Absalom, Absalom!* and after that we return to earlier periods with James's *The Ambassadors*, Twain's *Huckleberry Finn*, some Melville and Hawthorne. Even Fitzgerald's great rival, Hemingway, never wrote a book as incisive and brutally honest as *Gatsby*. Our first question in any Fitzgerald biography must be to discover how that man wrote that book; and here Meyers offers little.

A second question: if Zelda was so destructive of Fitzgerald's career, how do we explain that she was part of it when he did his best work? Meyers mounts a mighty attack upon her, citing many of her flaws, her flightiness, her need for excitement, her spendthrift ways, her adultery with the French aviator Edouard Joanzan, her spiraling into madness, her jealousy of Scott's talent and success. But he fails to account for what Scott needed: that he somehow required Zelda and the kind of woman she was—destructive to nearly all who saw her (Hemingway, in particular, saw her as a female from hell), but precisely what fitted into her husband's needs. In an almost parallel case, William Faulkner married Estelle Oldham, someone he came to both need and revile; and yet she provided what Faulkner needed, apparently, when he wrote his finest work in the late twenties and early to late thirties.

Third, another question is how Fitzgerald's drinking was a necessary part of his perception of himself: not that it was merely pathological, but that it was contributory to his talent in the period when he wrote *Gatsby*, some short stories of permanent value, and *Tender Is the Night*. Alcoholism is an enormously difficult subject, since it can be the result of a psychological factor, or else a matter of choice, or, as Meyers suggests, have a physical cause (p. 147). But the important factor in a major writer's drinking habits is not that he indulged, but what it all meant to him. It is insufficient to cite how it prevented him from doing his work, or how it impeded his greatness and weakened his resolve and performance. None of that works: it is too neat, too contradictory. All we need do is observe that Faulkner was a heavy drinker, both continuous and in binges, when he wrote his most significant fiction.

For the biographer, the difficult step after citing the alcoholism is attempting to blend it with the talent, so that the two do not conflict, but work in tandem in ways not at all easy to discern.

Fourth, Meyers asserts that his biography offers elements missing from previous biographies—although this reader feels there was no need for still another Fitzgerald life before some major material has even surfaced. Meyers quotes Jay McInerney on the deficiencies of previous biographies (p. xiii), as though this clinches the case for a new life. Meyers should have commented in his own voice that Bruccoli's study was "hagiographic"; Mellow's "peevish, sordid"; Scott Donaldson's "folksy" and psychoanalytic; Mizener's "grim" but excellent; Milford's *Zelda* "feminist revisionist"; Turnbull's memoir limited. No mention of LeVot's biography, in French—which does the job well, and more than enough until new material emerges.

What we have in Meyers's life is a smooth narrative that has little literary reason to exist, no more than did his biography of Conrad. This is simply the work of a professional biographer sweeping the field for books to redo, turning them out with a kind of rapidity which makes real insight impossible. For example, with a novel as significant as *The Great Gatsby*, why doesn't Meyers go through the manuscript, drafts, typescript, even proofs in order to determine how Fitzgerald worked, how he improved the book sentence by sentence, how ideas were shaped and reshaped, and how, finally, he came to the novel he published in 1925? All of this would transgress on the narrative, but it would also provide a real way into the author and into a great book; instead his few desultory pages of commentary, with no real grip on the text's possible meanings, do nothing but repeat what previous biographers have done. Furthermore, is it possible to discuss major novels in this old-fashioned way of descriptive remarks without some larger sense of critical and aesthetic concepts, without some notion of literary criticism?

Meyers is not alone, for most other biographies in this article-review also eschew critical positions, a critical vocabulary, and a critical perspective. We don't need the jargon, but we could use a critical perspective. One area to work in, for example, is to examine Fitzgerald's use of narrative. It is possible, even probable, that an author's narrative devices have biographical implications. How the writer tells his/her story has resonances for who and what he is, how he uses his literary influences, what makes him original, how he shapes his material, and what that means in terms of his life. Certainly narrative was significant for Fitzgerald's contemporaries: Dos Passos, Faulkner in particular, Hemingway; and it could be useful for Fitzgerald.

Narrative, of course, is not the only area of critical thought; instead of merely identifying the real people behind the fictional characters—as Meyers does with considerable energy—it would be biographically fulfilling to have read Fitzgerald intertextually, to understand how he developed certain tropes through repetition, emphasis, overlappings through his body of work, creating a kind of mosaic. Or else, identify and intertextualize, both. The latter method is especially useful with a writer whose body of longer fiction is rather small, and whose basic methods seem fixed from the start. Fitzgerald must not be made into Faulkner, by far the more innovative and greater writer; but some of the critical procedures now being applied to Faulkner could well be used with Fitzgerald—all in the name of more textured biography.

Meyers has a penchant for the spicy tale, the *Vanity Fair* aspects of his subjects' lives, and Fitzgerald and Zelda do not fail him in this respect. As a result of relying so heavily on these anecdotes—usually retold two and three times removed from the source—the narrative seems held together by brief episodes. Each episode has a mechanical quality: the introduction of a new person in the couple's life, with the introduction falling into formula (born, some oddities, and so on), then reportage of an idiotic act by Fitzgerald or his wife—for example, when confronted with James Joyce, Scott got down on his knees and pleaded for recognition; then on to another episode, often not too different from the previous one.

This characterizes much of the book up to 1930, when Meyers begins to tell Zelda's story, one of madness and commitment to various retreats, hospitals, asylums. At this point, Fitzgerald's life becomes almost an appendage to Zelda's, as he tried to deal with her recurring bouts of what was possibly manic depression and which was being handled as schizophrenia. Long before medication could help such a condition, her bouts were brutal on everyone in her circle, and Meyers's telling of this is compelling.

Yet even here there are problems. Fitzgerald must remain at the forefront, and he does not; Zelda's mental condition must not be viewed as isolated from other factors—too much pathology here, not enough contextualization; and "decline" is too much on Meyers's mind. He seems almost eager to get on with how these people ruined their lives, how they connived in some kind of Greek tragedy to bring themselves down. No question they were seriously flawed, and in Zelda's case unbalanced—in Fitzgerald's, also unbalanced in his drinking—but they were creative. Through all the mess, Fitzgerald wrote *Tender Is the Night*, then *The Crack-Up*, and, finally, *The Last Tycoon*, plus a few of his best stories. Zelda painted, wrote sketches or stories, danced. Somehow, one can justify still another Fitzgerald biography if it provides a synthesis of creativity and morbid, even pathological, behavior. Meyers relishes Fitzgerald's messes without adding any dimension to what we know. The accounting of his years in Hollywood could be more amusing; like Faulkner, he was so terrible that he brought screen writing to another level. Meyers makes little of why.

What persists in this reader's mind is the lack of strategy. There is no psychological energy, although there is plenty of pathology. There is little social commentary, although Fitzgerald, especially in *Gatsby*, is saturated with class. There are no political dimensions—what were Fitzgerald's beliefs? What issues struck him? What leaders? As to literary dimensions, the criticism is "pleasant" but cursory, in most instances little more than retelling the plot, showing who the real people were behind characters, and reveling in the messiness of it all. Meyers is better around the edges than on matters of substance.

One other factor remains: special pleading. In Meyers's presentation, Fitzgerald and Hemingway are the two giants of American fiction in the later twenties and throughout the thirties. Meyers asserts that with Fitzgerald's death in 1940, Hemingway had become the "preeminent American novelist" (p. 324). This follows Meyers's earlier narrative in which the two writers duel for who is bigger (as a writer, as a man, as having the grander penis). But by 1940, the preeminent novelist was neither; it was Faulkner, as Hemingway recognized. What Meyers misses is that as Fitzgerald played up to Hemingway, the latter played up to Faulkner. Faulkner had written four or five novels and several short stories in a twelve-year period which no one matched; and even if Faulkner is for the moment dismissed, there was Dos Passos, a little earlier Dreiser. Meyers is carried away by Hemingway's celebrity, but by 1940, the writer's reputation had long since shrunken into newspaper headlines. If chest thumping is "preeminence," then Hemingway was indeed the man.

AS FOR HEMINGWAY, the procession goes on. After Carlos Baker's flawed biography became outdated, we had Kenneth S. Lynn's *Hemingway* in 1987, which deepened our understanding of the tragic elements in the writer that Baker had skimmed over. In particular, Lynn revealed that behind Papa's super macho image there lay someone quite fragile, vulnerable, and, on innumerable occasions, self-destructive. Lynn's would seem to be the Hemingway biography for the eighties and perhaps the nineties. Just before that, we had Jeffrey Meyers's, in 1985, which revealed new material through interviews, letters, and manuscripts. It tended to be balanced, but lacked sufficient psychological probing, a point one could also make with the Lynn and now with the Mellow (*Hemingway: A Life without Consequences*). James R. Mellow's life, in 1992, was the final part of a trilogy of biographies, the first being on Gertrude Stein and her "company" (*Charmed Circle*), the second a double life of Scott and Zelda Fitzgerald. Mellow saw the three volumes as part of a "Lost Generation" cycle, but the lack of a cultural context for the Hemingway makes that designation seem more like an afterthought than a fully conceived plan.

The Hemingway industry has also been worked by female authors, with Bernice Kert's semi-biographical *The Hemingway Women: Those Who Loved Him—The Wives and Others* in 1983. This is a familiar type of biographical writing in which the forefront figure is really being shadowed by another subject altogether, so that whoever the women were, they are inevitably defined by what Hemingway expected of them, or how he used them. In this respect, they are like so many other people in the Hemingway chronology, male and female, dependent on their usefulness, then discarded or badmouthed, as the Hemingway need for ego glorification went on apace. The same kind of story exists for Picasso.

Mellow's biography of Hemingway has many solid points in his favor. It is balanced, without animus toward his subject, yet willing to reveal some of Papa's worst features (although not his anti-Semitism—cited only once). Most of all, it presents evidence for Hemingway's need for male company, whether younger men who could be disciples, or older men who could be mentors. It shows him in conflict between hero worship (early on he lavishly praised Mussolini) and his need to denigrate, even degrade, nearly everyone in his life. It does establish firm chronologies, coming up, for example, with new material on Hemingway and Agnes, the nurse who became his model for Catherine in *A Farewell to Arms*. Mellow shows that the two met to say farewell in Milan just before Hemingway left for America, not three weeks previously at the field hospital at Treviso. The further meeting suggests that possibly some closure could be made to the "affair" (sexual or not). Nevertheless, very few of Mellow's new points are particularly helpful; except for the detail itself, they reveal little. Even suggestions as to Hemingway's homoeroticism, or possibly homosexuality, have been plumbed and replumbed previously.

After so many biographies of a particular writer, a new life must justify itself in several ways: discovery of new material—obviously so; more accurate uses of older material—obviously so; but, more than anything, a way of looking at the subject that justifies the new biography. What is happening with the

Hemingway industry is that while new (and relatively minor) material surfaces as to his journalistic career and his married life, the biographies repeat each other. In nearly all the lives cited, but mostly in Mellow's, the footwork is excellent, but the material is static. The biographer, we can say, is so caught up in the chronology of his subject that pieces which do not fit are not absorbed; they are merely mentioned, and the march of time goes on.

Mellow seems to recognize this very late in his already quite long biography when he cites Freud's remark that at some point every life becomes unfathomable, that at this point there is an unknown (p. 590). This is certainly true of nearly all major writers; and it should be a given, not simply a remark tossed off and unassimilated to the very working of biography. There are great unknowns in Hemingway, unfathomable parts. Mellow works hard here and there to bring them up, especially Hemingway's battle to assert his masculinity, as against his fear that some feminine component would emerge, or that someone would cite him for being less than the macho creature he acted out.

But Mellow never gets into the role-playing, the acting out, the personae Hemingway took on as part of a disguised personality: he misses the way Hemingway staged himself, and of course he does not relate the staging to the novels and stories. The latter are treated straightforwardly, not as the twisted objects to emerge from a tortured human being. Connected to this: the Hemingway biographer must deal with his subject's decline when he still had half his life to live. After the early stories and *The Sun Also Rises*, Hemingway lost much of his characteristic style and tone; whatever talent remained was buried beneath all the roles. Mellow has it that celebrity began to do him in, but it was something deeper—and while that may be unfathomable, as Freud suggested, it must be probed. Papa came off the blocks like a sprinter, unlike Faulkner, whose career developed slowly, then emerged into something awesome. By the time Faulkner declined, his career had shape. Hemingway's was like a rocket even as his fame grew. Mellow's effort to keep the talent going forces him to overpraise as a major novel *For Whom the Bell Tolls*, a major failure with attractive parts.

Furthermore, Mellow does nothing with the Hemingway-Faulkner rivalry. He mentions Faulkner here and there, glancingly; but the two knew each other's work, shadowed each other warily, sensed that they were the two kingpins of American fiction; and in the background, each admired and feared the other. Hemingway went for immediate gratification: his enormous appetite for visible success, his quest for celebrity. Faulkner lay back, waited for it all to come to him. In some peculiar way, they complemented each other, two mama's boys: Hemingway with hatred and disdain, Faulkner with devotion. Their rivalry cannot be sidestepped.

Mellow's subtitle is "A Life Without Consequences," derived from Hemingway's remarks to his friend Krebs that he would never play it safe, that he would always challenge the odds. It is an excellent title, an excellent point; but its full potentialities must be examined, especially the psychological implications. These implications, perhaps unfortunately, take the biographer into the very areas Freud considered unfathomable. Are they special for Hemingway? Did he mean the remark to point to his art? Or to his life? Was it his way of arranging events so as to call attention to himself? It was his very inability to move along in his art that Virginia Woolf criticized—so that "without consequences" may not have been for the artist, but for the man; and, therefore, we have an evident division within the subject.

Hemingway himself seemed made up of bits and pieces, those early ones when he was willing himself into an original artist, those later ones when he layered himself because the artistic vision was fading. By *For Whom the Bell Tolls*, the talent was gone; the language is already becoming a parodic version of Hemingwayese. His language always led the reader along the edge close to parody, as did Joseph Conrad's prose; often, the mockery and the real things were separated by a small tone, a minuscule matter of style. When tone and style worked, they functioned at a high level, but by *Tolls* Hemingway had lost his distinctive voice; and he was like a fake Hemingway shadowing the real one, using the language of the fake because he had lost contact with his own real one. This is part of the Hemingway story—terrible decline, personal failure amidst international acclaim, an American story which shadows Fitzgerald's Gatsby. As Hemingway mocked and belittled Fitzgerald, little did he realize that Fitzgerald had his type located in the American scene and was simply waiting for the curtain to fall.

AS THE TITLE indicates, *William Faulkner and Southern History* (1993), Joel Williamson's book will differ from previous biographies of Faulkner, Joseph Blotner's and this writer's. The latter two were shaped as literary biographies; that is, Faulkner's achievement as a great American novelist was foremost, and the details of his life, especially for this biographer, were merely ways of highlighting the literary achievement. As an historian, Williamson had a different biographical agenda, and his distinct focus would at first seem to justify still another biography of Faulkner.

For Williamson, Faulkner can be taken as a canonical writer, his place secure, and, therefore, details about his background and life as significant in themselves, in the way that any detail we discover about Shakespeare is significant. There is no need to justify the historical details; they can simply stand. It is an interesting concept, but it does lead to problems in biographical writing. One of the first problems has to do with Faulkner's emergence as an artist, in the later 1920s and early 1930s, with *The Sound and the Fury, As I Lay Dying, Sanctuary, Light in August*. To what degree has he willed himself into an artist, or to what extent is he a product of that carefully worked historical context Williamson has provided for him?

If "Southern History" was Faulkner's fate, then how do we talk about him as a creative artist? Related to this, to what degree is Faulkner an "artist" rather than a "product"? Does historical context, the Southern connection, commodify him, so that what makes him distinctively Faulkner is dispersed amidst a good deal of historical detail? These are only the beginning questions which such a study raises.

Williamson encouraged and went along with publisher's claims that his life provided new views of the writer, when in fact much was old hat. As examples, no one ever claimed he was a slave-holding aristocrat or planter. Further, we all know about Faulkner's maternal grandfather, a seemingly respectable man who turned out to be a thief—he stole the town's money. What we didn't know was that Faulkner's great grandfather "possibly" cohabited with a black woman by whom he had a child whom he protected, educated, and launched into a successful career. The key word here is "possibly."

Let us back up. Early on, Williamson offers an interesting statistic as part of his argument: that in 1850 in Mississippi when the Falkner (original spelling) family was settling, more than half of the population were slaves; and this large number—about 435,000—was legally owned by perhaps one-quarter of the white families. As a result, two-thirds of all people in the state were involved in slavery, either as slaves or as part of slave-holding families. Williamson then extrapolates from this to the economic condition of the state, the type of agriculture, the ways in which slaves were kept in line with terror, fear, intimidation, and, in some instances, with care and concern.

All of this and related data are of interest, since much of it in some form does enter into William Faulkner's thinking, *but* it has little to do with the writer's best novels. *As I Lay Dying* has nothing to do with this background in slavery, except through some huge stretch; *The Sound and the Fury*, even with Dilsey, cannot be explained by historical contextualization; *Light in August*, in part, can perhaps be explained this way, but the essential dimensions of that novel lay in created situations which are matters of color, and this is "American" as much as Southern; but even *Absalom, Absalom!*—perhaps the most closely located of all of Faulkner's novels in the historical background—gains its momentum not from historical detail but from narrative devices which, in fact, question every aspect of history, the past, memory.

Consequently, Williamson's book draws us into one of the most difficult problems in biography. To what extent do the writer's origins and genealogy matter when we must justify the subject on the basis of his or her craft? How can craft, art, creativity, whatever, be connected to a past which lies deep in the most deceptive areas of all: memory, historical recall, family backgrounds, social and political data? We enter a wide disconnect.

An attempt at linkage occurs well into the First Part, called "Ancestry," which lasts for 138 pages. An episode comes late in the segment and was apparently Williamson's need, or his recognition of the need, to blend ancestry with Faulkner. For in most of these 138 pages, we do not see how the infinite details of the background have any relationship to the creative artist Faulkner. In this episode, Williamson details how Charlie Butler, Faulkner's maternal grandfather, stole the town's money and, possibly, ran off with an octoroon. The octoroon belonged to one Jacob Thompson, and with this Williamson feels he has the "original" Southern tale. He tells us that this story gets us into real Yoknapatawpha County history. "This is not the world that William Faulkner created; it is, rather, the world that created William Faulkner, and it encompasses the universe of race, class, sex, and violence, of family, clan, and community that affected him so profoundly" (p. 124).

Here is the historian speaking, justifying the history, but downgrading Faulkner's arrangement of his material, his own deceptions which were creative acts, his reshaping of the realities, such as they were. And once Williamson gets into the Faulkner texts, he has little to offer. All his remarks are based on ancestry, and even here, there is the usual hedging. In finding a Faulkner "shadow family" in the Ripley cemetery, the shadow belonging to the Old Colonel, Faulkner's great grandfather (William C. Falkner), Williamson is forced to qualify with "maybe," "perhaps," "probably," "possibly"—which means he has an idea, but the evidence is flimsy. Similarly, in his biography of Joseph Conrad, Jeffrey Meyers attempted to link the monogamous Conrad with the promiscuous Jane Taylor, but Meyers was forced to hedge every one of his statements with "possible," subjunctive mood verbs, and other conditionals—indicating that a speculation was being turned into a fact without any hard evidence. Williamson's find that William C. Falkner fathered children by a slave servant, then took care of the children when they entered the "mulatto elite," depends, mainly, on conjecture. It's good conjecture, but even if it were evidence, to go from that detail to Faulkner's use of miscegenation—as in *Light in August* and *Absalom, Absalom!*—is a leap.

When the second segment, "Biography," begins, the two parts are separated by insufficient linkage, as is the brief third part, "The Writing." In the "Biography" segment, which fills three-fifths of the book, Williamson writes of the place of black churches in Mississippi and then how Faulkner reflected their presence in *Light in August*. But this is a stale topic by now, another example of how the historian provides solid information but does not see how Faulkner reshaped that material artistically. The black churches in the state, or even in and around Oxford, are not the black churches of Faulkner's novels, not even the black church, Dilsey's, which ends *The Sound and the Fury.*

Faulkner's shaping serves not historical purposes, but creative ones; and the distinction must be drawn. The question is not what shaped him only, but the reciprocity between received information (which we can never really know) and his shaping of it; finally, his reshaping of it when memory and pastness change the forms of everything, until we have the "created" scene, event, individual, custom, practice, ceremony. This is what biography must reveal, or else we enter an "as if" land where so many stem ends end. Further, Faulkner's re-creation of a lynching, of Joe Christmas, in *Light in August*, does not derive from those that took place specifically when he was growing up, but from the way things were, how the races responded to each other, and how whites treated any black who they felt had abused, no less murdered, a white woman. Williamson had no valid way of connecting specifics to Faulkner, especially to the writer's creative and imaginative use of this material.

The residue of Williamson's otherwise careful study leaves us in a gray area between historical restructuring and the subject's work. Once Williamson comes to Faulkner's major fiction, the biography becomes a series of spearheading movements or parallel lines which fail to join. The critical apparatus he brings to bear on the great novels— *Absalom, Absalom!* in particular, but earlier, *The Sound and the Fury* and *As I Lay Dying*—is perfunctory; while all three novels are driven by inventive narrative strategies, we would never discover that from Williamson's telling. And yet narrative experimentation and innovation are a profound part of Faulkner biography; they do not exist separately from the events of his life. And to be incisive and trenchant, a biographer must attempt to discover why that writer used those techniques, or, put another way, how that narrative technique is wedded to the particularities of that subject. Faulkner's use of telling and retelling, of shaping and reshaping, is not bound up with the facts of his historical beginnings in the Falkner-Butler families; but in elements of Faulkner himself: what he willed, what he learned, what dangerous strategies he undertook in the face of the marketplace. This is psychological and critical territory; Faulkner's biography lies in the seams and interstices, not solely or mainly in beginnings.

Each subject obviously carries a different set of circumstances, and it should be clear by now that biographical writing cannot be uniform. While most reviewers and critics still seem to favor a neat, sequential, chronological frame of reference for the subject, the genre makes different demands on the biographer. Jerzy Kosinski is a good example of someone who needs an original, more creative kind of treatment than James Park Sloan's *Jerzy Kosinski: A Biography* (1996).

Sloan's life has many virtues, most of them located in his research into Kosinski's early life, and his own revision of the writer's revisionist view of himself as a young outcast thrown into a primitive, barbaric world of peasant Poles. Sloan unravels the facts of the case, as far as they can be determined at this point; and he is careful not to indict Kosinski for mere lying or deception, seeing him as someone crafting his life so as to give him material for his books. Sloan also examines Kosinski's possible links to the CIA or to related intelligence agencies, to the deceptions involved in his first two books, nonfictional works assailing the Soviet system. Sloan demonstrates how Kosinski is a "created" character, one who was acting out various roles which he felt he could control; there were, of course, roles he acted out which were beyond his control, and some of these helped to bring him down.

Where Sloan's book lets us down is as coherent biography; as history, even cultural history, it works, especially in the early sections. Sloan is particularly strong about Kosinski's father and about both father and son's relationship to their Jewishness, denied by the son until well into his career. The name itself, Kosinski, is a typical Polish one, far removed from Lewinkopf (lion's head), his birth name. And Sloan is quite convincing in showing how that change of name foreshadowed the deceptions, disguises, and hiding the son developed, the persona he affected so as to keep himself hidden behind secrets. But the life wound and circled; it was not a consecutive, chronological life—no one's is, but Kosinski's was even less than most. It required some biographical strategy, some approach or tactic which would help the reader enter into a life which was as much playacted as it was "lived."

In *Biography and Source Studies* III, an article by Lin Harris-Seares on Kosinski biography indicated one approach; and that is, to start with the, for him, traumatic attack upon him in 1982, in the *Village Voice*, an attack that in effect accused him of not writing his own work. Sloan keeps reminding the reader of this upcoming event, but he does not fit it into the strategy of the biography itself. Despite the proleptic observation, he keeps the episode sequential or chronological. Harris-Seares, on the other hand, sees the episode as central to Kosinski's life, to the extent that she can find it resonating in his early life and work *before* it actually occurred; she observes that as trauma it functioned both backward and forward: that such divulgation of his ways of working with other writers to produce his novels was part of an uncovering of himself waiting to happen long before it happened. She posits a biography of Kosinski based on such working back and forth, mainly in psychological terms, where psychological insight becomes narrative strategy. The value of this way of looking at Kosinski biography is that it attempts to match the biographer's story to Kosinski's own, instead of imposing on this most resistant of subjects a kind of journalistic, reportorial narrative.

Not that such a psychological reading need be the only one. Instead of this traumatic episode in which his concealment was blown, the biographer might have latched onto the role that Kosinski's Jewishness played in his life, from the early deception to stay alive in Poland to his later denial when he was home free and clear. Much of this was not simply dissembling or shame. It went very deep, inasmuch as on one hand Kosinski made it seem as though the young boy in *The Painted Bird* was himself and yet, on the other hand, the young boy could not be Jewish because Kosinski was not himself Jewish. Yet the boy is described in classic or stereotypical Jewish terms, although he possibly could be a gypsy; but the latter was unlikely, and surely readers took the boy to be Jewish, especially when Kosinski floated stories that he and the boy had shared nearly identical experiences. The matter of denial and self-denial was still another way in which Kosinski biography could have proceeded. Its advantage would have been to provide an abiding theme with a twisting story, one based on concealment, uncovering, further secretive dissembling, further unmasking.

Another way into this kind of biography would have been through the subject's politics. Just what was Kosinski? His seemed to be a politics of self-management: whatever was good for him was good for the country, for the world. His early years in America were filled with compromises made by way of governmental agencies; he could have been a spy, a secret agent, a double agent, or provocateur, paid by the CIA or comparable organizations. And if the political equation remains opaque—Sloan never does make any real sense of where Kosinski stood on anything—then there was his sexuality.

Sexuality is never a great hook on which to hang a long biography; it is both too private and too public to allow for any definitive point. But Kosinski had a sexual life of some variousness: usually a steady woman friend or companion, intermixed with sex with prostitutes, bouts of mate swapping, sexual activities with another man present (along with one or two women), possibly some desire for homosexual sex. Although Kosinski denied any homosexual inclinations, he did seek sex with a male for the "experience," for trying out something new and different.

In this range of activities, we have a compulsive sexuality, a need to impress lovely women, but also to carry on a life on the wild side, where violence, disease, and even death were possible. Kosinski gloried in black prostitutes, their life styles, their pimps, the sleazy places they took him; and nothing apparently happened to him. When he felt threatened, he made believe he had a gun and bluffed his way out. This, too, energized him—the famous author who, while moving in high society, was able also to move in outlaw circles. Had he not killed himself, would he have contracted AIDS? How did he avoid sexual diseases? The entire question of his sexual life could have been another way "in," perhaps not definitive, but sufficiently powerful to provide a shaping force to a more strategic narrative line.

Every biography, obviously, requires manipulation of the story line: even with a contemporary figure, there is the biographer's different time and agenda; and there is the subject's "messy" life which must be ordered and controlled by the biographer. There are the works, literary or otherwise. The works fit into a different time frame and do not in themselves easily adjust to biographical data. Further, the subject's letters, diaries, journals, jottings, and notes do not fall easily into the biographer's narrative. The result is an artificial story line. And when we have a subject as elusive, as psychologically complex, as full of denial and self-denial as Kosinski, the usual tricks of the biographical trade are insufficient. If we fault Sloan, it is not for lack of solid research, or insightful commentaries, or perseverance with a maddening subject, but for not finding a suitable voice, a suitable narrative strategy for a Jerzy Kosinski.

This biography, like so many published on celebrities (Huffington's on Picasso, for example), seems like a first draft. Sloan achieves closure on Kosinski, but the book itself does not cohere. Many of the reasons why can be applied more generally to biographical writing itself. The editing seems nonexistent, so that Sloan was permitted to keep lists, phrases, and analogies which repeatedly undercut a serious study.

One element of this is the endless array of famous people whom Kosinski knew and moved among, although the biographer should somewhere question Kosinski's need to mingle with the likes of Kissinger and other government officials. Sloan celebrates his subject's entrance into high society, but the people listed sound more precisely like those Kosinski should have avoided. Mailer could have provided an analogy of a once serious author whose literary achievements fell as his social aspirations rose. In any event, Sloan should explain Kosinski's passion for getting his name on lists, instead or merely repeating the lists.

As for jejune phrases, Sloan has Kosinski begin to sink once his past unravels, when he knew "he would go down with a whoosh like the *Titanic*" (p. 331). The *Titanic*!—it didn't even go down with a whoosh; it took some time. Or Kosinski came to learn, as Thomas Wolfe said in his "wistful lament" that "you can't go home again" (p. 57). That worked once, not now. Or else Sloan calls Kosinski "a sort of Audie Murphy of the Holocaust, a man who had been to Hell and returned to write it up" (p. 227). Such vulgarisms, and there are many, make it difficult to accept Sloan's more astute comments. "Audie Murphy of the Holocaust" clogs our thoughts. Overall, such solecisms could have been excised from the manuscript by a good editor; and then Sloan's book would have seemed sharper. But more seriously, the author's failure to apply a more psychological treatment of Kosinski makes the narrative line seem like a collection of episodes. Like so much biographical writing, Sloan's does not achieve coherence; which is unfortunate, given the amount of useful background information he had dredged up.

RICHARD LINGEMAN HAS written old-fashioned biography at its best, on Theodore Dreiser: *At the Gates of the City, 1871–1907* (1986) and *An American Journey, 1908–1945* (1990). His life reveals careful scholarship and a blending of life and work—with the aim of showing how the life, especially early poverty, repeats itself in the work. But Lingeman is less strong on Dreiser's intellectual roots, as though he had to list them and get through them expeditiously. We see this particularly when Lingeman blends Herbert Spencer's evolutionary theories with Dreiser's thought. Lingeman stresses Spencer's movement from evolutionary principles to theories of human behavior, without noting how all this was rooted in other aspects of nineteenth-century thought—in Positivism, in racial theories of mankind, in ideas of progress, in ideas affecting women and women's issues.

Once we introduce those dimensions, the quality or texture of Dreiser's thought inevitably becomes more complicated. Lingeman has emphasized one strand in Spencer's thought—the drive to power of human energies as part of a machine-like process driving all human behavior—and neglected the more thickening aspects which drove Dreiser. To put it literarily: by straining to fit Dreiser into particular parameters of thought, Lingeman has removed from Dreiser those aspects of his work which fall outside the Spencerian influence. That is, those aspects which do not derive from evolutionary theory and which have symbolic-mythical import as well as socially realistic ones.

While this does not subvert the main thrust of Lingeman's book—which becomes the standard life of Dreiser—it does what many biographies have done; it tends to homogenize the subject, making him (or her) subject to singularities, without consideration that the subject comes at the confluence of several elements. We must take this into more serious account in biography as a whole, whether Dreiser or otherwise. There is the tendency to settle on certain influences or presences in a writer's life and development, and then to lose sight of how the writer is a series of contradictions which do not fit into patterns or presences. There is no reason why the subject should be consistent. In fact, the drive for consistency weakens any discussion of the fiction—as we see with Lingeman. The fiction is accommodated, becomes part of a cultural narrowness, rather than revealing clusters of symbolic, mythical, metaphorical, tropic elements.

Put another way, the biographical dimension in its thinnest sense is strengthened, while the critical part becomes supernumerary. With this, we head into one of the paradoxes of biography, not simply with Lingeman's *Dreiser*. There is the biographer's penchant for consistency and coherence, even homogenization; and this immediately clashes with the subject. For the sake of consistency, the biographical dimension is emphasized—the nature of the life and its facts—but at the expense of the work and its multiplicities. Also, when life and work are interwoven, as sometimes they are, it is often reductive. This does not mean that Lingeman has to solve this problem. It is endemic to the genre at its highest levels: how to maintain the variousness of the works while at the same time intertwining the work and the life, which has itself been brought to some level of consistency. There is an unequal equation.

After we sift through Lingeman's careful amassing of facts and his intelligent application of them to Dreiser, several questions do remain. There is little or no sense of Dreiser as a psychological creature: a man full of self-hatred, hatred of others (often manifest in his anti-Semitism), and hatred of America itself as seen in his attachment to the Communist Party long after it was clear the party had its own agenda. The relationship of Dreiser to the party must be examined not only in the terms of surface occurrences—as Lingeman handles it—but at the subsurface level, where the party provided Dreiser with family, with loyalties of a sort, with a justification of the kinds of hatred his background conditioned him to.

Along with the lack of a psychological profile is any psychological reading of the major works. *An American Tragedy* has several of its roots in Dreiser's own life—that "murder" of the old self which would allow him to rise socially. But the Clyde-Roberta relationship must be analyzed in other ways as well: culturally, as the "murder" that lies below the surface in Dreiser's anger and self-hatred, in the need to kill the self, to be reborn, not only as the suitor of a rich young woman but as someone who would slay everyone in his way.

There is the need to see this as a mythical event: Jason seeking the golden fleece; Medea seeking revenge on him: the death of a former way of life, the move toward rebirth, and the tragedy that lies not within the system only but within the character, Clyde, who has assimilated it all. Similarly, *Jennie Gerhardt* must be viewed not simply as something based on Dreiser's sister Mame, not simply as a act of "showing," but as something negative, hostile, full of anger, denial, and hatred. Jennie may appear sympathetic, but underlying her are other, less accommodating feelings.

The Lingeman life is a weighty piece of work which nevertheless bypasses many key problems in literary biography. It moves along as if biography were a rational, logical process, when, in fact, it is a kind of puzzle which resists being put together. All good biography has innumerable loose ends, pieces which do not and cannot fit. Lingeman is of the school—the dominant school—which assumes that the parts make up the whole; but in literary biography, the point must be that the whole resists being the sum of the parts, that the whole is unknowable no matter how may details are accumulated. This is a given, and it should be the assumption of every literary biographer: that when he or she is finished, the subject has eluded biography as much as the work itself, if at a high level, eludes definition.

BOTH THE STRENGTHS and weaknesses of Ann Hulbert's biography of Jean Stafford *(The Interior Castle: The Art and Life of Jean Stafford*, 1992) can be located in a key passage near the end of the book. Stafford's health and writing career were winding down, and she was in a sense fighting a rearguard action to protect her kind of writing: meticulous, stylish, even elegant. Then in the later 1960s and on into the '70s, she was concerned that language itself was being traduced by so-called literary types; and Hulbert incisively sees Stafford's attack on the uses of contemporary language as "an extension of her fears about her own future." Stafford:

> Besides the neologisms that are splashed all over the body of the American language like the daubings of a chimpanzee turned loose with finger paints, the poor thing has had its parts of speech broken to smithereens. Setting the fractures and the dislocations has been undertaken by tinkers with tin ears they have fashioned for themselves out of old applesauce cans . . . ; and upon its stooped and aching back it carries an astounding burden of lumber piled on by the sociologist and the psychologists and the sociopsychologists and psychosociologists, the Pentagon, the admen . . . . The prognosis for the ailing language is not good. I predict that it will not die in my lifetime, but I fear that it will be assailed by countless cerebral accidents and massive strokes and gross insults to the brain and finally will no longer be able to sit up in bed and take nourishment by mouth. (p. 359)

What this passage cries out for is not simply Hulbert's association of the remarks with Stafford's physical and mental condition but a contextualization of the diatribe. For many of these new literary languages were fresheners of American colloquialism, from writers who were giving new life to the language: John Hawkes, Flannery O'Connor, Joseph Heller, Donald Barthelme, and other minimalists. If we locate Stafford's commentary in a context, we recognize how off base she was; how personalized she had become so as to defend a type of work she could no longer produce. Repeatedly, Hulbert shies away from the cultural impact of Stafford's remarks, unless she, the biographer, can relate them to someone close to the novelist, like Robert Lowell or the *Partisan Review* crowd. Consequently, this highly intelligent biography in other respects does not convey what Stafford was accomplishing within an historical frame of reference; there are almost no other novelists of note moving on the periphery of her world—except the poets and writers she met at conferences, and then rejected.

Stafford's accomplishment as a novelist was secure, from three longer works (*Boston Adventure, The Mountain Lion, The Catherine Wheel*), and from her collected stories. Yet we do not find her located among her contemporaries, many of whom were moving into areas making her seem closer to Edith Wharton than to Flannery O'Connor. None of this has to diminish Stafford's achievement, but the biographer must give her the historical context her high order of work demands. It is not simply a matter of length; Hulbert spends an inordinate amount of time discussing Stafford's novels and all of the important stories, as well as many of the minor ones.

A related problem is that, lacking grounding or a critical vocabulary, the discussions are often pedestrian. While we applaud a biographer who becomes so deeply enmeshed in her subject's work, there is always the question of how the effort is carried out. Unfortunately, Hulbert's comments are not integrated, whereby the biographer uses the work to move the narrative along. Hulbert stops all traffic as she goes into detail about novels and stories, most of the time with plot summaries, even then the summaries are not critically positioned. We learn about the fictions as they come along, but we do not get deeper glimpses into them as texts which validate Stafford's stature as a writer. An example: in the midst of an exhaustive analysis of *Boston Adventure*, Stafford's first novel, Hulbert says, "The stereotypical quality of Hope's character highlighted the contrast between her and Sonie, whose reverse aspirations—to join precisely the Bostonian gentry that Hope revolts against—were played out so unconventionally." The passage is impenetrable, and it may be unfair to single it out; but there are others which create opaque blocks of response rather than the kind of critical analysis which turns the works into biographical narrative.

This aside, Hulbert is particularly good on Stafford's torturous relationship with Robert Lowell, as he moved in and out of one obsession after another. And she is very sound in discussing A. J. Liebling, the hedonistic journalist, the expert on food and boxing, whom she married, two husbands after Lowell. Yet solid as she is here, Hulbert does not try to see Stafford through Lowell's eyes. There is no question Lowell was a brute, violent, manic, physically a roughhouse, a man in desperate need of medications which were not yet developed to control his mood swings. But Stafford, also, was tortured by her own past, especially by her lifelong anger at her father for his failure, his lack of insight, his self-serving life, so that all her relationships with men were tainted. As a mate, she drank, carried on, moped, was depressed much of the time or working. *That* made her Stafford, but it also made her relationships impossible, and Hulbert scants that side.

The biographer here is very careful to avoid "pathography," which Joyce Carol Oates ascribed to the previous biography of Stafford, in which the emphasis is on sickness, breakdown, depression, various neurotic bouts. Hulbert avoids this by underscoring Stafford's creative work, and this is all to the good: the life is really about the making of a fiction writer. But, surprisingly, Hulbert does not connect the recurring illnesses—even apart from the alcoholism, Stafford was a physical and mental mess—to the creative gift, except when Stafford herself addresses it. Such an intimate linkage required a more demanding subtext to the biography, associating illness and art, in some subtle way. Further, Hulbert does not discuss Stafford's almost lifelong drinking and subsequent alcoholism to her inner life as an artist; while this would require some speculation, it would put into perspective something that is pervasive among American writers. Any discussion, for example, of Faulkner's inner life as an artist cannot ignore his persistent heavy drinking; how the two are linked cannot be documented precisely, but that the two must be linked is essential.

Hulbert's biography of Stafford, nevertheless, is the strongest one to date. She does probe the recesses of her subject's mind and her creative gift; she does provide coordinates for the emergence of this gift in Stafford's own recognition of who and what she was. And the life themes are covered in the critical discussions of the works, even though the fictions are insufficiently opened up. The criticism is too tame, too traditional, too "expected." What the Hulbert life reveals is something rather profound about the genre itself: that while a real intelligence is at work here in carving out a meaningful Stafford, the biographer needs additional tools: critical, psychological, and an ability to assess contexts.

FINALLY: FOR ANY literary biographer, Nathaniel Hawthorne is a test. Having come under the Freudian scalpel, he was waiting for a judicious, even-tempered, well-argued biography, and in this respect Edwin Haviland Miller has done the job, in *Salem Is My Dwelling Place: A Life of Nathaniel Hawthorne* (1991). The great arena of Hawthorne biography has always been the nature of the "secret" he was believed to be clutching to his chest, or else so concealed within him, he was not fully conscious of its presence. According to this, the secret only emerged in his stories and novels, where some enormous blot on the escutcheon seems to exist and which cannot be erased. As the descendant of the hanging judge Hathorne (original spelling) in Salem, Salem was indeed Hawthorne's dwelling place, the location of himself and his family; but, more importantly, the place of his secret—whatever it was. Was it incest in the past with the Manning uncles, or incestuous feelings he harbored toward his sister Elizabeth? Was there some other form of lust, molestation, or a combination of incest and molestation in connection with those uncles, those male figures who dominated his early years? To what extent can we work back and forth between the allegories and symbolic or emblematic nature of Hawthorne's work and his personal life, or from the latter back to the work?

For Miller, a critical story for Hawthorne biography is "The Gentle Boy," an early tale. Miller writes that "No biographer is able to recreate adequately the most important years of a subject's life, the formative period when the child is seeking tactilely, emotionally, and verbally to cope with the seemingly gigantic puzzles of existence" (p. 37). The passage recalls William James's comment about the child confronting the big buzzing world. The early years are truly full of speculation for every biographer; for no matter how intense and meticulous he or she is about documentation, the puzzles are far greater than the results. Miller hopes that by drawing on "The Gentle Boy" he can find the etiology of the mature writer's depression, his loneliness and feelings of rejection, his perception of a lifelong low-spiritedness. Yet even here in this seemingly archetypical story, there is speculation, not certainty, that the beautiful youth, Ilbrahim, already marginalized by his name, can bring us closer to Hawthorne. Without denying Miller's brilliant reading of the story and his linkage of it to the young Hawthorne, the puzzles remain; and it is just possible that the sole way to bring Hawthorne's childhood into focus is through theorizing not about fictions but about theories of childhood. That is, the biographer—and certainly not just Miller—must make several critical choices.

In this way, the biographer creates or designs several scenarios for himself, using of course as many of the facts of the subject's life as he possesses. But these are usually few, combed from the subject's own musings, or letters, or diaries, and, therefore, unreliable, more fiction than fact perhaps. Once these scenarios are worked through, whether they are Eriksonian, more purely Freudian, social and political, or familial and drawn from eclectic sources, or simply deeply personal, they afford a way into the subject. But the way evidently depends on the biographer's choice of his means. And very often the biographer's choice depends on elements of his, or her, own childhood, or development, or more mature outlook: he "uses" his subject to confirm aspects of life meaningful to him, the biographer, in a kind of countertransference, while all the while posing as an independent or neutral observer.

Miller well knows there is nothing neutral about the biographer's craft; it is deeply personal, and it contains private elements which the biographer may reveal only in the guise of his writing about someone else. Because of these considerations, Miller has chosen to look at Hawthorne's childhood and early development through the writer's own fiction, although, admittedly, there is a selection process at work. Almost immediately it becomes clear that Miller has rejected both Frederick Crews's intense Freudian study and Gloria Erlich's familial study with its dependence on the Manning side of the Hawthorne family. Miller emphasizes the Hathornes in the seventeenth century and downplays the Mannings, who more or less supported Hawthorne's mother, herself a Manning, and her children. This is a decision, although to this reader, it is not completely clear why one must choose between families. It appears that both are quite significant: the seventeenth-century Hathornes with their intense religiosity and furious witch hunts; the Mannings, with their dominant male figures during Hawthorne's childhood, and the possibility—just possibility—of some kind of homosexual contact between the youngster and one of his uncles. None of this is conclusive, but Nathaniel Hawthorne, we can speculate, might be the recipient of several contradictory elements, all of which helped form that inward-looking, depressive, shadowy vision which invades his best work.

If the biographer uses the contradictory impulses coming to Hawthorne through paternal Hathorne side and maternal Manning side, there is little symmetry, and there may be chaos. But both possibilities open up areas of probing and examination, in which the developing writer is a battleground of conflicting forces: some of them profoundly personal and immediate (the Mannings), some historical, part of origins and stories and heritage (the Hathornes). John Hathorne, for example, tyrannized helpless women; we can see the Hathorne record as mainly persecution of women, as Eve and Lilith figures, although some men did fall in the witch hunts. What one makes of it will of course drive the biography. A third factor, as Miller recognizes and handles so well, is the matter of the literary work, the craft itself, the stylistics which determine what Hawthorne was not only as a writer but as a person behind the writing.

This dimension needed opening up, since Hawthorne developed a unique style or manner, one based not only on a low-spirited persona, but one profoundly linked to secret practices. This, too, winds back to the personal life, depending on how much the biographer wishes to make of it. One of the so-called secrets has been discussed among critics and biographers as incest between Hawthorne and his sister Elizabeth, which reaches into the work, as Miller points out, in incest between siblings, between fathers and daughters, and sisters. The same kind of discussion had grown up around Faulkner, because of the incestuous relationships in *Absalom, Absalom!* among others, although in Faulkner's life it was difficult to pinpoint who the combatants were in his own life. As for Hawthorne, Elizabeth (the name of both sister and mother) *was* present, as well as the Manning uncles, with one of whom the writer shared a bed when he was small. But Miller rejects this as Hawthorne's great "secret"—Melville believed he himself knew what that secret was, although to him it may not have been incest but a lack of manliness. In any event, the secret remains a trope, a metonymy, an emblem for Hawthorne's self-possession; Miller speculates that his secrets were that "he was in quest of a father, a mother, and perhaps even a brother to find security in a cold universe" (p. 36).

This becomes, for a good part, Miller's own quest: to find in Hawthorne those elements which would provide him some security even while he recognized there would be none. Surprisingly, this emphasis does not lead to a deeply psychological probe; instead, Miller is insistently literary, offering up, wherever possible, Hawthorne's own works as evidence, "The

Gentle Boy" being the first and one of the most significant. In this pursuit, Miller finds the terrible tensions within Hawthorne reflected in the work. As for "The Gentle Boy," its portrait of an outcast boy mourning the death of his father is "the most detailed account of his [Hawthorne's] recollections of his perceptions and depressions during his earliest years" (p. 43). Miller acknowledges the need for deep psychological probing—Hawthorne's attempt to enclose himself, even enwrap himself in self, to close out others, to become passive and otiose, what he practiced for years after being hit on the leg while playing with a bat and ball. The passivity and otiosity become almost a kind of Oblomovism. The writer's desire for withdrawal and retreat, his "hiding" in his attic room, all, indicate a rejection of life even while he was probing these qualities in his fiction. The dualism here goes much further than Hathorne and Manning divisiveness; it indicates a deep personality or character trait which must somehow be unraveled.

Miller's main strategy is to unravel it, as noted, by way of Hawthorne's own fiction. To his credit, he avoids simplistic dichotomies of head/heart or either/or; he insists on complexity, which leaves his book more open-ended than most. Too many biographers seek resolution or finality in their subjects, when, in fact, there is no such thing. It becomes imposed, and complexity, which can run from messiness to chaos, might well be more appropriate. Miller rejects formulas (p. 108), or historical-social significance as such—he insists on the full range of possibility, which goes beyond the treatment of original sin as Hawthorne's major trope. "Some critics," he writes, "seek to resolve his [Hawthorne's] inconclusive conclusions, when his obvious intention is to posit several possibilities, sometimes even contradictory" (p. 109). Yet open-endedness is in one respect antithetical to biography; but still, paradoxically, it is necessary for all good lives. One cannot wrap people up, obviously, but the biographer, as we know, is impelled to create chronologies, sequences, narratives, and these inevitably lead to imposed resolutions. They, too, are part of choice, the biographer's choice, even countertransference, and they, too, suggest symmetry or neatness where there is none.

One of the areas Miller handles well is the murderous division between parents and children (p. 110). Fathers are frequently sadistic—Miller sees Cotton Mather hovering over this, especially in such a well-known Hawthorne story as "My Kinsman, Major Molineux." In a related area, these sadistic men try to destroy women, as we observe most evidently in *The Scarlet Letter*. Miller pulls together many of these cross-currents of what he calls "authority and virtuosity," especially in his discussion of "Young Goodman Brown."

Yet even such a successfully thought-out biography as Miller's raises several questions, many of which cannot be successfully answered. We do not quite learn the etiology of what Miller calls Hawthorne's "sexualized environment, the almost prurient interest in sadism, voyeurism, incest and male terror of sexuality and marriage" (p. 116). As we suggested above, it is uncertain if even a deep psychological probe would have uncovered the layers of fear, disguise, desire for concealment which characterized Hawthorne, even when we use the work as a reflection of the man.

In another regard, would a more concerned socio-political-cultural grounding have explained Hawthorne, in a way David S. Reynolds, in *Beneath the American Renaissance*, reveals how popular culture underlay, among others, Hawthorne, Melville, Poe, and Dickinson? To what extent should biography explore what are, in effect, areas of sociology, history, and anthropology in order to arrive ultimately at literary decisions? Further, can the biographer resolve the diversified material in order to suggest a particular reading of his or her subject, when that subject is clearly not resolvable, not unified—such as Hawthorne, Poe, or Melville? Perhaps, as suggested above, the best the biographer can do is to indicate the opposing lines, the paralleling of ideas, the contexts as they converge, and then step back, with a deconstructed subject rather than a finished product.

Miller acknowledges this when he contrasts Whitman, who "flaunted his contradictions," with Hawthorne, who "hid furtively behind his" (p. 189). One area we would like to know more was in the extreme hostility Hawthorne showed to women writers. He wrote that he wished they were forbidden to write, "on pain of having their faces deeply scarified with an oyster shell." Such ferocity and sadism seem separate from the way he presents many of his women characters; but it does lead us to speculate that possibly Hawthorne's depiction of hard, sadistic men who treat their women cruelly is not an attack on such men but a way of engaging in the suffering of women. In this respect, Hawthorne would be reveling in "scarifying" these women under the guise of showing how they are brutalized by husbands or fathers. In reality, it is the women he is focusing on, not the masters.

If we carry this argument still further, we discover another seeming contradiction, that while the writer condemns the Judge Hathorne type of man, he nevertheless enjoys the spectacle of women being humbled. If we do reflect this view, we must account for that extreme hostility to women writers: it must be more than the fact that many, like Stowe, were highly popular and financially successful, while he found only a small audience. We must speculate that Hawthorne's attitude and remark has bearing on his artistic views, helping to explain, for example, a story like "The Artist of the Beautiful." Entering this is like encountering a swamp; every step involves quicksand. Miller more than touches on this, revealing that Hawthorne "apparently pledged himself to chastity at forty-seven" (p. 397). Given the above, we wonder how he practiced any sex at all, and how sex, art, and personal hostilities were linked.

Miller's *Salem Is My Dwelling Place* asks most of the relevant questions, but in raising so many fundamental dilemmas in Hawthorne studies, it also raises other problems having to do with biography itself. Can someone like Hawthorne be more than glimpsed? We ask this knowing that such uncertainty can be associated with many other figures—Melville is enigmatical, Poe is beyond us—but it is essentially meaningful with Hawthorne because of his penchant for secrecy which no biographer seems able to penetrate. The way in, apparently, is not so much "in" as it is in surrounding Hawthorne with cultural contexts, psychological scenarios, familial issues, and then teasing out of these all the irreconcilables which made him the author of *The Scarlet Letter*, *The House of Seven Gables*, and fifteen or twenty classic shorter fictions.

ARTICLE-REVIEWS

In the course of writing biographies and analyzing how they came into being, I also wrote several article-reviews on contemporary biographers of nineteenth-century English novelists, like Peter Ackroyd and Fred Kaplan on Dickens, Ruby Redinger on George Eliot, Michael Millgate on Hardy, and several others. This was not for me a very different experience from my work on more contemporary matters, since present-day biographers working on earlier subjects confronted most of the problems and choices I encountered with Faulkner, Kafka, and Conrad. And I had, of course, written a biography of a nineteenth-century novelist, Eliot, and discovered how difficult it is to capture the life of even a traditional subject, no less one as varied and complex as Dickens.

My other article-reviews concern the "brief" biographies being published by Viking Penguin under the editorship of James Atlas. I found that while some worked well within this format—for example, Mary Gordon's *Joan of Arc* and Garry Wills's *Saint Augustine*—most fell far short of what biography should be, even in its truncated form. Their function is clearly to provide readable narratives of famous subjects in literature, science, the arts, and history, but also to provide information on these subjects without undue complications and in short, television-like segments. Nearly all lack adequate historical contexts, psychological insights, or analyses of the subject's language; and we find few if any notes, no indices, little if any bibliography. Also, the assumption that any writer—novelists, historians, scientists—can, as long as he or she is well known, be a biographer cannot go unquestioned.

Finally, I have written at some length on biographies of contemporary American figures, such as Norman

Mailer, Mary McCarthy, and Saul Bellow. Of particular interest is the James Atlas biography of Saul Bellow, inasmuch as Atlas, general editor of the "brief" biographies, while insisting that the shorter versions will revitalize a dying genre, yet writes a biography with the length and heft he otherwise disapproves of. The contradictions of one biographer are compelling, but not so important as is the consideration of the product itself, whether longer or briefer, or just plain middling.

Four Brief Biographies

I DO NOT know if a "brief Whitman" is in the planning stage, but let us assume that it is, and that it distills Whitman's life and times in the 140 to 150 pages devoted to each subject. Can such a life possibly fulfill the promise on the flap copy of each brief biography under review here that "[such biographies] will introduce to a new generation of readers this once-popular genre"? What good can a brief life of Whitman do after David Reynolds's 650 pages (including extensive notes and index) of cultural biography and history? What skeletonized version of Whitman can be caught in less than one-quarter of that space with few or no notes and no index, and surely no new archival work? Can such a short project regenerate biography, or will it drive a stake into its heart? Will this become part of a new bull market in biography, or will it lead to bankruptcy?

One suspects that in such a Whitman narrative all the famous lines from *Leaves of Grass* will be there, but lacking a context, historical depth, or the play of ideas only a longer work can give. The life, we assume, will become a series of "stories," lacking the cultural linkages without which Whitman's often ambiguous poses or role-playings are difficult to comprehend. Further, while elements such as Whitman's homoeroticism or, possibly, homosexuality will be noted, significant social and political contexts which make Whitman's ambiguous sexuality more compelling and less easy to categorize will be excluded. What conflicts in Whitman can be presented? Can the brief biography delve into Whitman's tortured position on race? His shifting attitudes toward slavery and abolitionism? His embrace of Lincoln? His effort to resolve intense individuality with equally intense community? One fears that all these matters, and others, will be given a linear narrative which irons out conflict, complexity, and ambiguity. The brief Whitman will be truncated, reified, and reduced.

What is the reasoning behind such brief biographies, four of which have appeared as of this writing—*Crazy Horse* by Larry McMurtry, *Proust* by Edmund White, *Mozart* by Peter Gay, and *Saint Augustine* by Garry Wills? Most obviously, they fit a reading audience with the attention span conditioned by television, whether news reporting, sports, or sitcoms. They blur the distinction between journalism and biography—even the simplicity of the titles, which do not indicate any direction or theme, appears closer to a newspaper headline than to a book title. They may grab the reader's eye, but they do not provoke curiosity. By turning biography into a pop form, they may attract an audience that would not consider reading a six or eight hundred page book. Yet the question is whether anyone who will not read longer works will read at all; the question that remains an enigma is just how many readers are out there, and will they read a book on Mozart, or one on Saint Augustine, or a forthcoming one on Andrew Carnegie, at any length?

If they are not readers, will they come to the brief version in order to revitalize a once-popular genre, as the editor solemnly puts it? Possibly, but if one examines reading habits, best seller lists, mass market publicity, and notes how publishers are narrowing down to predictable lists, one wonders if anything but celebrity books (not mainly about dead white males) makes any sense. In one area, however—and this may be the key to their appearance at this time and place—brief lives are viable, in economic terms. They save on paper, print, and labor costs, and can bring down the spiraling cost of books—longer biographies are nudging forty dollars, whereas the briefer versions come in at half the price. In this regard, they make commercial, not intellectual, sense.

These are all gray areas. One thing, however, is clear, and that is the brief biography is part of a cultural drift that turns everything into entertainment. The long biography was, of course, also put forth to entertain, but it educated in the uses of history, in the application of psychology to complicated problems, in the meaning of original materials, in the very way a difficult life could be defined. A brief biography aims at only the high notes, emphasizes the big hits, and valorizes a simplistic or reductive narrative. It minimizes analysis or psychological probing, as well as literary or other criticism. It scants historical backgrounding and contextualization. It skips over original research. By any means, it turns nearly all lives into fictional narratives.

Yet the Penguin Lives series of brief biographies, under the general editorship of James Atlas, is quite ambitious. Besides the four volumes already published, two dozen more are in the planning or writing stage. As I write now, in the summer of 1999, I am struck by how few of the books will be by biographers, by how many of them are by authors well known for anything but biography. More seems to be involved here than merely a brief life of a famous subject; there appears to be an attempt to match up a celebrated writer with a given life, whether that person is a biographer or not. The implication of that is unfortunate: that biography really does not depend on any specific skills or practices, that anyone who is a "writer" can write biography; or else the implication goes even deeper, that biography is so trivialized that any successful person can write one. Thus, we have Edna O'Brien (a fine short story writer) on James Joyce—at least both are Irish; Janet Malcolm (she of the bizarre ideas about biography) on Anton Chekhov—is she a Russian scholar? Mary Gordon (a fine novelist) on Joan of Arc—is she a military expert? Jane Smiley (a novelist) on

Charles Dickens—is she a Victorian specialist? Paul Johnson (a right-wing social writer) on Andrew Carnegie—the confusion of realms here is complete; Peter Gay (a cultural historian) on Mozart—was it because Gay is a Freudian? Roy Blount Jr. on Robert E. Lee—a military matchup? Louis Auchincloss on Woodrow Wilson—Wall Street lawyer and gentleman novelist meets complicated president? The matchups are bewildering.

Beyond bewilderment, the indicators for this enterprise are not attractive; for behind the celebrity authors lies a more jejune view of the brief biography. All of these subjects have been done, often several times, in books of considerable skill—Maynard Solomon's densely ordered Mozart, Richard Ellmann's compelling Joyce, Taylor Branch's extensive work on Martin Luther King, Peter Ackroyd's magisterial Dickens, among others being rerouted. These are established biographies: if not definitive, then at least authoritative, well researched, closely argued, the gold standard for the genre. They were not written to revitalize the genre; they were the genre. Why would anybody want to replace them with books one-fifth to one-tenth their length, unless biography must now enter the world of the sound bite, unless the publisher is courting the audience for television and movies, rather than readers?

The answer lies, possibly, in the latter, a new audience, one that does not read yet covets information in small bits. We find some clue to this in the name of the enterprise: "Lipper/Viking Penguin Lives." Lipper is Kenneth Lipper, a businessman interested in films, and brief biographies make almost perfect fodder for simplified, reductive films of famous people—like the Mozart of *Amadeus*. In such an enterprise, all the denser and intellectual qualities which make the subject into a compelling figure can be deleted, in favor of a narrative which spells out the subject's greatest hits. The high points of the life may be reached, but the subject's real work—the reason for a biography in the first place—will be marginalized, as are literary values in White's *Proust* or musical values reduced to familiar high points in Gay's *Mozart*.

An example: White writes of Proust's being "frightened" by George Eliot's portrait of Casaubon in *Middlemarch*, a desiccated figure "who labored all his life on an insignificant and absurd work, as Proust put it." White adds parenthetically that Proust was "haunted" by this figure who, everyone assumes, is writing a Key to All Mythologies, but who is, in actually, confused and incapable of going forward. White then drops the matter. What he loses is how different Proust was, how Proust could marshal his observations, how Proust had all technical matters in hand (Casaubon does not know German, something essential to his project), how Proust did not have to pretend about his work to satisfy a young bride, as Casaubon had to do with Dorothea Brooke. The dimensions become altogether different; the analogy is only meaningful if it is fully explored.

The brief biography can do no other, since its very existence depends on cutting through swathes of material. As noted, there can be no original research or archival evidence, no new theories or visions; there simply isn't space within the 140 or so pages of the format. What has been done before will become the main foundation for the present study. The author will sift through this and that, so as to give a patina of meaning to his subject—even McMurtry's *Crazy Horse*, which works relatively well, depends on previous studies, to the extent that McMurtry is always referring to Sandoz or Evan S. Connell, or some other work on the Sioux warrior. He lacks the space in which to sort out his own theories or ideas, except that obvious point that we treated Native Americans very badly. In this respect Crazy Horse paradoxically becomes the sum total of what we *don't know* about him, since McMurtry is careful to avoid speculation or assessments without documentation. His Crazy Horse is, as a consequence, impenetrable.

Made for movies or made for television, these brief biographies in a sense nullify the genre. The planners thinks so little of biography—although Atlas is himself penning a huge biography of Saul Bellow, who has now become in the reading public's eyes more a neoconservative scold than a richly endowed creative writer—that they provide a kind of fictional format. By fictionalization, we get the life of someone divorced from that deep immersion in the work, whether writing, musical composition, painting, or whatever. Once the work is disconnected from the life, then the life becomes a fiction, a source of speculation, a sequence of ups and downs. Fortune rather than talent drives the engine.

Janet Malcolm (she is listed for Chekhov) has argued, in *The Silent Woman*, that the only valid tool for the biographer is letters: that all else "the biographer touches is stale, hashed over, told and retold, dubious, inauthentic, suspect." Although one may dispute quite strongly her negative assessment of the biographer's tools, as well as her trust in letters, she has, serendipitously, touched on precisely what the brief biography can do. *Retelling* is right on target.

This is less apparent in McMurtry's *Crazy Horse*, which evokes an entire culture rather than simply the life of a singular man. McMurtry is particularly apt in capturing the relationship between the U.S. army and Crazy Horse, more generally the military and Indians as a whole. He demonstrates how suspicion on both sides and broken promises on the army's side created a divide that not even the most resilient of Indians could bridge. Delicately lying behind this back-and-forth raiding and killing of each other lies a large ideological question; we move ahead, by analogy, to the Cold War, where there was not the actual killing, but the back-and-forth of killer weapons between the U. S. and the Soviet Union. McMurtry has, in this respect, created an American archetype, from the Indian Wars fast-forward to the Cold War.

He also tries to penetrate the legends surrounding Crazy Horse. He freely acknowledges his sources—Stephen Ambrose's *Crazy Horse and Custer: The Parallel Lives of Two American Warriors*; Thomas Berger's *Little Big Man*; Mari Sandoz's *Crazy Horse, The Strange Man of the Oglalas*; Ian Frazier's *Great Plains*, among others—and yet warns that most writers about Crazy Horse have speculated and provided undocumented, invented dialogue.

McMurtry, in fact, is very careful not to overdetermine Crazy Horse's role, since so little is known of him. Of course, the best-known aspect of the Indian came in the Little Bighorn massacre of Custer, perhaps the highpoint of Crazy Horse's campaign to maintain the integrity of the Oglala Sioux. But Crazy Horse was not a chief; rather, he was a leader by example, a man who retained a certain purity of vision at a time when Indians were beginning to recognize the end of their way of life. McMurtry comments:

> Perhaps the tribes recognized that they were likely never to have such a one-sided military victory again, either—a victory that was thrown them because of the vaingloriousness of one white officer.
>
> Or perhaps they didn't think in these terms at all—not yet. With the great rally over, the great battle won, they broke up and got on with their hunting.

Whatever the tribes felt, Crazy Horse refused to capitulate to the loss of the Great Plains, to the loss of the buffalo, to the degradation of an entire culture. In McMurtry's hands, he is more a tragic figure—a man reminiscent of those in Greek tragedy who confront what will destroy them—than a warrior or a hero.

McMurtry makes a good deal of how Crazy Horse died, whether at the hands of the military, or as the result of resentful members of his own tribe, or with the help of Little Big Man, or even with his own acquiescence. The ambiguity of his death is part of the ambiguity of his later life.

> From the time that Crazy Horse handed over his rifle and his horses to the white officers at Fort Robinson until his death just four months later, he was a confused, stressed, off-balance, and, finally, desperate man. For almost the first time in his life he had done something he really didn't believe in, something that went directly against his nature. Even though he knew he had done it for the right reason—the welfare of the people—it did not feel right. (p.114)

But whatever the death—and McMurtry explores all the possibilities—the end of Crazy Horse only enhanced the legend. As we shall observe, nearly all biographical subjects need legends, from Crazy Horse to Mozart and Proust. The legend gives the biographical subject more than historical or cultural significance; it creates an aura that biography must somehow reveal—Mozart's precocity, Proust's supernal use of time, Hemingway's physical prowess, Conrad's mysteriousness, Fitzgerald's drunken bouts, Woolf's depressions and recoveries. Yet in most instances, the brief biography cannot work through such legendary revelations, since the latter, to seem valid, need context, space, extended discussion.

Edmund White's *Proust* suffers from a failure to penetrate the Proust legend. For those who are Proustians, there is something preternatural about the subject. In his hands, passion surpasses passion, love transcends love, attachment overrides attachment. His intensity is unmatched in literary history, and part of the legend is Proust's ability to infuse density and intensity into less than extraordinary events. White makes valiant efforts to catch great moments in Proust—tea and madeleine are the most often points of reference—but there is a reductionism also at work. We observe this in White's commentary, for example, in a passage relating Swann and Odette in "Swann in Love," part of the first volume:

> One of the most memorable scenes in *Swann's Way* occurs when Swann cannot find his mistress, Odette, and rushes in his coach from one closing café to another; at last he finally spots her and realizes that during this frantic search something has crystallized in him, a true passion for her, so different from the boredom and indifference he had felt just the day before. This famous scene had its antecedent in Proust's life when he was unable to find Reynaldo [Hahn, the composer] and nearly went mad. (p. 64)

Such a passage is inadequate on several grounds. It fails to probe Swann's ambivalence about Odette, a woman presented as unworthy of his passion. Swann dislikes her as a person even as he feels an obsessive passion for her as a woman. And his passion is an irrational impulse, not one he can ever explain to himself. Further, Odette does not fit into Swann's social ambitions; she is socially marginal, and yet he, a climber, must pursue her. Finally, White analogizes Swann and Odette to Proust and Hahn, implying that behind this great obsession of Swann's lies Proust's with the composer. This loses sight of the fact that the created relationship in the novel is far different from the personal one, and that Proust, far from merely shifting gender roles, understood the nature of heterosexual passion and obsession. Much more needed to be done here. This is not the place for a superficial gloss, but for extensive analysis, without reductive examples.

At some point, perhaps in the planning stages, White decided that Proust's "gayness"—the biographer's choice of word—was paramount in any discussion of his life; and this becomes his hobbyhorse. No one disputes Proust's homosexuality as an integral part of him and his vision of French society, but it can also be misleading to make it the sole force; and "gay" itself has so many contemporary references it suggests a life style which was not accurately Proust's. To insist on gay was to introduce a later twentieth-century term with all its diverse possibilities into a discourse that should be more nuanced. Everything about Proust was nuanced, even muted; and all the interpretations that turn girls into boys, or boys into girls, have to be folded into a view of sexuality that is far from being gay and is closer to being a distinct later nineteenth-century kind of ambiguity. White might have used a little Foucault here to probe into social and sexual codes.

White's analysis lacks, most of all, any psychological sense, any effort to penetrate Proust's work and to link up the work with the subject himself, so that, inevitably, the man and the work are indissoluble. This lack of any psychological penetration seems endemic to the short form of biography, not only for lack of space, or for larger contextualization, but in the very choice of biographer: those not noted for psychological and critical acumen. Further, the short form needs clean lines and uncluttered narratives, producing a linear he or she did this or that. The short form is nearly all narrative bones, with little flesh; it is all shaping of anatomy without any heaviness. Heaviness means clutter, and this must be avoided. Such a life is viewed only empirically, as if a life can be comprehended once the skeletal remains are examined. One thinks of a medical lab, where the body is dissected, the illnesses and accidents chronicled, the wounds, fractures, and breaks measured, while the life that once inhabited that skeleton is minimal. Anatomy is all.

The following passage, which establishes the relationship between Proust and Hahn, is all bones—simplistic, reductive, misleading:

> In 1894, when Proust was twenty-three, he met the composer Reynaldo Hahn, with whom he would have a passionate and (given the period) surprisingly open affair for the next two years. Hahn was just eighteen years old. Thanks to Hahn, Proust plunged into the world of music; his writing soon betrayed a new interest in contemporary composers.
>
> Hahn was the son of a Catholic woman from Venezuela and a German-Jewish father; like Proust, he was half-Jewish, gay, and artistic. (p. 61)

To take the latter assertion first, Proust's mother was Jewish, as Hahn's father was. This created for each quite a different dynamic from the stated "half-Jewish." Proust was, according to Jewish tradition, Jewish; Hahn was not. But beyond that distinction, what Jewishness, half here, half there, meant to each was quite different, as was what being "gay" meant. The first part of the statement is also misleading—the "surprisingly open affair" in Paris was not scandalous; this was not the England of Oscar Wilde. And, finally, to use "betrayed" is not on target; music became a means for Proust, not the betrayal of a new interest.

The brief biography is to biography as journalism is to creative work, or as television is to real news and real reporting.

We may never know what really happened, whether in the life or in public affairs, but analysis, probing, and careful definition can get us close to something which we feel may be right. The brief form, on the other hand, must deal with all the old stories, and that accumulation becomes the life. The subject has almost no other air to breathe. White's *Proust* works valiantly to counter these problems—we recognize that the biographer is intelligent enough to understand his predicament. Get in, get out, keep linearity; and yet this is hardly what one wants in a Proust biography. For if any writer deserves ambiguity—not in thought but in possibility—Proust does.

White attacks George Painter's classic two-volume biography of Proust, ostensibly on interpretive and gender grounds, but really because Painter's volumes make White's effort supernumerary. The latter characterizes Painter's work "as so amusing that it could be used as a source for a stand-up comic." This once again proves there are no editors anymore—who would leave that in? One may disagree with Painter as White does about his handling of Proust's homosexuality, but one should use language suitable to the subject's level. White's repeated use of "gay," as already noted, is another jarring note: a perfectly fine term for here and now, but not for the nuanced Proust.

White acknowledges that he owes most, not to Painter of course, but to Jean-Yves Tadié's *Marcel Proust*, published in 1996, but not as yet in English. Tadié, he says, "discusses Proust's sexuality without having any Freudian biases," as though to avoid Freudian analysis is essential to superior biography, when, in fact, Freudian analysis is simply one of many tools, neither to be avoided nor to be overdone. Why the hostility, especially in the light of Proust's relationship to his mother (his Jewish side)? But White then asks Tadié to excuse him for his own "homosexual bias" in his "little book." White's purpose is to bury Painter, as though in a reenactment of Harold Bloom's anxiety of influence.

His take on Proust focuses on two elements: Proust's use of involuntary memory, which is somewhat short-circuited, and his homosexuality. One might, in fact, cite this as a homosexual life of Proust, when a more considered position would have been a biographical and critical portrait of the artist who was homosexual, not a portrait of a homosexual who was an artist. In the positive sense, White does demonstrate how French intellectual life in and around the turn of the century was dominated by a homosexual culture; but in so doing, he makes it appear that Proust gained his strength as a great writer from his homosexual identification—which he tried, unavailingly, to hide. Here is a much more compelling theme: what he tried to hide rather than what he was. Yet Proust's greatness moves beyond his gender—although that is not of course to be minimized—into areas of imaginative creation and vision; and here White cannot follow, because he lacks both the desire and the space. To discover the imaginative recesses of a major figure, the biographer needs room to lay a multiplicitous foundation and then to build. There are no shortcuts.

In summary remarks at the end of his brief biography, White says that Proust is popular because he writes about glamour, and about love, comments which make him sound like some Harlequin romantic. The final remarks are so perfunctory because the brief biography has not created sufficient foundation to support even 150 pages of text, and the commentary is added on. White concludes that Proust "is the first contemporary writer of the twentieth century, for he was the first to describe the permanent instability of our times." Proust the first! With the implication that he was the most significant? How about Kafka, Musil, Joyce, Yeats, Eliot, and if we want to dig deeper, we should add pre-moderns such as Baudelaire and Mallarmé. Such remarks cheapen the greatness of Proust by making him a contestant, a competitor in the twentieth-century sweepstakes for who arrived there first. At nearly every level, this brief biography has been miscalculated; White took on an impossible assignment and then failed in most of his strategies.

Peter Gay's *Mozart* has many of the flaws of a brief biography. Intelligent in its formulation of Mozart's career, it nevertheless does not offer any language in which to present the music. Gay's way of speaking about the chamber music and orchestral works is, in the main, to exult in their beauty; but he fails to tell us what Mozart did musically to create that impression. We already know his music is exultant, and we want the biographer to search his subject's life to discover precisely what made him Mozartian, that is, unique. We encounter the problem early on. Gay speaks of how by Symphony No. 19 in A Major (K. 201) Mozart's "true genius as a symphonist emerged." Mozart was then all of seventeen. Gay's language for Mozart's important shift toward maturity is that the work is "rich in original thematic material," that it "stands out as an arresting move beyond earlier exemplars," that, further, it would be at home in the repertory of any modern orchestra.

Gay returns to this symphony several times in his account, but he never informs us what made No. 29 mature, engrossing, or compelling. The language he uses to describe it can be moved around to apply to dozens of other works, and not only by Mozart. There is nothing special about this as a descriptive language, and certainly nothing specific for the work itself. We observe this when Gay takes up Bach's possible influence on Mozart:

> . . . how strongly his exposure to Father Bach resonated in his last compositions remains open to discussion. This much, though, seems plain; it augmented his compositional ammunition, powerful as it already was, and called for real mastery of the technical vocabulary. But Mozart was not just a follower of Bach: whatever counterpoint he employed, notably in the great G-Minor Quintet and the equally great C-Major Symphony, he adapted to his style and made his own. (p. 103)

That is, essentially, spinning wheels, using vague adjectives ("powerful," "great" twice, "real") and inspirational nouns and verbs to leave us wondering what Mozart did.

Gay—a fine intellectual historian and a biographer of Freud—is best when he writes about the Mozart operas. He can balance out his perfunctory remarks about the greatness of the music with closer analysis of the text. He has, as it were, a literary text to deal with, and he makes the most of it (although, unfortunately, he keeps referring to *Le Nozze di Figaro* as *Le Nozze de Figaro*; editing isn't what it used to be).

Besides his inability to draw upon language to describe his subject's work—a necessity in biographies of composers, painters, or any figures who don't trade in words—Gay relies almost completely on previous biographies, which he cites. Most obviously, he relies on Maynard Solomon's *Mozart*, the most recent and most authoritative of the biographies; and here we find a language. Solomon presents examples of the music (he includes a passage from Symphony No. 29) and shows how certain passages work, how they are original or derivative, what makes them Mozartian. On No. 29, he writes:

> These are works [including the G-minor Symphony K. 183 and two other pieces] that are studied for the ways in which they bear upon the evolution of classical style in general and the sonata forms in particular, seen primarily in terms of such issues as formal symmetry, thematic development, harmonic trajectory, cyclic integration, coherence, organicism, and motivic work. (p. 122)

Gay also uses Solomon's exhaustive analysis of father-son relationships between Wolfgang and his father, Leopold; but, surprisingly, he shies away from any deep psychological probing, surely because of limitations of space. Thus, once again, the brief biography provides the outlines of a career without giving us the very thing that makes that career so intense.

At this point, we might ask who the audience is for a brief book on Mozart. It is, assuredly, not for the Jerry Springer crowd, or for those who take the book club selections. Will it appeal to those who read seriously?—estimated at perhaps

50,000–100,000 people in the entire country. Will it help create another audience for biography? After all, the jacket copy, as noted, haughtily states that this economic offering "will introduce to a new generation of readers this once popular literary form." One could argue that it is the final nail in the coffin of a once-popular literary form; that the advent of the "brief" is always the end of something, not the beginning of something else. One ingredient it will surely end is biography that contains sustained argument or sustained point of view, any analysis that goes beyond a dip in and out of major events. That audience, too, is hard to find, and we may wonder that even if these brief studies do find readers whether we are doing anyone a favor. Is a truncated Mozart better than no Mozart at all? That question remains open.

The makeup of audience for Mozart differs from that for any of the other subjects so far published. The reason is that an audience already "knows" Mozart—or at least knows many of the stories and some of the music: the Salieri factor from *Amadeus*; the salaciousness of Mozart—now part of the legend; the dictatorial, unbending Leopold—a slave driver, as it were; the amazing genius of the young Mozart; the tragic, perhaps demonic, death. And then the music: some part of the operas (*The Marriage of Figaro*, *The Magic Flute*, *Cosi Fan Tutti*, *Don Giovanni*) and fragments of the symphonies (the Jupiter, for example), and the piano concerti (the "Elvira Madigan," for example). With the other subjects, the audience is less obvious, since these subjects are not so thoroughly part of the general reader's culture; Proust known more by reputation than in the reading; St. Augustine probably misread and misunderstood, if not confused with the city in northern Florida; and Crazy Horse, at most a name to those who have seen westerns or watched television versions of the Indian stories.

I exaggerate, perhaps, but none of the subjects has the easy cultural access that Mozart has provided, both the Mozartian Mozart and the manufactured Mozart—the figure all pundits cite as the pure genius who never experienced doubts. There are Mozart festivals in many cities, and Mozart performances even for those not solely identified with "high culture." There is Mozart in one's face, perhaps a debased Mozart; and one of the paradoxes is that a brief biography aimed at this somewhat knowledgeable audience is inadequate because it adds little to what that audience already knows.

For the more experienced Mozartian, Gay's efforts to enter into a musical language are simplistic. When he comes to counterpoint, one of Mozart's technical resources, he cites the composer Walter Piston's definition. Why should that suffice? And this is Gay's practice throughout. Musical analysis consists of what another composer, critic, or biographer said. Gay rarely enters directly into the music, or offers commentary that is original, or subversive, or even mildly unaccommodating. Mozart is always at the top of his game, once he has emerged from his childhood years as a composer; he was no follower of Bach, according to Gay, but someone who reinterpreted Bach and made him "his own." How? In what musical terms? What forms were involved? If Mozart's music is the reason for the biography, the biographer must interpret the music.

Gay is sound in penetrating some of the various Mozartian legends and myths. He reveals that so-called inspiration, usually cited as endlessly flowing in Mozart, was almost always accompanied by commissions; thus, inspiration was associated with moneymaking. And Gay does not disguise Mozart's salaciousness, his pornographic letters, his celebration of excretion and fixation on anality. Yet Gay makes little use of this, although it might have proven useful to provide more context for such behavior, or to link it to other elements in Mozart; instead, he lets it all stand as some parallel universe to Mozart's musical triumph. We receive a bifurcated individual, undigested. None of this material is biographically easy, but the short form disallows the very kind of expansive linkage of elements which justifies still another biography.

Even in the discussion of the operas, something seems missing. In *Don Giovanni*, for example, Gay cites Leporello's famous "catalogue" aria, the aria in which he enumerates on the Don's conquests. Gay speaks of the aria as part of the lewdness and vulgarity of the Don's manservant, but omits the irony, the boastfulness, the psychological need Leporello has to vaunt his master, and his master's need to let his reputation precede him. The irony of the aria is multifold: Leporello's expression of being needed to enable his master to compete sexually; the Don's need to be perceived as a great cocksman, if not lover; and, overall, a need for the opera to create an outrage, a subversion, a dent in conservative taste. Gay cites only the latter, not the psychological dimensions of the boastfulness on both master and servant's part.

That, too—the lack of space to develop psychological (not psychoanalytic) dimensions—is a failing of the brief biography. The less such a reading is needed, the more effective the shorter form can be, as we shall see with Gary Wills's *Saint Augustine*. That is perhaps why a literary or purely creative subject—Mozart here, Proust elsewhere—is least helpful in salvaging what the editor considers a moribund form.

ON THE OTHER hand, *Saint Augustine* is made to order for a brief biography. Here we have a subject about which the layman knows little or nothing, in which the author must do considerable historical contextualization to account for his narrative, and, in the end, in which there is limited reader interest. I say "limited" when I exclude those religious believers and historians who are eager to learn new details about Augustine; clearly, most of the readers of Wills's book will be an audience that is probably secular, as well as those with a passing interest in historical reconstruction. What such an audience desires—and for once a brief biography is in order—is an intelligent overview of the Augustinian legacy. That legacy may be religious or simply historical, for either the believer or the secular cultural critic.

What makes this short book so appealing is that we sense Wills's own need to work through Augustine's legacy for his own enlightenment. As his subject struggles to deal with Rome's "City of Man" and to establish his own "City of God," we see Wills struggling to affirm what is clearly something dear to him: his belief in certain absolute principles which lie outside the transitory values of a secular society. When Matthew Arnold wrote of "ignorant armies clashing by night," nonbelievers thought of the death of God; when Augustine, however, spoke in similar phrasing, he was weighing God's triumph over ignorance and violence.

Saint Augustine, 354–430, as we know, lived most of his adult life in North Africa, chiefly as the Bishop of Hippo (what is now in Algeria). What most of us know far less is that North Africa was a crucial part of the Roman Catholic empire as Christianity had spread and as Rome was being buffeted by foreign, even barbarian, forces. Augustine had to balance several critical factors: the pervasiveness of the Roman Empire itself, with its centralization, its subjugation of its colonies, its sense of order, its basis in legal proceedings, as well as its despotic elements; a split Catholic Church, divided over loyalties, over religious and ideological practices, and, in many instances, split because of heretical or renegade priests; the Donatist rebellion, what we might characterize as the ulta-orthodox, the pharisees of the Christian Church, who refused to defer to the more mainstream church represented by Augustine.

Then there were the conflicts within Augustine himself, conflicts he outlined in his "Confessions," which Wills retranslates and redefines as "testimony"—these include sexual matters, questions of marriage and family, adultery, as well as personal relationships to the city of God. By retitling Augustine's Confession as Testimony, Wills hopes to regain the ancient meaning of the word, as testimony to God's goodness and grace when measured against man's frailty. This retranslation is essential to Wills's presentation of Augustine's ideology: that while man may consider himself strong, even invincible, when measured against the infinity of the godhead, he must bow in deference to God's grandeur. As we read Wills, we think of the nineteenth-century poet of God's grandeur, Gerard Manley Hopkins, much of whose ideology is Augustinian.

For Wills, this formulation of Augustine's life takes on added significance when he acknowledges that his subject was a man of words, not only an excellent speechmaker but a creative spirit. "He had, all his life," Wills writes, "been building a palace of words in which he lived; this antirhetorical rhetorician who yet saw the divine Word reflected in every word men speak or write (or even mentally formulate)...." (p. 144). Wills often cites Augustine's punning nature, his use of Latin words which are close in sound or meaning to create an ironic or sarcastic dimension to his remarks. He couples, for example, pain and Punic, uses catch phrases, what Wills calls "bubbling up in self-indulgent echoes or assonance." Augustine as phrasemaker or wordsmith surprises the lay reader, who possibly knows only something of the bishop from his "Confessions" or from fragments of *The City of God*.

The sole criticism one may make of Wills's effort is that he too readily accommodates Augustine's positions. He tries to create a dynamic, even dramatic, situation, so that Augustine becomes heroic in the confrontation with the Donatists for the soul of the Catholic Church in North Africa. Here, the bishop can do no wrong, as he attempts to persuade the stubborn Donatists that he represents mainstream Catholicism, that they are a narrow tributary; and while he does the persuading, he is, according to Wills, flexible enough to make room for them in mother church, if only they will come. In all such power plays, as Wills relates them, Augustine was insistent and yet generous, offering love and forgiveness, as part of his view of God's charity and ultimate offer of grace. Yet here, in the confrontation with the Donatists, not nearly enough is made of their position, a position which while we may disagree with it wholeheartedly, even mock it, was something pure. The entire question of purity, which often becomes intolerant and despotic when put into practice, needs further exploration, as does Augustine's ability to maintain his position of power when so many conflicting forces were operating. Here the brevity of the biography—145 pages of text—mitigates against explorations into larger historical and cultural contexts.

For the nonbeliever, Augustine as victor in the church power plays is surely of interest. But of corollary interest is an examination of what the bishop's role in Catholicism meant for future development of the church. Surprisingly, Wills has little to say about free will and determinism, about choice and fate or destiny, about what a celibate clergy would come to mean (Augustine favored it), what insights into family and children Augustine would have, all in terms of how his influence helped to redefine the future of the church. Wills touches on such matters here and there, but once again brevity prevails.

Finally, in all four brief biographies, there is the question of sources. Like the others, Wills depends heavily on his predecessors, in Wills's case on Peter Brown, professor of history at Princeton and author of a biography of Saint Augustine (incidentally, in the June 24, 1999, *New York Review of Books*, Professor Brown gives a highly enthusiastic review of the Wills book). While there is nothing intrinsically wrong with this reliance on previous work, the practice does say something about the brief biographies: that, even at their best, such as with the Wills, there is something second-hand about them, books not part of original research or insight, but books based on previous ones. In Wills's case, he has organized his material originally, giving the reader really two perspectives of Augustine: first, from the *Testimony*, then from the life itself, as it unrolled. The conciseness and originality of the presentation help disguise the fact that much or most of the material is indeed not freshly excavated but merely redesigned. The brief biography offers a tantalizing question: Will it help people to read more because it spoon feeds knowledge? And if so, do we gain a larger informed or uninformed audience? Is there any substitute for full, not derivative, reductively contextualized books?

The Long and the Short of It

WHILE THE PUBLICATION of Viking/Penguin's brief biographies goes on apace, longer biographies are still accumulating, not the least James Atlas's *Saul Bellow*, the 686-page kind of monster he has chastised in his editorship of the briefer ones now appearing. The advent of such contradictoriness allows us a long look into what each type of biography accomplishes, to which we may add very long books on Mary McCarthy by Frances Kieran (2000) and on Norman Mailer by Mary V. Dearborn (1999). In the jacket copy for the early ventures into brief biographies, we read that the shorter form will revitalize an aging genre; and yet the aging genre seems to hold its own against the latest form of quick entrance into a life and equally quick exit, with sound bites of about one hundred fifty pages as the median length.

With the "aging genre," we get notes, often lengthy ones, an index, and a more leisurely pursuit of what is important in the writer's work. In the brief forms of biography, we find no notes or else notes that are very skimpy, no index, little or no bibliography, and, most importantly, no new material or new archival research, no expert in the field, but instead, a well-known writer (see Auchincloss on Woodrow Wilson, Peter Gay on Mozart, Edmund White on Proust, Edna O'Brien on Joyce).

The fault line here is the assumption that any established writer can "do" biography, without necessarily possessing the tools of biographical research and writing. The belief that this can lead to a successful result is a sad commentary on celebrity culture overwhelming literary and historical values, since the writers were selected not for particular expertise, but for name recognition as novelists or historians or cultural critics. Sometimes, a writer can overcome what might seem a mismatching, as Mary Gordon does with Joan of Arc or, in part, Edna O'Brien with Joyce. But just as often, the writer gets lost, repeating previous writers on the subject and making only negligible effort to move past received wisdom, as in Elizabeth Hardwick's very brief *Herman Melville*. Hardwick reads Melville well, but depends completely on Hershel Parker and previous biographers for details and even basic assumptions.

As I observed in my *Biography and Source Studies* (5) review of the first four, the more successful brief biographies are those not about literary or creative figures like Proust and Mozart, but those concerned with nonfictional subjects such as Saint Augustine and Crazy Horse. The same point holds for the next group of five biographies: *Joan of Arc* by Mary Gordon and *Mao Zedong* by Jonathan Spence, although far less so for *Woodrow Wilson* by Louis Auchincloss. What makes the nonfiction biographies more successful and those of creative and imaginative figures far less of an achievement can be explained. The other book in this recent batch of five, besides Elizabeth Hardwick's *Herman Melville*, Edna O'Brien's *James Joyce*, falls somewhere between, a mix of compelling writing and well-worn comments.

An obvious difference between the two types of biography here is that creative figures require far more of a discussion than the brief version allows. We saw this immediately in the Proust and Mozart, as well as in the recent batch, the Joyce and Melville. Whether Proust's *Remembrance* or Mozart's major operas and symphonies or Joyce's *Ulysses* and Melville's

Moby-Dick are under scrutiny, some imaginative reach is an evident requirement. The brief biography simply does not permit the space for this. Another distinction is that nonfiction subjects—Mao, Crazy Horse, Saint Augustine, Wilson—are more focused, their lives led along by facts, movements, often a rather narrow range of ideas. They may change and zigzag, but there is a thread running through their lives, and if the biographer catches that, the life can be more neatly organized. Even here, nevertheless, there is the danger of reductiveness. For creative figures, the thread is complicated, imaginative thrusts leave the biographer in mystery, and change is more apparent than stability.

Creative subjects require some psychological probing, not necessarily psychoanalysis, but eclectic psychological tools. While this is clearly also useful with leaders, statesmen, and generals, it is not so essential, since many leaders—Mao, Wilson, Crazy Horse—are often actors performing roles dictated by social, political, and economic circumstances, and what we call contextualization. Creative figures work in and out of circumstances, and what they achieve is unique. Mozart picked up from all the music surrounding him in the latter eighteenth century, but he made it his, and that uniqueness, which we find in all major creators, needs space for probing, discovering, and even speculating. One need only compare the brief Mozart in this series with the lengthy, stately biographies by Maynard Solomon and, more recently, by Robert Gutman.

The argument of the brief biographer is that he or she does not diminish the value of the lengthier version—although the series is headlined by the statement that the brief biography will resuscitate the genre. The idea is to furnish the hurried and harried reader with something accessible, those who would never take the time to read six hundred, or more, pages. Yet this argument collapses on itself, since the brief treatment of creative figures does not offer us the true greatness of the subject, only a capsuled, highlighted figure who went from one success or failure to another. The Mozart, or Proust, or even Joyce, of this shortened form is not Mozart, Proust, and

Joyce, but a televised version, a *Reader's Digest* sense of how things are, great figures who can readily be fitted into a busy schedule when the very point of their greatness is that, unlike pop figures, they cannot be shoehorned in. And for historical figures, the history is simplified and reduced; the complexity of a Wilson is brought down to a formula.

SOMETIMES, THE IDEA works. Mary Gordon and Joan of Arc are an excellent paring. Gordon's sympathy for Joan—her feminization of the woman-warrior, in fact—works well even within the contexts of two such different eras as our own and Joan's fourteenth century. While recognizing this gulf, Gordon identifies with Joan's quest for validation of her voices and the disturbance she created as a feminist: not only as a female, but as a cross-dresser, since Joan, as we know, dressed like a man when she led her troops against her enemies. We may at first be disturbed by Gordon's ahistorical reach for common feminist ground, but she convinces us her pairing makes sense. In the following passage, Joan is certain of her own invincibility, whereas the newly crowned Charles wanted to relegate her to a vastly inferior place. "Charles and Joan illustrate a phenomenon that occurs when young women want to move from the realm of the symbolic, where male imagination has placed them, to the realm of the actual, where they want to be" (p. 66). Gordon continues: "A girl can be an ornament, but if she wants to act rather than be looked at, if she wants a scope and autonomy rather than the static fate of the regarded, even the well-regarded, object, she becomes dangerous" (pp. 66–67). Joan, she says, has not changed; she was, instead, "misread."

Gordon is splendid in her pursuit of Joan's effort to validate herself and what her voices were telling her. And the question of the cross-dressing, the transvestism, makes sense within the context of her mission. Male dress of course helped protect her against very possible rape, which on several occasions, almost came to pass. It also gave her the symbolism of male power—while making her one of the boys, it further sustained her position as an army general or leader. It was obviously also more comfortable, since all activity took place on horseback; it made it possible for her to wear heavy armor (weighing up to sixty pounds), whereas female vestments would have interfered with armor. Male dress, additionally, gave her not simply male power, but counteracted the deficits that would have accrued to her as a female. While all of the above elements came into play, cross-dressing made it possible for other leaders to negotiate with her; they could reason they had lost to a man, not a woman. At the same time, Joan was playing a dangerous game, with the cross-dressing leading into the world of witches, magic, alchemy, myth-making, some of which could be punished by burning.

What is lacking here—although not a huge omission—is some psychological insight into Joan. This is a difficult task, since the farm girl turned leader of an army and crowner of a king does not lend herself readily to deep probing. Personal information is hard to come by. Gordon seems content to treat Joan as a phenomenon: she happened, she was special, she had the clairvoyance of an artist, and she remained fully integrated in who and what she was. In this respect, any effort to analyze her would be considered presumptuous; it would be like attempting to explain a great artist's genius, which always remains out of reach.

Gordon is half right in not trying to do the impossible, but at the same time the reader wonders why Joan performed as she did. Did the voice indicate she was an imaginative genius? Or half-crazy? A schizoid young woman who "heard voices"? How did she personally deal with what was a no-win, self-destructive situation, one whose outcome was foreordained? Did her sharp wit indicate she was satisfying some inner compulsion to denigrate her adversaries, or was it her way of calming her fears? These and dozens of related questions occur, as we marvel at Joan's successes in the field and her ability to sustain herself even as her situation implodes.

But such matters are secondary; primary are Gordon's insightful use of her materials—she is clearly synthesizing the material of others, particularly Marina Warner's *Joan of Arc: The Image of Female Heroism,* Edward Lucie-Smith's *Joan of Arc,* and the translation of the proceedings of Joan's trial, a volume edited by W. S. Scott. Gordon also draws on images of Joan in Shaw, Brecht, and other playwrights. Of particular interest is Gordon's take on Warner's comments, in the segment called "The Narrative of Joan's Virginity." Gordon's point here is that Joan's virginity was frequently at risk of being violated, and yet men drew back, so that her virginity remained unviolated. She wonders why or how Joan's power was able to overcome what would have been routine: the rape by the military of a captured or helpless female. Gordon speculates that Joan's virgin body created fear, and she implies that something magical was at play. As a person who has herself gone through Catholic indoctrination about the female body and virginity, Gordon is particularly sensitive to how Joan's virgin body was not a marginal matter, but part of "every act of hers."

Finally, Gordon as a fallen away believer finds her attitudes toward Catholicism triggered by everything about Joan. There is an agon here of some complexity: the author unable to believe, but still sensitive to former teachings, confronted by a powerful, charismatic young woman who embodied every dimension of the Church—except its prohibition against precisely the role Joan chose for herself. Joan incorporates the Virgin Mary, the female warrior, the suspicion of being a witch, the believer who willingly tests God—the panoply of female roles which tempt grief and, ultimately, bring on self-destruction. The portrait is compelling.

On a technical note, the lack of an index is criminal.

DESPITE A SPATE of errors and the fact that there is nothing new or original here, Edna O'Brien's "brief" *James Joyce* is so well written that the reader is "Joyce-ful" to have it in hand. The book does suffer from all the problems we associate with these brief biographies—the details are derivative, the narrative skips the deeper analysis the subject requires, the text is not carefully edited for errors, and overall it appears hastily done, often full of undigested material. And it was assigned to a "writer," not to someone with much sense of biography.

Withal, O'Brien's close identification with Joyce as an exile from Ireland gives her short book a passion and an intensity which serve her well. In several respects, she has written a portrait of the artist as a seriously flawed but dedicated individual who suffers not only the slings and arrows of fortune, but intense internal pain which makes him, or her, a martyr to his craft. We get this from the first page with the image of Daedalus, our archetypal artist, and his son, Icarus, falling from the skies with wings that melted in the sun's heat. The image, cast by O'Brien into a simulacra of the exiled Irish artist, is followed by a piece of writing in the Joycean style. None of this is startling, but it works well because of O'Brien herself as the latest in a chain of Irish literary exiles.

With this, she has created several layers: she takes on the identity of both subject and biographer; she has moved into the very nature of romantic art—the artist as martyr; and she has "Irished" Joyce, reinvented him as an Irish writer subject to provinciality and misunderstanding. In Ellman's expansive biography, Joyce is a European, an international, universal writer. Most other commentary sees him in such a light, citing his return to the Greek classics, his knowledge of several languages, his diverse reading, his mastery of narrative techniques. O'Brien wants us to envisage a Joyce who both rejected the Roman Catholic Church and never left it; who abandoned Dublin and never forgot it; who put the lilt of the Irish "sound" into his prose and never stopped hearing it. One of the great successes of her "life" (not biography) of Joyce lies here.

Another success is paradoxical. As O'Brien moves along with episodes from Joyce's life, the reader loses sight of when such events are occurring. She does not provide dates, merely topics, and in so doing negates what the reader usually expects of a narrative with solid anchoring in dating. Here we find the distinction between a "life" and a biography. O'Brien skips much significant information; she barely touches on the political background to Joyce's work, with a brief mention of Parnell and Kitty O'Shea and the 1916 insurrection against British rule. She incidentally mentions Yeats and Synge; for the most part, she has excluded any cultural reading of Joyce which we expect in more traditional biographical writing. Some of this can, of course, be traced to the briefness of such a biography, the need to stay in or around the 150-page limitation (she comes in at 179 pages). But O'Brien has her own plan to create a sense of Joyce through a life journey: the Irishman as artist, the Irishman as a tortured individual, the Irishman as a martyr to his craft. In this way, she eschews more conventional biography.

Repeatedly, she returns to what is generally true of all Irish writers: the greatest never lose sight of Ireland even as they can function only in exile. Joyce is the most exemplary of exiles, but the others are of almost equal stature: Beckett and O'Casey as well as, earlier, Shaw, and the latest example, Edna O'Brien. She and Joyce have been drummed out of Ireland for salaciousness, for flouting the Church and authority, for fostering secularism. It is, obviously, a great theme, and O'Brien hits it whenever she can. Joyce becomes her cause. In an early chapter, called "Rebellion," she lays out her premise: that of all Irish writers, Joyce's relationship to his country "remains the most incensed and yet the most meditative." She continues: "No one who has not lived in such straitened and hideous circumstances can understand the battering" (p. 15) of his upbringing, and, by implication, the upbringing of every Irish child.

None of this, however, excuses the problems which inevitably invade every brief biography. O'Brien's hit-and-run comments on Faulkner are nonsense: "Faulkner thought himself Joyce's spiritual heir and while the breathlessness of language in Faulkner is sometimes comparable, Joyce's characters are more graspingly human and Dublin not merely backdrop for their venality but as rich and musical as themselves" (p. 96). The reader is breathless: Faulkner never thought of himself as "Joyce's spiritual heir"—there is, in fact, no evidence he was familiar with Joyce before he wrote his own "stream" novels,

The Sound and the Fury and *As I Lay Dying*. T. S. Eliot and "The Waste Land" were more his thing. To speak of "breathlessness" of language in Faulkner means what? And his characters are not only human; they reap the whirlwind. Further, Quentin Compson is at least as complex as Stephen Daedalus, and Faulkner's Yoknapatawpha County is at least as intricately woven as Joyce's Dublin. There are no winners here.

Other problematic areas arise in O'Brien's mathematics in connection with Joyce's siblings. At the beginning, she states that Joyce's mother bore sixteen children; but as the book goes on, this number fluctuates, and at one time she speaks of fifteen, with one unaccounted for (p. 17). She is, however, very good on Joyce's mother, May—"writers and their mothers—the uncharted deep," she writes, but does not go far enough, fearful as she seems to be of any psychological probing. She is often equally sound on John Joyce, the patriarch, the drinker, back slapper, and ne'er do well who helped destroy the family; but she fails to pick up sufficiently on the hatred the son felt toward the father. Lack of space hobbles O'Brien, but one senses she is withholding her anger, pulling her punches, letting go too easily of her own rage. In this same tradition of writing, Frank McCourt in *Angela's Ashes* does not spare the father who twins John Joyce.

Particularly strong, still in family matters, is O'Brien's understanding of the relationship between Joyce and his deeply troubled, angry, and eventually mad daughter, Lucia. She was to be the light of Joyce's life and turned out to be the shadow. O'Brien attempts to defend Joyce's self-imposed distance—"Writers are a scourge to those they cohabit with" (p. 103)—but cites his concern, his wooing of Lucia as well as his mothering of her. She is also fine in her portrait of Joyce's ruthlessness, his use of friends and benefactors—especially Harriet Weaver—his sponging, and his assumption that as a writing god he must be deferred to. She understands that this destroyed nearly every relationship he had: his wife Nora, his children Giorgio and Lucia, even those who devoted themselves to his welfare; and yet his genius excuses him, in an agon between his craft and civil life. The man who assumed he was king of the hill and owed deference was the man who wrote the premier novel of the twentieth century in *Ulysses*, and the man who attempted the impossible in *Finnegans Wake*. O'Brien's Joyce, withal the flaws, seems the man who could have done that.

WHAT STRIKES THE reader of Elizabeth Hardwick's *Herman Melville* is the paucity of commentary, given that so much space in an otherwise very brief biography is taken up by quoted material from Melville. While Hardwick strives hard to achieve a free-floating or even poetic language, she simply does not have enough to say about Melville. Most of her space is taken up with discussion (often brief) of the major fiction.

Hardwick's *Melville* reveals she can be a shrewd commentator on literary texts, but is in no way a biographer. She has no real take on her subject—admittedly a difficult and always retreating, reclusive figure—but in a short book she is obligated, it would seem, to provide some thread for her seriatim discussion of life and work. She relies heavily on Hershel Parker's monumental *Herman Melville*, the first volume of which appeared in 1996. To this, she adds her own commentary on homoeroticism in Melville, both in his life and his work, citing *Moby-Dick, Pierre*, and others. But this appears insufficient, since it is not integrated into a holistic view of the writer.

Although the book jacket no longer carries the presumptuous statement that these brief biographies will "introduce to a new generation of readers this once popular genre," we do still expect some greater life narrative than we find here. How can a genre be reinvigorated when there is so little biography at hand? As we see with the use of homoeroticism, most detail is hit or miss, accumulated rather than absorbed. In a letter to the *Times Book Review*, responding to a harsh review, Hardwick validates her effort by indicating she "studies all of Melville's writings." What she offers as biography is slim pickings, hasty references to Hawthorne and his relationship to

Melville, second-hand material on Melville's son, a suicide, a little more on Melville's religious thought. She apparently had great difficulty with her subject's long, clotted poem, *Clarel*, and yet it is a rich storehouse for Melville biography. It is a test for both biographer and critic.

One theme that recurs—although it, too, seems insufficient—is what we might call the Philoctetes theory of Melville as the wounded warrior-writer, licking his wounds, going into deep depression over his marginality when his later books were maligned, planning his revenge which he is unable to wreak, and finally producing a masterpiece like *Billy Budd* as a final statement of his heroic endeavor as an unappreciated writer in late nineteenth-century America. It is not a novel theme, and it does not account for Melville's social conscience, his keen awareness of the cultural and political context in which he wrote, nor of the philosophical influences upon him. Race plays a huge part in early Melville and continues through *Moby-Dick*, and Melville on race needs more than a brief notice; it needs contextualization. And to what extent is race intermixed with sexuality, and to what degree does Melville fall into stereotypes, that nonwhite races are more charged with sexuality, or practice it with less sense of guilt? And, further, to what degree, in Melville's masterpiece, do questions of power prevail, and how is that sense of power linked to themes of power in the larger culture?

We find that Hardwick has not delved deeply into others' research—which would have been necessary, since while she can be a sensitive reader of the fiction she is not an original scholar. If these sensitive readings of the novels were to serve as the backbone of the biography, the reader asks for more, for the integration of work and life which would give us a more compelling Melville. The intense creative power that went into Melville's fiction goes unexamined; clearly, while he seemed a fast worker in the early stages of his career and then withdrawn in the later, after 1850 he was not a facile writer. We wonder if the fact that Hershel Parker's biography which ends in Melville's 1851 meant that Hardwick had no one to depend upon, and, therefore, she has little to say about Melville in the second half of his life—understandably a life lived under wraps. Here we run into the nub of the brief biography: that lack of archival research which would provide more, had the writer both the space and the will.

AT ONE HUNDRED seventy-eight pages, plus ten pages of notes, Jonathan Spence's *Mao Zedong* is one of the longest in the series. Spence makes good use of the greater length by going into some detail about the political issues confronting Mao: not only the division between communists and nationalists under Chiang, but divisions within the communists, competing warlords, and the inevitable struggles in a country of, then, over half a billion people.

Mao presents certain problems a biographer does not have with most other subjects. Since Mao's "story" is also the story of China for a good part of the twentieth century, the biographer must write a profile of Chinese history. Mao and China are made to appear inseparable, in ways that the United States and, for example, Woodrow Wilson can be separated, except for eight years of his administration. But Mao was intertwined with Chinese history from the time he was old enough to move through the administrative ranks, starting in the 1910s.

What this means is that biography and history interpenetrate, and it is understandable if the biographer gets caught up more in historical data (civil wars, internal struggles, administrative decisions) than in personal analysis. Inevitable in such biography, the focus is on deeds, not personal agonizing, not even questions of morality and immorality in decision-making. Such is Spence's treatment of the Great Leap Forward and the Cultural Revolution. While he cites the devastation they wrought, they are not connected to any doubts or misgivings in Mao but, instead, become part of the historical record. They occurred, and then Mao, and we, move on.

What takes place within a leader's life when he, or she, recognizes that decisions have led to great disasters—loss of life, destruction of an economy? Probably, very little, since by the time of decision making, the leader thinks of himself as invincible or as a savior—at least that is how Mao is presented. The leader has so intertwined himself with the fate of the country that he and the country are indistinguishable; and since there is a certain immortality bestowed on him as leader, he feels no blame for failure. Thus, generals can send thousands to their deaths; presidents can declare war, knowing that multitudes will die; and dictators by their decisions can consign millions to doom. For the biographer, this obviously creates enormous problems, since invincibility, once noted, does not permit much penetration; and the subject simply "does" what he or she does, and that's that.

Spence, accordingly, is content to present Mao and the history of much of twentieth-century China as one and the same. After the Second World War, Mao *is* communist China, and everyone else is a player in his life. To some extent—and here Spence does not speculate—Mao becomes a player in his own life. Given more space and the inclination, the biographer could have assessed more profoundly how the seeming leader is really caught up by events and circumstances that make him, or her, a role-player; what seems to be a position of leadership becomes one of subservience to forces one may have unleashed and which, then, become unpredictable and inexorable. This is the interesting and compelling part of biography, mainly missing here; such a positioning of the biographer allows for more than speculation, although less than documentation. It provides a wedge by which a psychological and political probe can enter, as the forceful leader becomes swept along by elements he can no longer control.

We observe this occurring in Mao's later career, once he has consolidated his power and he proposes and oversees through his administrators the Cultural Leap Forward and the Cultural Revolution. The Cultural Revolution in particular, in the '60s and early '70s (it more or less ended in 1976), found Mao at his most assertive; and yet it gained its own momentum and ultimately carried him along in its sweep. It was, in some respects, a forerunner of Pol Pot's "revolution" among the Khmer Rouge in Cambodia. It forced a penetration of Mao into every household, ordered his picture on the wall, his sayings at hand, his thoughts on everyone's lips, his quotations in every bookstore. People had to dress in a certain way—no jeans, tight clothes, or special hairdos or shoes. No pets of any kind were permitted. Those who were not peasants—such as landlords, capitalists, professionals—had to wear a sign identifying themselves as such, recalling the star Jews in Germany had to display. Every room in a house had to have at least three people in it; children were told to criticize and report their parents' derelictions. So, too, were students ordered to report their teachers. Medical treatment would be streamlined; complicated procedures were outlawed. As Spence indicates, doctors were to write their prescriptions without using English. All education was to include farming and laboring. The aim—as later with Pol Pot and the Khmer Rouge—was to transform China into a nonintellectual, non-middle-class agrarian and laboring country; and to punish along the way all intellectual and non-peasant classes.

This, then becomes a biography in a somewhat different mode, and to the limited degree Spence illustrates the various contexts in which Mao sets into motion what he can no longer control, the biographical portrait is appropriate. Yet the brevity of the presentation creates only high points, and disallows any complex sense of contemporary Chinese history, eliminating many of the very elements which propelled Mao and then overtook him. For these reasons, Spence's "biography" reads like an extended encyclopedia entry.

LOUIS AUCHINCLOSS'S *Woodrow Wilson* is the shortest of the brief biographies, one hundred twenty-five pages, with a two-page bibliography, and one of the least carefully done. The brevity alone undercuts several aspects of Wilson's life, not least the complex tensions that undercut his long and mixed career. Also, Auchincloss does not help his presentation by creating analogies between Wilson's actions and attitudes with those of the recent Clinton administration. Auchincloss offers a torturous passage in which he quotes Henry Cabot Lodge, writing to Teddy Roosevelt, that he never hated anyone in politics with the hatred he felt toward Wilson. Auchincloss then quotes historian John A. Garraty, who has cited Lodge's grandson as glossing the word *hatred* as something only intermittent in his grandfather, not something malevolent or malignant. Auchincloss follows this with Bill Clinton's quibbling over "embarrassing terms"—sex!—at his impeachment hearing. The sequence is bewildering, especially in such a short narrative, where every word, sentence, and paragraph should count.

Historical analogies in the best of cases are a dangerous procedure, and here the contexts are so different, so opposite, that analogy creates useless diversion. The practice, fortunately, does not dominate, and for the most part Auchincloss gives a straightforward, albeit tepid, account of Wilson's career, from university professor and president of Princeton to president. The narrative is by now well known, as are the main personages in Wilson's life: Colonel House, his advisor; Henry Cabot Lodge, his nemesis in the Senate; and Wilson's second wife, Edith, who chose to protect her husband through secrecy and deception when he was ill.

The feel to this particular brief biography is unmistakably a paste and scissors job. The material is clearly taken from a few major sources, such as August Heckscher's *Woodrow Wilson* in 1991 and John A. Garraty's 1953 book on Henry Cabot Lodge, as well as his 1956 study of Wilson. Except for those inappropriate analogies, Auchincloss shows little indication of independent thought, for what we learn we could have garnered from a long encyclopedia article. Here the selection of biographer and subject simply does not work, and the basic idea of the series, that any writer can write a biography, is challenged. We saw how mangled Proust became in Edmund White's handling, and here while Auchincloss does not mangle Wilson, he does give us little more than a high school primer on his subject.

For the nonhistorical reader, Auchincloss does not sufficiently probe his notion of "two Wilsons," since the dualities of his character and mind go much further than his moral sense on one hand and his positions which lacked moral substance on the other. The dualities, if mentioned, must be extended: for example, to a Northern and Southern temperament. Wilson carried over many of the South's positions, on race, for instance, while clearly living as a Northerner. In another respect, he seems divided as a passionate man who surrounded himself with pliant women and the man of rectitude who was ascetic and forbidding in his tastes, especially when it came to women. So much seems unresolved in Wilson, despite his considerable achievements, that we expect from the biographer more probing of character and temperament as the basis for his decisions—for example, Wilson's stubborn refusal to give ground on treaties following World War I. In Wilson, we need a more psychologically insightful probe that affords us a lens into a far more complicated and tortured individual than Auchincloss's "realism" gives us.

The problem is not only lack of space, but the disposition of the biographer to plant Wilson in difficult decision-making and political events without contextualization, this for a man who was president of Princeton, governor of New Jersey, and then a two-term U.S. president. Also, in his race through Wilson's years, Auchincloss has almost nothing on the presidency during the war; after all, two million Americans landed in Europe, and casualties were high. We know how other presidents before and after Wilson agonized over casualties, but for Wilson the war does not appear to have troubled him. Even in such a brief biography, an additional forty–fifty pages (bringing it up to the length, for instance, of Jonathan Spence's *Mao*), would have given us some of what is now missing.

Some examples follow that needed clarification:

Teddy Roosevelt tried to subvert Wilson's war efforts by saying the president did not represent the American people and that Congress came much closer to speaking for most Americans. This attack, almost treasonous in its implications, needs much more commentary than simply reportage.

Lodge is given a segment, and Auchincloss says that just as there were two Wilsons, so there were two Lodges. But we get little sense of how the divided Lodge, as alluded to, managed to resolve himself in his blockage of the divided Wilson. The idea is attractive, since we are now dealing with four personalities, but the working out is lacking. It may not have been only lack of space, but part of the hit-and-run manner of the narrative which precludes probing.

Finally, another casualty of brevity is that Wilson is forty-five by page 17. Everything moves too rapidly, and we need more of his development, his obsessions, what Auchincloss labels his divided self, to understand him at forty-five. Another ten or fifteen pages in this area might have given us a more textured early life, less the sense of a narrative on the run to get at the big stuff. We need more agony and torture in the inner self of a man so split between repression and passion, so seething with moral obsessions that he would allow them to destroy him and subvert the fate of the western world after the war. In Wilson's case, we have the paradox of a man whose idea of a moral order and a peaceful world clashed so brutally as to destroy the chance for either. Biography at any length has to capture this.

Once again, the reader deplores the lack of an index in these political biographies.

Now the longer biographies:

Frances Kieran's method in *Seeing Mary Plain: A Life of Mary McCarthy* is to thread her narrative of her subject's life with comments from McCarthy's own books and from those who knew her or wrote about her. The idea, Kieran says, is to see "Mary plain"; somehow, as she was. This is, of course, an impossible biographical endeavor. We never see the subject "plain"; we can only recreate what the subject may have possibly been. The biographical subject is always a metaphor of the real. Kieran, then, is attempting what cannot be done, and once that is admitted, she does a good job of giving us a McCarthy who in parts does come alive. But the book is sadly lacking in any psychological profile, and the author accepts whatever is on the surface as the "life." We find no analysis of details, events, circumstances which would put the external voices into a more intimate context, or that would challenge their own veracity, just as one would want to challenge Mary's own veracity in her recollections (*Memories of a Catholic Childhood, How I Grew,* and *Intellectual Memoirs*).

When the biographer fails to provide larger context, including analysis, historical anchors, or even theory, then the life unfolds solely on the subject's terms. This, too, is a misreading. By offering external commentaries, Kieran does attempt a broader context, but those commentaries, often acute, do not cohere. They come from people who, in the main, want to vaunt McCarthy; or if not exactly praiseworthy, they want to establish their own agendas about her and her literary work. Inevitably, the biographer knows more about the subject than anyone except the subject, and in many instances the biographer can see the subject more clearly and honestly than can the subject herself. When the biographer squanders her opportunities, the subject takes on the aura of "heroine" in her own narrative; hagiography results.

As an example, we consider the excerpts from Vassar graduates who observed Mary at the college, from Mary's own memoirs, from reviews and other sources, or letters published and unpublished—all of this part of the aleatory nature of biographical writing. The real question is whether this type of "external" arrangement is more prone to chance than the more conventional way of handling such material. In the latter, the conventional way, a biographer assumes a control which he or she may, or may not, have. Nearly everything except hard data is random—where to put this or that, how to disguise the lack of coherence, how to create a narrative where there are huge lacunae, how to account for elements which do not readily fit into a sequential story line. But in Kieran's way of proceeding, as we shall see shortly, a biographer creates only the aura of control, of making the narrative appear valid. With this excerpted type of biography, the arrangement of the materials—however well-intentioned and thought through—cannot but seem random, since pieces come floating in from every direction and could, often, easily be fitted in sooner or later. The distinction between this method and the conventional one is validity. The biographer using excerpts and contemporary observations to fill in can create only a far more random narrative.

The distinction is important, since one senses that as the long biography comes increasingly under attack—as it has been by writers as disparate as Janet Malcolm and John Updike—"solutions" will include more excerpted, oral types of life studies, as it has in spawning the brief biography series. This should not suggest that new methods should be scorned; sometimes they work, even in the brief biographies, as in Garry Wills's *Saint Augustine* and Mary Gordon's *Joan of Arc*. Yet they cannot replace the real thing, and they may, in fact, smudge the distinctions—that only the controlling hand of the biographer, ready with contexts, some theory, some psychological analysis, can come close to a life.

Fairly early in her biography Kieran quotes an excerpt from McCarthy's review of Aldous Huxley's *Brave New World*, which she wrote for the Vassar undergraduate magazine *Con Spirito*, in 1933, while she was still an undergraduate. In the review, she notes that Huxley fits well into the literary scene: a "collapsing Lawrence," full of "sentimental mysticism," Joyce deflating into a "comfortable intelligibility," Woolf lacking "hard thinking" and lapsing into a simple "pretty femininity of *The Second Common Reader*." In this milieu, Huxley reveals snobbery, easiness, and superficiality. McCarthy goes on to castigate the simplicity of Huxley's thought, the point being that any reasonably educated person could duplicate it.

After this lengthy excerpt, Kieran validates it as an indication that McCarthy was finding her voice, and that she "had a gift" (p. 81). Yet such excerpts, we might suggest, do not show her developing a voice as a gift, but as an indication of her limitations. She is here a very young person going after her elders and accomplished artists with no understanding, only a desire to treat them as objects blocking her own path. She will achieve status not by insight or even comprehension, but by way of attack.

McCarthy's objectification of people in her fiction is foreshadowed here by her rejection of Joyce, Woolf, Lawrence, and Huxley. Kieran requires here a far longer look. Part of the difficulty of using such excerpts is that the biographer lets them stand as validating commentary, when in fact excerpts from others and from the subject herself must be put to the test of sensibility and intelligence, as well as to the test of subversive motives. McCarthy's desire to objectify everyone, including writers far greater than she could ever hope to be, was not a growing maturity, but part of a complicated need to assure her own superiority, even when it had not yet been established.

An additional factor in building a biography by excerpts or by oral reports is the sneaking suspicion that, as in the Kieran—or the Manso of Norman Mailer, for example—the biographical work is a display of laziness. In this respect, the author takes an unenergetic view of his or her material, and by using external blocks forgoes the difficulties of a continuous narrative. Additionally, this type of biography permits the author to get around previous lives, in Kieran's case the one by Carol Brightman in 1992. With little new material, the author can provide a different slant, and also reveal indisputable data, documentation that cannot be challenged. Space is cleared for still another biography, an oral history, as it were.

What counts, finally, is whether or not the process works, whether the subject is further clarified than she would be by a more conventional means, as in the Brightman study. One positive element is that the author can incorporate more material than in a consecutive narrative; since there is more maneuvering space, the reader comes to expect interruption with oral excerpts, reviews, and commentaries. The downside is a certain arbitrariness of selection, a loss of narrative drive, and a suspicion that the biographer is letting excerpts do the work. But most significantly, the reader has the sense that the material is not only arbitrary but excessive and subject to authorial manipulation, more so than in more conventional narrative. Further, it allows for even greater vaunting of the subject, that praiseworthiness which is already a factor in the genre.

McCarthy is a forlorn figure now in American letters, her fiction relegated to a minor mode, her criticism excavated as a relic, and only some of her short stories cited, and that less for literary quality than for their daring at the time. Her wit, her cynical remarks, her sexual daring (in fiction and in life) are all but forgotten. By the time she died, in 1989, she had fallen behind the standard for postwar fiction, the Gaddis, Pynchon, O'Connor, Bellow, Roth world. Even in terms of strictly female novelists—an artificial grouping created by journalists and reviewers—she does not hold up well with Flannery O'Connor, Toni Morrison, Eudora Welty, Joyce Carol Oates, and others. As a feminist, a label she rejected, she seems perhaps to have made her way too much through well-placed men: Philip Rahv at *Partisan Review* and then Edmund Wilson. There is, of course, the beautiful McCarthy, the canny, intelligent McCarthy, the promiscuous, almost nymphomaniacal McCarthy (she boasted of two or three sexual encounters in a single day), the sharp-witted McCarthy, but not an enduring literary McCarthy, except, perhaps, in the genre of memoirs.

What, then, remains? For one thing, Kieran's retelling of the McCarthy-Wilson marital warfare, which brings home the shifting allegiances of such an alliance. In Kieran's insightful retelling, one hears echoes of another strange alliance, never consummated by marriage: the on-again, off-again relationship between Franz Kafka and Felicia Bauer. As with McCarthy-Wilson, Kafka-Bauer brought together two completely unsuited people who could not let go: two engagements, even while Kafka yearned for marriage, but not a union or an alliance, and Bauer demanded a conventional husband while she was fascinated by the unconventional Kafka. They pulled back and forth, each reaching out for the other while denying what the other was. Kieran's selection of excerpts, combined with her own narrative, captures that sense of two people hugging themselves while still trying to hug the other.

Yet the piling on of excerpts even at its best palls, such as in the bombardment of commentaries on how much McCarthy adored Hannah Arendt. We have remarks from Isaiah Berlin, who thought both were overrated, also from Irving Howe, Alfred Kazin, Saul Bellow, William Phillips, Barbara Dupee, and others, sometimes doubled as they commented on each and then on both together. This brings up another, related matter, not only the proliferation of commentaries past the exhausting point, but the fact that several are not either well-written or well-spoken (if part of an interview), or even well-considered.

Linked to these problems is the point that such excerpts, commentaries, remarks, are all unfiltered, raw, and, therefore, not always in focus. The reader senses that the biographer has failed in the mission we expect of biography, that digestion of source, raw materials, and data, whereas here the excerpts become a transgression. Some of this might be advantageous, breaking up the inevitable boredom implicit in most biographies' recital of facts, and that is not to be ignored. But overwhelming all is that transgressive voice which excerpts inevitably bring, the lingering feeling that the biographer is not assimilating the materials into a metanarrative. One of the glories of the long biography—as distinguished from the brief one—is the metanarrative, a distinctive voice in which the biographer assures the reader of control and validity. The metanarrative to the biographer is what seeming sincere means to the politician.

There is another dimension here that needs emphasis. An oral biography or one with extended excerpts inevitably contributes to a gossipy view of the subject. The remarks from friends, enemies, and even neutrals reinforce rumor, gossip, not analysis, not literary or social criticism. That much is ordained. Excerpts lighten up the narrative and translate into sexual behavior of the subject, social missteps, and related matters, all linked to *People Magazine* gossip. The latter virtually takes over the narrative and feeds the reader's appetite for something "inside," or else feeds the reader's own agenda, often bringing the subject down to the audience's level. Whatever actually takes place, the material so presented is not so much enlightening as it is part of the kind of journalism practiced in the tell-all magazines, whose methods it recalls.

The increased practice of the oral biography, or modifications of it, is a relatively recent phenomenon, and it cannot be viewed in a cultural vacuum. Its appearance is part of the shift to the gossipy nature of news rather than the news itself; and it is not unconnected to celebrity worship which has overtaken all the media. The excerpts are frequently used to turn the subject into a celebrity, a method Kieran employs. McCarthy, who wrote well but was a low-level novelist, is presented as a celebrity when she visits Italy, for example, and writes her books on Venice and Florence. Since she knows little or nothing about either place, her assignments are based on celebrity, and their success on the gossipy nature of her books and her racy personal life (up to then three marriages and the famous discord with Edmund Wilson).

Given, then, the immense negativity an oral biography entails, Kieran does well in sections, especially McCarthy's stay in Venice, spread out over three summers while she was researching her book on Venice. She catches several aspects of the writerly life very well: the cheap, uncomfortable accommodations; the difficulty of dealing with people in a foreign language; McCarthy's reliance on the few contacts available—on the hospitality of Bernard Berenson, for instance, whom she was not fond of—the loneliness of the individual living alone in a bustling, tourist-ridden city; the feeling of smallness in a place so full of beauty and history; the inability to separate the real from the counterfeit; the recognition of one's ignorance even as one is preparing a book on the subject; the feeling of hostility from friends she has satirized in her novels; and on through all the maladies of isolation. Here the biography succeeds.

But there are some questions which this reader at least must ask of a book running over eight hundred pages:

How can Kieran let McCarthy's views on fiction—her attacks on James and Woolf, for example—pass as givens, or call them "common knowledge"?

Why doesn't Kieran probe further into McCarthy as a teacher, since her literary tastes seem so self-serving?

Why doesn't Kieran give us more on McCarthy's antiwar position in World War II, since as it stands she took this position without any understanding of any of the issues?

How can Kieran let McCarthy's views on theater stand without comment, when the latter trampled both *A Streetcar Named Desire* and *Death of a Salesman* and called *The Iceman Cometh* worthless?

Does Kieran ever clarify whether McCarthy was truly an intellectual or merely clever at posing as one by seeming critical of everything?

And, finally, why doesn't Kieran examine more critically McCarthy's rather nasty stand against feminism, since her remarks are short-sighted, unenlightened, and self-serving, based mainly on the assumption that women like her don't need a feminist movement?

WHILE WELL PUT together as narrative, Mary K. Dearborn's *Mailer: A Biography* fails in several respects as serious biography. It rarely takes the measure of Mailer's ideas, for it seems more energized by Mailer's own take on matters than on establishing how and why he succeeds (or fails) as a novelist. His verbal energy, which is indisputable, often hides the overwhelming idiocy of many, if not most, of his ideas. Among other things, during his fifty years as a writer (he was famous at twenty-five, with *The Naked and the Dead*), he has proclaimed the following and invested his fiction with these ideas:

A hatred of the idea of women (while a womanizer) that is almost pathological

A believer in sex that connects to reproduction, which is another form of giving women all the trouble

An opponent not only of abortion but of all contraception, also part of his antifemale bias

An obsessive need for violence—head-butting (like long-horned rams), boxing, creating havoc at parties, his own and others'

An egocentricity which borders on pathological

The need for control as a display of his superiority, whether with other writers or with women

A paranoia about enemies and competitors, whom he sees everywhere

A belief in a life force which gives him virtually Nietzschean powers to make decisions

A mysticism which goes well beyond the reasonable sense that there are mysteries in life—for example, the embrace of Wilhelm Reich

The lack of remorse at the destruction he has cast—his mixed feelings, for example, after his protégé Abbott murdered the waiter

The need to be the Jewish Hemingway

While Dearborn touches on much of this ground, she does not create a profile which synthesizes someone often out of control. Her method, instead, is methodical and formulaic. She moves along Mailer's life chronologically, and at each publication she comments, or at each event (six marriages are events in themselves) she stops to analyze it; but she fails to put it all together. Except in the case of *The Prisoner of Sex*, Mailer's "response" to the women's movement, she does not understand how it is Mailer's ideas which fail and which weaken nearly all of his books. *Why Are We In Vietnam?* is his most successful novel because it is most nearly a verbal artifact, and it has one basic idea cast in a satirical mode. The novel reveals Mailer's considerable verbal gifts without the impediment of his pathologies (except perhaps his anal fixation). It is all language, Mailer's own invention in the main, and it carries one basic idea—that Texas machismo has carried us into the Vietnam mess, an idea of limited breadth in itself, but of significance given Mailer's verbal dexterity.

Yet in other works, especially the much-acclaimed *The Executioner's Song*, Dearborn cannot put together arguments which measure the book's failures as well as its occasional successes. The reader seeks in vain in the bibliography for items which would have given Dearborn literary or psychological tools and provided a deeper probe into Mailer and his work. It is insufficient to keep hitting at Mailer's need for male dominance and his testosterone-driven energies; the question of paranoia, however potentially cliché-ridden, must be explored. Questions of self-esteem deserve probing—Dearborn mentions it without pursuing the point. Mother love and devotion must be factored in more forcefully and then integrated into an overall analysis.

The point is not to psychoanalyze Mailer or even to find some all-explaining pattern; it is to create more coherence, to give some basis for the idiocy and savagery of many of his ideas, to examine his penchant for violence, for being a nasty, cruel drunk, for seeking competition even when it is not called for, for twisting every relationship into obsessive control. And then, parallel to these probes, is the need for some literary point of view to assess his work, some basic positioning so that contexts, analysis, intertextual readings are possible. In a life about a significant writer, it is surely necessary for the biographer to possess some fundamental literary ideas.

The Executioner's Song, as already suggested, becomes a case in point here. Dearborn's sympathetic reading involves almost exclusively a retelling of the main ingredients of the book. Along the way, she comments that Mailer provides Gary Gilmore's complexity; her argument is that he, Gilmore, reflects on karma and reincarnation, profound reflections that mirror Mailer's own ideas. But admittedly, Gilmore does not connect this to anything, and Dearborn's claim for his complexity rests on shaky ground. She has hit a dead end, but in point of fact, the chief failure of the book is its inability to create complexity. What works at the documentary level fails at the novelistic; and Mailer, perhaps more cognizant than Dearborn about this, called his book "A True Life Novel." Why it fails at the novelistic level is quite clear: when Mailer is through with his analysis of Gilmore as full of contempt for life, as consumed by self-hatred, as sensing personal doom, the more the murderer comes across as simply a punk; and as a punk he is unable to support the stature Mailer needs for a fully figured fictional character.

Gilmore may be Mailer's "White Negro," but for the reader, or at least this reader, he cannot sustain Mailer's vision of him. The more we try to understand him, the more he withdraws, not because he is so complex, but because he is so simple. Dearborn rarely catches in Mailer's characters—whether Gilmore here or Rojack in *An American Dream* or Hearn and Cummings in *The Naked and the Dead*—the fact that Mailer's efforts to dress them up with ideas, usually his own ideas, do not give them the texture of meaningful characters; and, accordingly, they cannot support Mailer's dependence on them to carry the ideological freight of their respective books.

These flaws do not invalidate the readability of the biography, nor do they subvert the advantages of the long biography, but they do undercut its intellectual validity. One suspects that when Robert Lucid, Mailer's authorized biographer, publishes (if ever) his three-volume biography of Mailer, he will not critically examine the nature of his subject's ideas; and he may, instead, allow them to stand as if valid because of Mailer's stature as a writer. That would be a mistake, for the glory of the long biography is the amplitude of space for discussion of ideas and the contextualization of the subject's vision.

Returning to *The Executioner's Song*, we can see that Mailer's use of Gilmore's letters to his girlfriend Nicole, while appealing in themselves, fail to create that complexity we look for in a thousand-page book. The reason novelistic contextualization is needed is that Gilmore's two murders are so brutal, so lacking in human rapport, so needless. Only an intricately woven context could have led us back from the murders to him. Because Mailer more or less abandons him as part of a fictional analysis, Gilmore becomes, like his victims, an object. The book never rises to *Crime and Punishment*, nor to Mailer's closer parallel, Dreiser's *An American Tragedy*. As a kind of irony, Gilmore is a marketing phenomenon, an American "tragedy" in the sense that he appeals only to consumer schadenfreude, quite unlike the sense of Dreiser's Clyde Griffiths, whose story is a real American tragedy of class, caste, and Faustian temptation.

I have cited *The Executioner's Song* as one example of how Dearborn fails to grapple with Mailer's work—*The Prisoner of Sex* is an exception—and settles mainly for surfaces, possibly so as not to subvert Mailer's significance. He is important as a writer who has grappled with all the major issues postwar America has faced, from his exploits as an existential hippy in the '50s, a protestor in the '60s, an opponent of feminism in the '70s, and a growing conservative in the '80s and '90s, what he called a radical conservatism. But what is necessary is a level-headed evaluation of the achievement based on the quality of the ideas, which were too often for Mailer's own good merely nonsense, or else simply provocative, not substantial. His belief, for example, in sexual power for the male, indebted as he was to Henry Miller and Wilhelm Reich, made little sense except as a means of empowering him. It fitted in well with his need to bed a variety of women; but it ill served his career as a novelist, since it appeared to give him one string to his bow. His corollary need to compete, to be number one, to overpower competitors both physically and intellectuality often came apart when he ended up with black eyes, bleeding nose and mouth, or in verbal conflict a loser to Gore Vidal and William Buckley, neither of them exactly rocket scientists.

One of Dearborn's best moments—and a validation of the long biographical effort—comes near the end of her book when she attempts to evaluate *Harlot's Ghost*—Mailer's paean to the CIA—in terms of the writer's career. Yet even here as she notes how the one-time provocateur identified with American establishment power, she does not sufficiently assess the literary qualities of the novel, which run from embarrassing to dismal. Any student of language can observe Mailer's verbal dexterity morphing now into blague.

IT IS ALWAYS of interest—and amusing—when a critic opens up huge contradictions between his, or her, views and his work.

For years, James Atlas went along with enthusiastic reviews of long, full-fleshed biographies, including my own of Joseph Conrad (which he called "A magnificent accomplishment . . . which I predict will become a classic of biography"), and then he became founder and editor of a series of brief biographies issued by Viking Penguin. In the first batch of these brief biographies, as we have indicated, he included on the jacket copy sentiments that indicated the short biography would reinvigorate a "once popular" genre, biography itself. And in numerous reviews and articles leading up to the brief biographies, Atlas bemoaned the state of biography left in the hands of the long-winded set. At the same time, and for the last ten years, Atlas has himself been working on a long, full-fleshed, inclusive, and exhaustive life of Saul Bellow, the very kind of biography he had for several years been hauling over the coals. He is, indeed, a man caught between conflicting ideas, and he begins to sound as if all he said was self-serving: praise for the big boys when he was entering the arena, then disdain for them when he edits the briefs, and finally positioning himself once again with the big boys when he publishes his Bellow life. Atlas always had his finger up to test the winds.

Now the product is available. And it is the very quality of lengthy biography which gives Atlas's *Bellow* its value. In other words, the long segments on Bellow's early life in Canada, then in Chicago, in the neighborhoods and schools, along with material about friends, neighbors, and relatives, all, need the very space the brief biography disallows. In fact, Atlas's *Bellow* could be longer. Here are some ways.

If we speculate about length, then we need to bring up several questions about the writing of biography. For example, does Atlas give us sufficient context for Bellow's fiction? The immediate response is that he does give us salient matters—the Cold War, the arms race, the disruptions because of various movements, America's runaway embrace of technology—but background material is not thickly textured, nor is it thought through. There is the tendency to list and to let it go at that. Since Atlas does not attempt more texture and context, his narrative of Bellow's last thirty-five years seems repetitious. His main argument, which he plays and replays, is that Bellow responded negatively to aspects of modern life, its schisms, divisions, disruptions, its lack of civility, and, most of all, its youthful rejection of meaningful, i.e., classical, culture. If we understood better Bellow's response, because of more contextualization and, therefore, greater length, then we could perhaps comprehend better his racist attitudes, his misogyny, and other areas that appear merely ugly.

This would not be to excuse him, but to see him as part of a widespread white, Jewish-male backlash against some anti-Semitic blacks, perceived threats of female insurgence, and the young who demand their own dissident cultural values. Bellow, then, becomes more solidly grounded in his culture and not simply a crank and chauvinist. Along the way, some of that repetition in the final half of the biography might have been mitigated.

Further, a somewhat longer biography—all part of Atlas's contradictory attitude toward the genre—might have afforded him more in-depth literary criticism of the major books. *Henderson, the Rain King*, for just one example, requires more than a few pages of commentary. *Henderson* is a significant pivotal point in Bellow's literary career, when his earlier, more controlled realism opened up to something wild, seemingly uncontrolled, and passionate. The novel becomes a compelling mirror of America as the fifties are shifting into a decade of self-centeredness, violence, and yes, passion for causes as well as for self. *Henderson* is, in fact, part of a conflict in Bellow, for after that, while he did not forsake the whirlpooled inner life, he did come down hard on social disruption and all it brings.

Moreover, the psychological reasoning is flat and needs extension. When Atlas attributes Bellow's five marriages to his inability to deal with the loss of his mother, the biographer has entered a treacherous area. In the writing of biography, there are always areas, some of them oceanic, which cannot be explained logically, and the biographer ventures in at a disadvantage. In Conrad biography, that time arrives when Conrad, at twenty, attempted suicide with a gunshot to his chest. All efforts at explanation of this event prove elusive and unsatisfying, especially since he never attempted suicide again. In Faulkner biography, the moment arrives when Faulkner leaps from his early novels (*Soldiers' Pay*, *Mosquitoes*, *Sartoris*) to *The Sound and the Fury* and *As I Lay Dying*, an amazing step for him which is impossible to explain. In Bellow's case, anyone who marries five times (amidst innumerable affairs) cannot be "explained" by mother worship, or any singular cause.

If the biographer does venture in, then explanations must be on a very broad front: mother perhaps, but a multitude of other reasons, none of which alone can ever prove satisfactory. The desire for sexual control of women must be weighed against the hatred of women, which must be weighed against the need for self-identification, which must be weighed against the compulsive need to assert masculinity and to use sex as a form of canceling depression, and so on and on. Whatever the reasons, they lie deep within the interstices of motivation, and are most probably unknowable to him or to her. It may simply be boredom, that tiring of sexual activity with the same person; and the boredom may derive from numerous other factors, which translate into numerous marriages, as we see with Mailer, Hemingway, and, here, Bellow, fifteen or so marriages among them. The adventurous biographer may see some connection to the need to "produce" work, to create, to activate the imagination, to keep language flowing, some linkage that D. H. Lawrence wrote about fervently, the linkage of sexuality and creativity. We can never know, but one thing we do recognize is that any effort to provide linear causation is doomed.

Someone so skittish about psychological analysis finds it difficult to pinpoint Bellow's compulsive philandering, both during and between marriages. Is the inability to be alone part of his mother problem? Is the choice of somewhat inferior women (in his eyes) a mother problem, or an ego problem which perhaps beggars analysis? Is his flitting from woman to woman related to his inability to sustain negative criticism? Is this a sign of a weak or a very strong sense of self? If a weak sense, then he was fearful of the damage negative reviews could do; if strong, he simply could proceed, no matter what anyone thought of him, from his feeling of superiority. Where does the biographer take his stand? Any final analysis seems impossible, but at least the measurement of an ego such as Bellow's requires a much more discriminating sense than Atlas reveals, although in terms of sheer narrative, he provides a readable and even compelling biography.

Atlas makes Bellow palpable. The natty clothes, the jokes and witty, catty remarks, the constant travel, the search for women, the marriages and divorces are all part of a commanding story. Yet when Atlas seeks meaning, as with the mother explanation above, he falls short and becomes reductive. About one-third through, he tries for deep meaning, saying that "*the* theme" for Bellow, personally and professionally, was to "elude categories of every kind." Atlas sees this theme as solidifying in the mid-1950s, right after Bellow had published *Augie March,* his breakthrough novel. Yet biographically such announcements are always dangerous, since they establish a vise from which neither the biographer nor the subject can escape. As the narrative develops, it is clear that Bellow did not avoid categories. In fact, he pursued, often compulsively, certain set stances—the serial adultery, the serial marriages to unsuitable women, the replay of conservative and frequently racist ideas in his fiction. One area in which the narrative flags is in the second half of the biography, when Bellow has become predictable; events double and triple themselves as Bellow falls into set categories.

The first half of the biography appears fresh, and the details which justify such a long biography are insightful; but in the second half, Atlas seems somewhat uncertain how or where to proceed. Since his strength does not really lie in literary criticism—he narrates what happens in the novels and identifies the real life figures behind the characters—he must work with his strong point, his ability to generate a narrative. Yet Bellow's life, compelling as it is, falls into repetition, and the later fiction itself cannot generate the excitement that *Augie March*, *Henderson*, and even *Herzog* did in the '50s and early '60s. The next thirty-five years or so are really replays of the earlier life, with a deteriorating literary product: segments on the new novels, which are of mixed interest, a rundown of the reviews, then a segment on Bellow's raucous personal life (affairs, marriages, divorces, alimony fights), then the loss of friends to anger or death, followed by another round of about the same. Even a carefully wrought and well-researched biography has a myriad of problems.

MISCELLANEOUS

These three relatively short pieces are outgrowths of panels in which I discussed "Faulkner and Alcoholism," "Naming in Eliot," and "Why Another Kafka Biography?" Like the longer pieces in this collection, they raise questions that perplex the biographer because they cannot be resolved in any clear narrative way. Was Faulkner's drinking helpful or destructive for him? Was Eliot's change of names throughout her life, both before and after she became George Eliot, a sign of weakness or strength? Was there room for another Kafka biography, or was his life so set in stone that nothing more could be said?

Faulkner and Alcoholism

We all know that Faulkner drank, but the circumstances in which he drank are less well known—it was often in binges that were suicidal. He was not a social drinker, but preferred solitary activity, alone at his desk or in hotel rooms. But establishing that is not much of a biographical discovery. What matters is how Faulkner's alcoholism and binging affected both his life and work. This means the biographer is less interested in whether his drinking was genetic or part of some emotional process we cannot quite interpret than in his drinking as part of a psychological and artistic process. The biographer is not concerned, primarily, with the science or pseudo-science behind an individual's alcoholism and, in that, may differ considerably from a social scientist's probe into drinking itself.

In Faulkner's case, alcohol becomes another unsettling element in a life full of stops and starts, complete with leaps which the biographer cannot really account for. Alcohol, in brief, sets up its own set of problems which must be coordinated with everything else. Since excess drinking is so much a part of the American literary landscape—Faulkner, Hemingway, Fitzgerald, Steinbeck, and on and on—it bleeds over in each instance into the very interstices of a writer's achievement, here Faulkner's.

Once we say this, we still have all the questions. We may ask if drinking itself was bad for him, or whether it enhanced his sense of himself, even to the extent of reinforcing his sense of personal identity. We must immediately put aside the usual explanation of excessive drinking as injurious or debilitating, for Faulkner was able to produce some thirty volumes of work, win the Nobel Prize for literature, and write several pieces of fiction which have entered the permanent canon of American literature. If drinking inhibited or slowed him down, then we would have to claim that without it he may have achieved more. That is unlikely, since his achievement was at the highest levels; with it, not without it, he became America's greatest novelist since Henry James. And he created *Absalom, Absalom!* his most considerable achievement, when he was most vulnerable, in Hollywood, and drinking heavily.

We have, here, to distinguish Faulkner's drinking from, say, Fitzgerald's, which undercut his capacity to write; or from Hemingway's, which debilitated him at a much earlier age than it began to affect Faulkner. When it comes to alcoholism, each writer is distinct, not part of any generalized pattern. Faulkner's "pattern" would appear to go against common sense, in that he gained rather than lost from it.

Yet as biographers, we are obviously also interested in the man, not only in what or how he created what he did. The man, or woman, in biographical writing should never be disengaged from the work, although the linkage is unstable and can be approached in almost an infinite number or ways. For Faulkner the man, the drinking may have helped reinforce him in a tension-filled family scene. When he and Estelle Oldham finally married—Faulkner had pursued her many years earlier and been rejected as worthless by her family—they had little in common except that earlier romance. After his rejection, she had married, then divorced, and returned to Oxford; he had turned from early efforts at poetry to novels and was moving into his most productive period with *The Sound and the Fury* and *As I Lay Dying*. They were two people pushed into each other's arms—Estelle's sister, Dorothy, did the pushing—who otherwise inhabited different planets. Estelle was already drinking heavily and very possibly on drugs (prescriptive and others), and Faulkner had found his career.

As a consequence, the domestic scene was messy and antagonistic; it even started off ominously as Estelle, while they honeymooned, attempted suicide at a beach resort on the Mississippi Gulf. Given to elaborate dresses even while on the beach, Estelle walked into the Gulf, while Faulkner was occupied with proofs of *The Sound and the Fury*. Someone noticed a party-dressed woman floundering in deep and dangerous waters, and she was pulled out. If she wasn't actually trying to kill herself, she was seeking attention—and their married life was set.

Two heavy drinkers came together and energized a marital situation that often seemed like a martial challenge. Faulkner's daughter reported that she could not bring school friends home because she never knew if her parents would be lying unconscious on the living room floor. There were also physical confrontations, fingernails to the cheek, bites, etc. The usual interpretation of this would be that such a home situation, like the drinking, would be an impediment to creative work; that what the artist needs is quiet and repose in his or her life; and that constant disruption might be a conscious or unconscious way of avoiding work. None of this applies to Faulkner. His personal turmoil—to this scene in Oxford, we should add his hatred of Hollywood, where he earned good money as a scriptwriter, and his intimacy with a woman who served as Howard Hawks's script girl—seemed, somehow, to focus him.

To this must also be added the frequent depressions, which might well have been brought on by the bouts of drinking—alcohol, for most, is a depressant. The biographer must take the depressions into account—were they debilitating or did they create the circumstances out of which Faulkner could resurrect himself and work effectively? In this respect, the depressions were not negative, but episodes from which he could extract himself strengthened. There was, clearly, a cycle of drinking and depression, depression and drinking; but intertwined with this was a steady production of highly imaginative work, especially in the most tension-ridden, anxiety-producing period, the 1930s.

Further questions arise, and they are critical to biographical writing. Is Faulkner's drinking somehow connected to his mature prose style? Or, put a different way, did his drinking enhance or inhibit a style that became known as Faulknerian? By this reasoning, his indulgence in long, punctuationless sentences could be ascribed to some kind of alcoholic-induced vision. The sentences could be part of a haze or hallucinatory experience in which words take on extrasensory dimensions. The lack of grammar or syntax in these sentences—or what we might call Faulknerian grammar—is not so much a conscious avoidance of rules, as in literary stream of consciousness, as it is a kind of automatic writing attributable to alcohol. Can such "letting go" with words be linked to the binges in which he almost let go of life itself?

Possibly, the alcoholism was genetic. After all, Faulkner's father, Murry, was a very heavy drinker until after several acts of violence he gave it up, and heavy drinking was systemic in the family. If genetic, how does the biographer handle it? For a genetic disposition to alcohol would make the subject an unconscious agent of something he could not control. And if not genetic, then we can suppose the drinking was socially induced—we know that drinking was the manly thing to do, part of the culture, not only manly, but also womanly. Drinking was, for many, a way of life. Where does the biographer come down in this, or can he even come down anywhere without heavy speculation?

A still further question: As Faulkner's work declined after the long pieces on *Go Down, Moses*, when he was still only forty-five, was it drinking that did it? Or Hollywood? Or a combatant personal life? Or some deeply rooted depression? Or simply the aging of an American writer who had exhausted his vein of experience and knowledge? What can be ascribed particularly to alcohol or to some other softening of the brain, or the wiping out of brain cells that nourished the creative part? To what extent did his drinking frustrate his will, and, more importantly, how did the drinking make him lose the earlier freshness of his prose?

The act of drinking itself has several compelling dimensions besides those connected to Faulkner's work. Not usually a social drinker, he did drink excessively when in the company of very masculine men—hunting companions, in particular. Was this socializing or something psychologically troubling for him that led to excess? He relied on them, we know, to save him from himself, as we observe from his hunting camp experiences; and on other occasions, he counted on companions to find him when he went into an almost suicidal binge. The intensity and severity of the binges, to the point of oblivion in shadowy environments, give pause to simply saying he was an alcoholic and leave it at that. Further, he did have the ability to stop, for months at a time. Even further, if the binges were indeed suicidal, what does this suggest about Faulkner as man and writer? Was he desperate, living with inner demons which dictated periodic desires to end it all? Can we connect this to family life, to a father he disliked, to his wife and daughter, or to some aspect of his career as a writer when he felt he had failed or deserved more attention?

Do we say, as a physician might diagnose, that it was disadvantageous; or, as a psychologist, that he needed the chaotic inner life, the demons, so as to find order when he sat down to write? The demons that led to the binges in some way reinforced the order he found at his desk, so that disorder was necessary to underlay the productive writer. All this is, of course, speculative. Even as the biographer burrows ever more deeply into causation, he or she is arranging variables, creating some kind of theory or assessment based on only some of the factors. For even the most penetrating of biographers cannot find certainties here; and yet any biographer would be foolish not to attempt to factor in something as important as alcohol and binges in Faulkner's life as a writer. They were not marginal indulgences.

Naming in George Eliot

ALTHOUGH A TRADITIONAL subject in several respects, George Eliot nevertheless poses several problems for her biographers; and, inevitably, these problems bleed over into any effort to connect her to her work and her work back to her. One of the problematic areas is Eliot's decision in 1854 to run off to Germany with George Henry Lewes, on the surface an unlikely choice of companions. Married, with four sons, with a reputation for philandering, he was involved in complicated arrangements with his estranged wife (she would have four children by Thornton Hunt whom Lewes accepted as his own). Lewes also had a reputation as a lightweight, a type of Frenchified flitterer. Yet if we try to understand why Eliot went with Lewes, really as his mistress, we must understand how she hoped to transform herself, and that is linked to name changes.

Prior to her meeting and "elopement" with Lewes, Eliot, born Mary Anne Evans, had dropped the "e" in Anne and had become, for reasons of her own, Mary Ann Evans. In time, that name gave way to Marian Evans, and with this—the first of several name changes—we observe the beginnings of transformational yearnings. She was, we can argue, struggling to emerge into something else—just what we cannot know as yet; but the French form, Marian, suggests she was seeking a life well beyond what she thought was a smothering existence.

The name changes this early, before she became George Eliot, suggest a major problem in biographical writing: to what extent can the biographer use hindsight as to what the subject became as a means of interpreting the earlier life of that subject? Can we work backwards, since with a dead subject we know what happened? Related to this is the question of whether someone like Eliot, precocious, intellectual, sensitive, capable of absorbing all forms of information, has within her the career as George Eliot long before she became George Eliot, itself a name change of great significance.

Does the career, then, unfold as part of what is already there, latent, resting in the unconscious or preconscious; or does it depend on certain circumstances for it to flourish? Could Mary Anne Evans, in brief, have been thwarted from becoming George Eliot, or was it inscribed within her own choices and sense of her destiny? Further, does this reading of Eliot apply to all creative artists, or is it peculiar to her because of will, determination, and intellect?

These questions may seem on the order of chicken-and-egg conundrums, but they present dilemmas for the biographer. Can the latter allow a series of name changes to go without comment? And related to this is the question of just when the biographer pounces on a name change and sees it as significant. In Eliot's case, we know that many other names will follow, so that from hindsight we recognize there is a sequence. At what point in the sequence do we acknowledge that something is happening, that some kind of transformational thought or will is operating? Can we really connect Mary Anne/Mary Ann/Marian Evan's decision to run off with Lewes as part of this transformational process, or did it originate from different factors altogether—that she was smitten, that she sought a sensual life, that she saw career possibilities in the elopement, and so on into areas of equal speculation? Name changing now becomes as dramatic for us, as biographers, as possibly it was for her, our subject. Dramatic in the sense that what we do with these changes will determine the biographical process, as much as these shifts in name determined her pursuit of self-fulfillment.

But further problematic name changes lay ahead, and not only the assumption of George Eliot as her pen name. Others came to call her Madonna (while many in society called her whore); Mother (she was childless, but proved a caring step-mother for Lewes's sons); Polly and Polian, and so on. Most compelling of all, Eliot insisted on being called Mrs. Lewes, when the legal Mrs. Lewes was alive and well; and while she insisted on Mrs. Lewes, she was known as George Eliot to her public and signed her letters to friends and relatives with earlier versions of her Evans name, Mary Anne, Mary Ann, Marian. In a period of a few months, we find a dozen or more name designations. This carries through most of her productive years as writer and companion to Lewes.

As the combination of names proliferates, an amusing question is how she kept track of what name she was using with each person. We know that she retained the George Eliot pen name throughout her writing career, but less well known is that in her early period as a writer she kept her real name and sex from her publisher; and that Lewes, who dealt with the publisher, Blackwood, said her first book was penned by a shy, retiring, reclusive clergyman. Here, the woman with whom he was living was kept closeted and presented to the outside world not only as a man but as a man of cloth. Eliot eventually revealed herself to Blackwood, who took it in stride. Dickens had already penetrated her disguise when he read *Scenes of Clerical Life*. But there was little need to disguise her sex, since women writers were in vogue, and a majority of the fiction published after 1860 was written by women.

Yet the disguises continued, and for the biographer the situation offers considerable potentiality. But even as it presents a rich texture, it becomes problematical. Do the name changes suggest security in herself—that she could prevail no matter what she called herself—or insecurity, that she had to disguise who she really was? Did the later changes indicate she was hiding from critics who, while admiring her books, maligned her for running off with a married man? What psychological factors are in play? Could the name changes be part of a disintegrating process which suggests she was breaking to pieces which only her fiction writing could allay? Her frequent depressive periods, her headaches, her generally poor health could all point to such disintegration, which found wholeness only in her writing. This is an assumption, a speculation. Did she know who she really was outside her writing, or did Mary Anne Evans somehow blend with George Eliot? Her celebrity came with George Eliot, whereas her personal life was Evans. Was she also Mrs. Lewes, in her mind, or who? No one called her George; no one called her Madame or Miss or Mrs. Eliot. George Sand, another name changer, was George to her friends, and Madame Sand otherwise—she lived fully within her pen name; in fact thrived within it. Eliot tiptoed around hers. She refused it in public and insisted on Mrs. Lewes—all the while contributing funds to support the real Mrs. Lewes.

Was she so divided between public and private that names were her metaphorical way of manifesting inner states? Or else moderating inner turmoil? Was Eliot confused, as the name changes might indicate, and did this confusion manifest itself in her novels and give them their textural strength and deep psychological insight? Did she see confusion emanating from personal values as a conduit for her unique voice, what I call in my biography the "voice of the century"?—in which confusion and ambiguity about religion, science, industry, mechanization, marriage, and all the rest were far more prevalent than the Victorians liked to admit? Perhaps in her name changes, Eliot was expressing the messiness of a century which while insisting on order and orderliness was all the while practicing something quite different. Under all the name changes, she took on different personae, different roles, and the changes enabled her to act out parts of herself which society did not sanction.

These are just a few of the questions related to name changes, but these uncertainties in biographical writing are not necessarily moments of frustration. Rather, they are indicators of what makes biography a worthwhile pursuit. For essentially the biographer deconstructs the subject's life, and then, confronted with the seemingly disparate elements, must put them all together to create the semblance of a narrative. I say "semblance" because a perfectly valid narrative is quite impossible, unless we foolishly believe that a life, real or reconstructed, follows a continuous line. As we have seen, even with such a traditional subject as George Eliot, the problematic areas—naming in particular—are immense and open only to speculation.

The one solid anchor the biographer may have, as I had with all four of my books, is the marginality of the subject, whether in reality or in the subject's perception of himself or herself. Kafka is an obvious example, and Conrad also always considered himself an exile, while Faulkner lived so deeply within himself that he remained unknowable. Even Eliot, as we have observed, never achieved that mainstream, the escape from marginality, which part of her wished to attain, although the rejection she experienced fueled the sense of conflict which made her fiction so textured. Marginality is a treasure for the subject's creativity, while possibly painful for the private individual; but for the biographer of a major figure it becomes not only a given but an essential tool.

Trying Kafka Again

What did I hope to accomplish in still another biography of Franz Kafka? What could I do that had not been done before? That is, obviously, a question all biographers ask themselves—can they possibly add to what their predecessors have accomplished, beyond bringing a more up-to-date sensibility to the enterprise? There was, in Kafka studies, the much-acclaimed Ernst Pawel biography from the early 1980s, and the less-acclaimed one by Ronald Hayman. There is little else in Kafka biography in English, except for the translation of Max Brod's early hagiographic work. In Germany, solid biographical work has been done by Wagenbach, Binder, and others—but this is inaccessible to the non-German reader. Also, I discovered that both Pawel and Hayman relied heavily on the German work, especially using Wagenbach's study of the first half of Kafka's life, up to 1912, when he made his creative breakthrough.

My plan was multifold: to do an end rush, so to speak, around previous biographies while meeting them head-on in interpretive matters. My strategy was nothing less than to capture Kafka's life amidst the entire artistic, cultural, political, and social history of the period, encompassing Central and Central-Eastern Europe. It was to recreate Prague and the Austro-Hungarian Empire as it began to emit its dying gasps. It was, in terms of historical development, a continuation of what I had attempted with Joseph Conrad's biography, in terms of Poland, France and, finally, England. Conrad had left Poland just short of his seventeenth birthday, and, therefore, that experience, while critical, was truncated; but Kafka was Prague-bound for his entire life, and Prague was, I found, the center of his world. Understand Prague, I thought, and I can grasp Kafka. It seemed that to comprehend a story like "A Hunger Artist," the biographer needed a very broad approach; for "hunger" resonates throughout Kafka's entire world. It is a Prague story.

Beyond even that, I wanted to understand how Kafka assimilated Prague, in his unique way, not merely how Prague lay heavily over him. Although the Prague Golem shadows his world, Kafka was himself not created out of dust, as was the Golem of legend. Further, there was, as mentioned in an earlier essay, my own sense of countertransference, my imposition of myself and my own background on Kafka's emergence from his background.

Several aspects of the subject came under scrutiny, and the strategy was, as in all biographical writing, to create a narrative that molded these elements into coherence. Yet I always entertained the idea that such elements might not blend in Kafka, only in *my* approach to him. We assume, we biographers, that the subject is the sum total of all the approaches we made toward him, or her, when in fact the subject might not have integrated these elements. Further, for someone like Kafka, what integration the biographer has taken for granted is part of the very struggle of the subject, who sees only incoherence. As several of my pieces here suggest, my interest in biography is founded on the belief that uncertainties lie at the center of all biographical writing, and that the best of subjects resist the very narrative I impose on them.

Kafka certainly trumped this idea. At every stage, his life, like his work, remained problematical. I found several elements that failed the test of coherence. In his Notebooks, for example—and here I refer to the German version of the Notebooks, much fuller than the English translation—we find repeated images of knife wounds, of knives twisting in his, Kafka's, body, of his being penetrated again and again by sharp instruments. It is an obsessive image, whether in the dreams Kafka reports, or in a more conscious desire to be stabbed, with the knife twisted in his guts. It is, in some respects, a variation of the story "In the Penal Colony" or the ending of *The Trial*. What do we make of such a repetitious image, a cruel and unusual trope? Do we say that the image is clearly homoerotic—being penetrated, stabbed, pierced, invaded? Or do we see it not only as part of his morbid view of himself as unworthy and sacrificial, but also as a particular kind of death, death by penetration which he identifies as ecstasy.

Yet there is nothing in Kafka's life to indicate he was anything but heterosexual in practice. Nor was there anything to view him as suicidal, however depressed and morbid. He visited prostitutes occasionally—although he feared disease and thought some sexual practices were too filthy even to think about. He had women friends, mainly unconsummated relationships. He did have a circle of male friends, the so-called Prague Circle, Brod, Werfel, and others; but none of this falls outside a heterosexual world of writers and artists coming together for talk and beer. The biographer is faced with competing forces: the homoerotic images, obsessively detailed, in the Notebooks; the life itself, with no hint of homoerotic or homosexual practice. These unresolved problems—and I could not myself come to any conclusion—work themselves through in several aspects of Kafka's life: contraries that do not link up into any coherent pattern. There are, of course, psychological explanations, which may or may not be valid: that the images in the Notebooks are not wish-fulfillments, but, as noted, Kafka's less than conscious desire to be a martyr of sorts; that these seemingly homoerotic images are projections, in some respect, of his desire to kill the father; even that he had delusions of being a god sacrificed, Jesus's Calvary experience, spear in the side, hands nailed to the cross.

Whatever I did, I recognized I could not impose on him the biographer's usual control or narrative. Kafka's story had to be the way he arranged his own life without regard for the consistency one expects in biographical writing. Clearly, the life and what is written about it do not pull in the same direction. What I saw in this was that the very contraries and unresolved conflicts which might destabilize the biographer were actually ways in which Kafka gathered himself and gained energy for the way his life worked. While this is true for every biographical subject, in Kafka's case, the silences dominated.

Still another large area in which linkage was impossible came between his professional life with an accident insurance company and his private life in which he was one of the most considerable anarchists of the century. He was the man who trashed everything he touched: marriage, family, home life, the bureaucracy, the state, the very nature of being as a coherent sequence of events. *The Metamorphosis*, everyone's favorite family story, is an ultimate subversion not only of bourgeois life but of all life, using a form from nature to indicate the incoherence of human routine. As an insurance man, Kafka handled industrial accident cases in which workers lost fingers, hands, and limbs, and then brought cases against the insurance company. Kafka represented the company, but attempted to broker the best deal for the workers. He arrived at his office on time, he worked diligently, he did not ruffle co-workers or management, and he remained a favorite employee despite the company policy of not hiring or promoting Jews. Kafka's work here cut through most of his adult life—until he became too sick to continue—and paralleled his most dire Notebook entries and, of course, his fiction. He worked in insurance, but in his writings questioned every aspect of that workaday life.

Another problem derives from the biographer's desire to psychoanalyze Kafka, to turn oneself into an analyst and him into an analysand, and by so doing, imposing some psychological order on anarchic impulses. Further, by putting Kafka on the couch, we broaden our probe and try to understand the role of the decaying Austro-Hungarian Empire, itself a patchwork of incoherent parts, and how that paternalistic, authoritarian monarchy becomes intermixed in Kafka's mind with an authoritarian household led by Hermann Kafka.

This links us to still another question, and that is whether Kafka's relationship with Hermann was really so loathsome as we extrapolate from his fiction and his diaries? Or was it part of Kafka's need to exaggerate the crudeness and cruelty of the father as a way of exaggerating his own weakness, so that he could gain strength from the perception of weakness and turn it into his own kind of power in his writing? Further, in pitting him against his father, as most previous biographers have done, they have tried to impose resolution on extremely complicated materials, when, in fact, Kafka, as I show in my earlier essay, was possibly angrier at his mother and her neglect of him than he was at the imperious Hermann. Are all efforts to impose some framework on Kafka doomed to failure, creating half-truths, if not downright distortions? To what degree are all attempts to write Kafka's biography efforts in futility, since he escapes whatever framework the biographer may erect? And related to this is the question: are there some figures, like Kafka notably, who cannot be caught in biographical writing, not only because of the immensity of their vision but because of the ambiguities which make up that vision? Or do the ambiguities simply prod the biographer to give it another try?

Acknowledgments

"In the Struggle between You and Kafka, Back Yourself," *American Imago* 55; and Johns Hopkins University Press.

"Writing Kafka's Biography," *Biography and Source Studies* 3; and AMS Press.

"Three Problematical Areas in Conrad Biography," in *Conrad Revisited: Essays for the Eighties*, University of Alabama Press, 1985.

"Conrad's Life & Letters, Letters & Life: The Final Three Volumes," *Conradiana* 31.

"Biography and Narrative: Faulkner's *Absalom, Absalom!*" *Biography and Source Studies* 1; and AMS Press.

"Writing George Eliot's Biography," *Biography* 22; and University of Hawai'i Press.

"Conrad's Letters and Biography," *Conradiana* 10; and Greenwood Press, 1999.

"The Biographical Dimensions of Conrad's Literary Theory," *Criticism: A Quarterly for Literature and the Arts* 2.

"A Mutant: Biography/Autobiography/Fiction," *Biography and Source Studies* 2; and AMS Press.

"Some American Biography," *Biography and Source Studies* 4; and AMS Press.

"Four Brief Biographies," *Biography and Source Studies* 5; and AMS Press.

"The Long and Short of It," *Biography and Source Studies* 6; and AMS Press.

Bibliography

Aaron, Daniel. *Studies in Biography.* Massachusetts: Harvard University Press, 1978.

Ackroyd, Peter. *Dickens.* New York: Harper Collins, 1990.

Ambrose, Stephen E. *Crazy Horse and Custer: The Parallel Lives of Two American Warriors.* New York: Doubleday, 1975.

Ashton, Rosemary. *George Eliot.* New York: Oxford University Press, 1983.

Auster, Paul. *The Invention of Solitude.* New York: Penguin Books, 1988.

Baker, Carlos. *Ernest Hemingway: A Life Story.* New York: Scribner, 1969.

Baker, Carlos. *Hemingway: The Writer as Artist.* New Jersey: Princeton University Press, 1973.

Benfey, Christopher. *The Double Life of Stephen Crane.* New York: Random House, 1992.

Blotner, Joseph Leo. *Faulkner: A Biography.* New York: Random House, 1974.

Booth, Bradford Allen. *Anthony Trollope: Aspects of his Life and Art.* Indiana: Indiana University Press, 1958.

Cheever, Susan. *Home Before Dark.* Boston: Houghton Mifflin, 1984.

Cockshut, O. J. A. *Anthony Trollope: A Critical Study.* London: Collins, 1955.

Dearborn, Mary V. *Mailer: A Biography.* Boston: Houghton Mifflin, 1999.

Edel, Leon. *The Complete Notebooks of Henry James.* New York: Oxford University Press, 1987.

Ellmann, Richard. *James Joyce.* New York: Oxford University Press, 1959.

Erlich, Gloria C. *The Sexual Education of Edith Wharton.* Berkeley: University of California Press, 1992.

Gay, Peter. *The Bourgeois Experience: Victoria to Freud.* New York: Oxford University Press, 1998.
Gay, Peter. *Education of the Senses.* New York: W. W. Norton and Company, 1999.
Gay, Peter. *The Tender Passion.* London: Oxford University Press, 1986.
Glendinning, Victoria. *Anthony Trollope.* New York: Random House, 1993.
Guerard, Albert J. *Conrad the Novelist.* Cambridge: Harvard University Press, 1958.
Haight, Gordon Sherman. *George Eliot: A Biography.* New York: Oxford University Press, 1968.
Hall, John. *Trollope: A Biography.* London: Oxford University Press, 1993.
Hughes, Kathryn. *George Eliot: The Last Victorian.* New York: Cooper Square Press, 2001.
Hulbert, Ann. *The Interior Castle: The Art and Life of Jean Stafford.* New York: Alfrd A. Knopf, 1992.
Johnson, Edgar. *Charles Dickens: His Tragedy and Triumph.* New York: Viking Press, 1977.
Karl, Frederick R. *Franz Kafka: A Representative Man.* New York: Ticknor and Fields, 1991.
Karl, Frederick R. *George Eliot: Voice of a Century, a Biography.* New York: W. W. Norton, 1995.
Karl, Frederick R. *Joseph Conrad: The Three Lives.* New York: Farrar, Straus and Giroux, 1979.
Karl, Frederick R. *William Faulkner, American Writer: A Biography.* New York: Weidenfeld and Nicolson, 1989.
Kiernan, Frances. *Seeing Mary Plain: A Life of Mary McCarthy.* New York: W. W. Norton and Company, 2000.
Langer, Susanne. *Feeling and Form: A Theory of Art.* New York: Scribner, 1953.
Lynn, Kenneth Schuyler. *Hemingway.* New York: Simon and Schuster, 1987.
Malcolm, Janet. *The Silent Woman: Sylvia Plath and Ted Hughes.* New York: Alfred A. Knopf, 1993.
Marcus, Steven. *Dickens: From Pickwick to Dombey.* New York: Basic Books, 1965.
Maynard, John. *Charlotte Bronte and Sexuality.* New York: Cambridge University Press, 1984.
McCarthy, Mary. *Memories of a Catholic Girlhood.* New York: Harcourt Brace Jovanovich, 1957.
McCourt, Frank. *Angela's Ashes: A Memoir.* New York: Scribner, 1996.
Meyer, Bernard C. *Joseph Conrad: A Psychoanalytic Biography.* New Jersey: Princeton University Press, 1967.
Miller, Edwin Haviland. *Salem is my Dwelling Place: A Life of Nathaniel Hawthorne.* Iowa City: University of Iowa Press, 1991.

Millgate, Michael. *Thomas Hardy: A Biography.* New York: Random House, 1982.

Myer, Valerie Grosvenor. *Jane Austen; Obstinate Heart: A Biography.* New York: Thorndike Press, 1997.

Painter, George Duncan. *Marcel Proust: A Biography.* London: Chatto and Windus, 1965.

Parker, Hershel. *Herman Melville: A Biography.* Baltimore: Johns Hopkins University Press, 1996.

Plumb, J. H. *Georgian Delights.* New York: Weidenfeld and Nicolson, 1980.

Ray, Gordon Norton. *Thackeray.* New York: McGraw-Hill, 1958.

Redinger, Ruby Virginia. *George Eliot: The Emergent Self.* New York: Alfred A. Knopf, 1975.

Reynolds, David S. *Beneath the American Renaissance: The Subversive Imagination in the Age of Emerson and Melville.* New York: Alfred A. Knopf, 1988.

Rhodes, Richard. *A Hole in the World: An American Boyhood.* New York: Simon and Schuster, 1990.

Sandoz, Mari. *Crazy Horse; The Strange Man of the Oglalas: A Biography.* Lincoln: University of Nebraska Press, 1961.

Sloan, James Park. *Jerzy Kerzinsky: A Biography.* New York: Plume, 1997.

Spilka, Mark. *Dickens and Kafka: A Mutual Interpretation.* Massachusetts: P. Smith, 1969.

Strouse, Jean. *Alice James: A Biography.* Boston: Houghton Mifflin, 1980.

Tadie, Jean-Yves. *Marcel Proust: A Life.* New York: Penguin Books, 2001.

Tindall, Gillian. *George Gissing: A Born Exile.* New York: Harcourt Brace Jovanovich, 1974.

Warner, Marina. *Joan of Arc: The Image of Female Heroism.* New York: Alfred A. Knopf, 1981.

Watt, Ian P. *Conrad in the Nineteenth Century.* Berkeley: The University of California Press, 1979.

White, Edmund. *A Boy's Own Story.* New York: Dutton, 1982.

Wideman, John Edgar. *Brothers and Keepers.* New York: Vintage Books, 1995.

Williamson, Joel. *William Faulkner and Southern History.* New York: Oxford University Press, 1993.

Wolfe, Tobias. *This Boy's Life: A Memoir.* New York: Grove Press, 2000.

Wolff, Geoffrey. *The Duke of Deception.* New York: Vintage, 1990.